Person Centred Planning and Care Management with People with Learning Disabilities

by the same authors

Intimate and Personal Care with People with Learning Disabilities
Edited by Steven Carnaby and Paul Cambridge
ISBN 978 1 84310 130 7

of related interest

Working with People with Learning Disabilities
Theory and Practice
David Thomas and Honor Woods
ISBN 978 1 85302 973 8

Deinstitutionalization and People with Intellectual Disabilities
In and Out of Institutions
Edited by Kelley Johnson and Rannveig Traustadóttir
ISBN 978 1 84310 101 7

Inclusive Research with People with Learning Disabilities
Past, Present and Futures
Jan Walmsley and Kelley Johnson
ISBN 978 1 84310 061 4

Quality of Life and Disability
An Approach for Community Practitioners
Ivan Brown and Roy I. Brown
Foreword by Ann and Rud Turnbull
ISBN 978 1 84310 005 8

Guide to Mental Health for Families and Carers of People with Intellectual Disabilities
Geraldine Holt, Anastasia Gratsa, Nick Bouras, Teresa Joyce, Mary Jane Spiller and Steve Hardy
ISBN 978 1 84310 277 9

Advocacy and Learning Disability
Edited by Barry Gray and Robin Jackson
ISBN 978 1 85302 942 4

Women With Intellectual Disabilities
Finding a Place in the World
Edited by Rannveig Traustadóttir and Kelley Johnson
ISBN 978 1 85302 846 5

Sexuality and Women with Learning Disabilities
Michelle McCarthy
ISBN 978 1 85302 730 7

Person Centred Planning and Care Management with People with Learning Disabilities

Edited by

Paul Cambridge and Steven Carnaby

Jessica Kingsley Publishers
London and Philadelphia

First published in 2005
by Jessica Kingsley Publishers
116 Pentonville Road
London N1 9JB, UK
and
400 Market Street, Suite 400
Philadelphia, PA 19106, USA

www.jkp.com

Library of Congress Cataloging in Publication Data
Person centred planning and care management with people with learning disabilities / edited by Paul Cambridge and Steven Carnaby.
p. cm.
Includes bibliographical references and indexes.
ISBN-13: 978-1-84310-131-4 (pbk. : alk. paper)
ISBN-10: 1-84310-131-9 (pbk. : alk. paper) 1. People with mental disabilities—Services for. 2. Learning disabled—Services for. I. Cambridge, Paul, 1952- II. Carnaby, Steven.

HV3004.P434 2005
362.3'8—dc22

2005010933

British Library Cataloguing in Publication Data
A CIP catalogue record for this book is available from the British Library

ISBN 978 1 84310 131 4

Contents

List of Tables

List of Figures

CHAPTER 1

Introduction and Overview

Paul Cambridge and Steven Carnaby

This book aims to be a departure from the discourse on person centred planning (PCP) developed since its promotion in *Valuing People* (Department of Health 2001) and subsequent implementation by the *Valuing People* Support Team. Indeed, it is a departure from the tendency to see person-centred systems in services as isolated from each other. This most evidently includes other micro-organisational arrangements such as care management and micro-budgeting arrangements such as direct payments, but also wider systems and processes at the macro-organisational level such as purchasing and commissioning. These broader issues include among others inspection and service standards, adult protection, risk management and partnership working. All such arrangements have potential relevance to how PCP works and what it can achieve for individual service users as well as for services for people with learning disabilities more widely.

Valuing People made the link between care management and person centred planning explicit and observed that organisations and their cultures would also need to change if person centred planning and services were to work well:

> care management will continue to be the formal mechanism for linking individuals with public services. Its systems must be responsive to person-centred planning and have the capacity to deliver the kinds of individualised services likely to emerge from the process. (Department of Health 2001, p.50)

However, it left social services departments and learning disability partnership boards to decide on the nature, form and extent of any relationship. *Valuing People* also recognised the need for wider systems links, stating that person centred planning must 'link effectively with other plans including vocational plans, Health Action Plans, housing plans and communication plans' (Department of Health 2001, p.50).

Such plans are also generally person-centred and should connect with PCP. They may also require systems level resourcing, suggesting important links with care management and commissioning more widely.

In exploring the links between person centred planning and care management and in reviewing ways productive PCP and care management can be taken forward, this book highlights the important role individual practitioners and managers play in making systems work well and in implementing change effectively. We believe that service managers and practitioners cannot hope to develop person-centred services simply through *introducing* the device of PCP, however that happens to be defined. Individualised or person-centred approaches are needed on a number of fronts in our work with and support of people with learning disabilities – individualised communication, advocacy and self-determination and the development of positive self-images and learning disabled identities. At one level it is evident that PCP cannot successfully operate in isolation of other work and at another that it has the potential to provide a vehicle or at least a route for fostering person-centred initiatives and action. User participation is now not only desirable or feasible, but essential at all levels of service and resource organisation, providing a prerequisite to successful PCP and a wide range of user outcomes developing from PCP. Chapters in this book are dedicated to promoting such an ethos and provide individual service and user case studies to illustrate how collaborative development and partnerships with service users can promote PCP and person-centred action.

One of the objectives in commissioning and collating the wide range of material presented here was to balance a general overview of PCP and care management with an exploration of key themes relevant to their joint operation and relationship. By using a combination of chapters looking at issues of structure and process, best practice case studies and key issues for implementation we wanted to generate useful lessons by encouraging contributors to share their ideas for policy and practice development. To be useful beyond learning about an effective way to work with and support a particular service user, lessons need to be transferable from one individual to another, from one set of local circumstances to another and from one service system to another. They also need to be generalisable at the policy level while remaining relevant to local practice and individual supports. As such they also need to be capable of being widely disseminated and specifically fed back to those involved in implementing and developing PCP in order to improve practice and achieve desired outcomes and goals. These include increased participation and decision-making by people with learning disabilities in addition to final outcomes such as improvements in people's quality of life, self-esteem, life satisfaction and self-determination.

Two common but polarised assumptions are often made when hearing about the work of others. These are that successful work from elsewhere can simply be replicated and that learning from individual cases or situations can be readily transferred. The messages in this book contradict both of these assumptions. We assert that much can be achieved if our practice is informed by an effective and thorough review of the evidence and circumstances, alongside the will to implement positive change. This is why most of our own research and that of others at the Tizard Centre is applied in its nature. We also recognise that evidence-led change is not always easy to achieve in services for people with learning disabilities, particularly with service organisations where institutionalised practices, set expectations or conventional attitudes predominate. All service users are individuals experiencing unique circumstances and, while this limits the transfer of learning, we also have the capacity to interpret differences and build constructive lessons.

This book therefore sets out not only to illustrate what can be achieved, but also how to achieve positive change. Our work as researchers, practitioners and service managers has amply demonstrated that PCP and care management are concepts about which we have much accumulated knowledge and experience – albeit redefined within the new policy paradigm of inclusion and the new language of person-centred services. Twelve years ago the Care in the Community initiative expected individual care planning (ICP) or individual programme planning (IPP), along with care management, to be part of each service, helping develop individual services and user choice but also as a means to manage the transition of individuals and resources from long-stay hospitals to community-based provisions (Cambridge, Hayes and Knapp 1994, Cambridge *et al.* 2002; Knapp *et al.* 1992). Yet even under a central policy spotlight, individual planning and care management developed in a variety of ways, based on ideologies, management and professional imperatives, operational expediency and wider demands from outside the service system (Cambridge 1992; Renshaw 1987).

We face a similar challenge now with PCP and care management. When measured against the original care management experiments in England (Challis and Davies 1986; Challis *et al.* 1990; Davies and Challis 1986), a wide diversity in care management practice emerged following its mainstreaming in the 1990 community care reforms (Department of Health 1989, Department of Health/Social Services Inspectorate 1991), including learning disability (Cambridge 1999; Cambridge *et al.*, in press). Care management has shifted from a carefully constructed intervention and process, where care managers conduct a series of core tasks with limited caseloads, to a general policy instrument where care management has become demand driven, determined by administrative factors and constrained by resources.

Unless we scrutinise and review the implementation of PCP long term we are likely to find ourselves in a similar situation, where approaches to PCP diversify and proliferate outside an understanding of the advantages and disadvantages of different approaches. We need to ensure that PCP is not hijacked by self-interested organisational or professional agendas, and that its potential is not deflected. While there are possibilities for an efficient and effective interdependence between PCP and care management, with care management providing a sound foundation, there is also a risk that care management will distort, dilute or at worst corrupt PCP. We discuss the possibilities and potentials of such a relationship in more detail in Chapter 14.

The last decade or so of community care has seen the development and implementation of a collection of variously named arrangements for placing service users at the centre of services or service planning at both micro- and macro-levels. These principally evolved from and had their roots in the philosophies of normalisation/social role valorisation (Wolfensberger 1972, 1980), an ordinary life (King's Fund Centre 1980), the five service accomplishments (O'Brien and Tyne 1981) and more recently the more ostensibly political notion of social inclusion (Department of Health 2001). They centred on or promoted lifestyle or cultural themes such as housing, community integration, participation, friendships and social networks, personal relationships and sexuality, skills and independence and so on – all things which remain important for everyone but which can also be introduced through PCP and its outcomes. We have over two decades of experience working to these traditions and it would be irresponsible not to take account of our accumulated experience in providing community support and developing person-centred work in implementing and reviewing PCP.

Some of the issues stemming from this body of work are indeed systemic – for example, the tension between resource-led care management and professional advocacy, the vulnerability of the service user within the contract culture and the tendency to see care management or individual planning as a device for organisations rather than service users (Cambridge and Brown 1997). Such conflicts have become evident in the very different approaches to and arrangements for care management in services for people with learning disabilities (Cambridge 1992, 1999; Cambridge *et al.*, in press) and, in relation to PCP, apparent in individual care planning arrangements in services for people with learning disabilities (Carnaby 1997, 1999).

While no one book or study can hope to address and resolve all such issues and questions, especially when those involved in developing and implementing PCP are only just beginning to learn from their experiences, the material presented here has been developed to help us make a start.

This book is structured into three parts. Part One in some ways can be seen as the heart of the discussion, as it examines the structural and process considerations underlying PCP and care management. Chapter 2 by Jim Mansell and Julie Beadle-Brown provides a baseline perspective on PCP and person-centred action, reviewing the policy location and practice and research evidence on person centred planning arrangements. This makes for helpful scene setting and an important reference point for later chapters. The authors discuss issues relating to the effectiveness of planning systems, the potential gaps between noted descriptions of planning models and their implementation and finally describe their vision for how services can achieve person-centredness in tangible ways.

Chapter 3 by Simon Duffy and Helen Sanderson explores the potential relationships between PCP and care management, as the authors debate ways in which care managers can support and enhance service user empowerment rather than hinder its development. Much of this discussion requires clarity with regard to the mechanisms of resource allocation and its distinction from the co-ordination of support, and this discourse is well articulated here. Central to the chapter's material is the proposal that an 'exchange model' of assessment, as described by Gerry Smale, is more likely to lead to a person-centred understanding of what support is needed. Duffy and Sanderson go on to discuss a 'Five Gear Model' of person-centred care management practice and propose that its adoption has the potential to yield radical results.

In Chapter 4, Tony Osgood combines personal experience with a review of the literature on individual planning and person-centred approaches to discuss the tensions between service-led and person-led cultures. Through the use of vivid case material and valuable insight, he gives an honest, frank account of the risks involved when services take up the language of PCP without managing to achieve genuine change.

Building on this foundation, Part Two takes the discussion points raised in these early chapters by focusing on best practice experience in PCP and care management. These middle chapters draw on service development experience and initiatives from across England. In their account of user involvement in Chapter 5, Doris Clark, Robert Garland and Val Williams outline an approach from the most important perspective of all – that of people for whom the rhetoric and practice of PCP is primarily intended. Privileged with these personal accounts of clearly effective person centred planning and support, we are able to see the merits of an approach that is seen to be listening to people in meaningful, non-tokenistic ways and, as importantly, enables action to be taken with regard to what has been heard. The very creation of the partnerships required to write the chapter also provides key messages in empowerment and real participation by people with learning disabilities in the PCP debate.

The concept of meaningful participation is also central to Chapter 6, which looks at involving young people with learning disabilities in their own transition plans. Steven Carnaby and Patricia Lewis report on the ways in which one particular school decided to review its approach to transition planning. In finding itself lacking in terms of effective, person-centred practice, the school set itself the task of developing a range of techniques and strategies to ensure higher levels of individual participation in the transition process. The chapter provides a number of innovative ideas for making the challenging time of leaving school less threatening and more empowering.

In Chapter 7, David Dick and Karin Purvis look at how the development of total communication can contribute to the PCP process. Using their experiences in Somerset as their material, the authors discuss the potential obstacles to establishing a culture that is committed to person-centredness and helpfully provide valuable ideas for how these obstacles can be addressed at a number of levels – both across and within organisations.

Jill Bradshaw in Chapter 8 explores the centrality of communication to PCP in more depth. She uses the experiences of a number of speech and language therapists in a range of services to discuss the importance of acknowledging the complexities involved in working with people with additional sensory disabilities, as well as other complex needs such as challenging behaviour or dementia. In an engaging and realistic account of the issues involved, Bradshaw emphasises the importance of careful assessment from communication partners who are able to commit time and resources to making the communication partnership work. The examples of good practice presented illustrate how these values and commitments can be made a reality when given adequate organisational support.

In Chapter 9, Robina Shah asks questions regarding an understanding of issues relating to ethnicity and culture that go to the very heart of what this book is trying to say about person centred planning and approaches. Her observations are enormously helpful and need to be read as underpinning all of the other chapters if those responsible for leading and supporting services are genuinely working with the individual in mind. In discussing the experiences of 'E', Shah states:

> 'Same' is not equal so the 'E' story goes
> Discrimination and racism still flow
> But what matters too is that 'E' is entwined
> With person centred planning both yours and mine!

Part Three of this book moves on to examine key issues for the development and implementation of PCP. First, Hector Medora and Sue Ledger in Chapter 10 provide an interesting case study of a systems approach to implementation and share useful experiences of a pilot study that highlights the need to drive concept of person-centredness throughout an organisation at every level. Their detailed discussion of implementation informed by prior reflection on values and outcomes suggests the need to look at existing processes and systems and consider how they can be reconfigured to meet the criteria required, rather than assuming that wholesale reinvention has to take place.

In Chapter 11, Julie Beadle-Brown reviews the relationship between PCP and direct payments, and gives a clear account of the barriers to take-up. She suggests that with greater creativity and flexibility within an expanded care management system, more individuals would be able to access this model and arguably achieve a more empowered lifestyle as a consequence. Clearly, the phenomenon of direct payments is still in its relative infancy with regards to research and the establishment of best practice, but this chapter does point us in the direction of available examples.

Helen and Andy Alaszewski look at risk management and PCP in Chapter 12. After reviewing the history and context of risk in the lives of people with learning disabilities, the authors discuss the role of PCP in enabling and supporting discussions and decision-making around risk. The authors show how the individualised nature of risk assessment and management is well aligned with the spirit of PCP, and also suggest that risk needs to be considered using a combination of PCP and other aspects of risk management such as health and safety.

Adult protection processes and the role of PCP are then examined by Hilary Brown and Karen Scott in Chapter 13. Here the emphasis is on the potential and limitations of PCP in this area, and the chapter uses pertinent case material to draw out the key arguments. Essentially, the chapter suggests that there is a case for integrating safeguards into PCP as a strategy to prevent abuse and neglect. Importantly, the authors warn against the tendency to view 'protection' as a negative perspective when striving to pursue person-centred outcomes with people.

Our final chapter attempts to be reflective in tone, drawing on some of the lessons that our contributors have shown us and combining these insights with our own observations to form our concluding remarks. In essence, this discussion indicates that the relationships constructed between care management and person centred planning processes and approaches appear to hold considerable potential for people with learning disabilities – but that it is the creative and flexible use of this potential that is likely to lead to real empowerment of individuals. We hope that the chapters in this book go some way in inspiring and aiding those charged with the task of ensuring that PCP achieves its stated goals.

REFERENCES

Cambridge, P. (1992) 'Case management in community-based services: organisational responses.' *British Journal of Social Work 22*, 495–517.

Cambridge, P. (1999) 'Building care management competence in services for people with learning disabilities.' *British Journal of Social Work 29*, 393–415.

Cambridge, P. and Brown, H. (1997) 'Making the market work for people with learning disabilities: an argument for principled contracting.' *Critical Social Policy 17*, 27–52.

Cambridge, P., Carpenter, J., Beecham, J., Hallam, A., Knapp, M., Forrester-Jones, R. and Tate, A. (2002) *'Twelve Years On': The Outcomes and Costs of Community Care for People with Learning Disabilities and Mental Health Problems.* Canterbury: Tizard/PSSRU/Durham, University of Kent at Canterbury.

Cambridge, P., Carpenter, J., Forrester-Jones, R., Tate, A., Knapp, M., Beecham, J. and Hallam, A. (in press) 'The state of care management in learning disability and mental health services twelve years into community care.' *British Journal of Social Work.*

Cambridge, P., Hayes, L. and Knapp, M. (1994) *Care in the Community – Five Years On.* Aldershot: Ashgate.

Carnaby, S. (1997) 'What do *you* think?: evaluating an established individual planning service for people with learning disabilities using qualitative methods.' *Journal of Intellectual Disability Research 41*, 3, 225–231.

Carnaby, S. (1999) 'Individual programme planning: where is the "individual"?' *Tizard Learning Disability Review 4*, 3, 4–9.

Challis, D., Chessum, R., Chesterman, J., Luckett, R. and Traske, K. (1990) *Case Management in Social and Health Care.* Canterbury: University of Kent, Personal Social Services Research Unit.

Challis, D. and Davies, B. (1986) *Case Management in Community Care.* Aldershot: Gower.

Davies, B. and Challis, D. (1986) *Matching Resources to Needs in Community Care.* Aldershot: Gower.

Department of Health/Social Services Inspectorate (1991) *Care Management and Assessment: Managers' Guide.* London: HMSO.

Department of Health (1989) *Caring for People.* London: HMSO.

Department of Health (2001) *Valuing People: A New Strategy for Learning Disability for the 21st Century.* London: Department of Health.

King's Fund Centre (1980) *An Ordinary Life: Comprehensive Locally-Based Residential Services for Mentally Handicapped People.* London: King's Fund Centre.

Knapp, M., Cambridge, P., Thomason, C., Beecham, J., Allen, C. and Darton, R. (1992) *Care in the Community: Challenge and Demonstration.* Aldershot: Ashgate.

O'Brien, J. and Tyne, A. (1981) *The Principle of Normalisation: A Foundation for Effective Services.* London: The Campaign for Mentally Handicapped People.

Renshaw, J. (1987) 'Care in the community: individual care planning and case management.' *British Journal of Social Work 18*, 79–105.

Wolfensberger, W. (1972) *The Principle of Normalisation in Human Services.* Toronto: National Institute on Mental Retardation.

Wolfensberger, W. (1980) 'The definition of normalisation: update, problems, disagreements and misunderstandings.' In R.J. Flynn and K.E. Nitsch (eds) *Normalisation, Social Integration and Community Services.* Baltimore: University Park Press.

Part 1

CHAPTER 2

Person Centred Planning and Person-Centred Action

A Critical Perspective

Jim Mansell and Julie Beadle-Brown

INTRODUCTION

Person centred planning (PCP) formed a central component of the 2001 White Paper *Valuing People* in England. The White Paper identified person centred planning as central to delivering the government's four key principles (rights, independence, choice and inclusion) and a high priority for management attention and resources.

> Given the importance of person-centred planning as a tool for achieving change, we will make supporting its implementation one of the priorities for the Learning Disability Development Fund and the Implementation Support Team. (Department of Health 2001b, p.50)

Guidance issued subsequently (Department of Health 2001a) was intended to create a large-scale programme of training and implementation. The White Paper set out an ambitious programme of targets for the introduction of PCP (figures, unless otherwise indicated, from *Valuing People* (Department of Health 2001b)).

By April 2002 the Learning Disability Partnership Boards were to agree a local framework. By 2003 'specific priorities' were set for:

- people still living in long-stay hospitals (about 1500 people)
- young people moving from children's to adult services (number not known).

By 2004 'significant progress' was expected for:

- people using large day centres (about 50,000 people)
- people living in the family home with carers aged over 70 (about 29,000 people (Mencap 2002))
- people living on NHS residential campuses (about 1500 people).

Developed over nearly 30 years in the USA, PCP is represented by a family of approaches and techniques which share certain characteristics (O'Brien and O'Brien 2000). It is intended to reflect the unique circumstances of the individual person with learning disabilities both in assessing and in organising what should be done. It shares this with other approaches adopted in learning disability services, such as individual programme plans (Accreditation Council on Services for Mentally Retarded and Other Developmentally Disabled Persons 1983; Blunden 1980; Houts and Scott 1975; Jenkins *et al.* 1988) or individual service plans (Brost *et al.* 1982; Emerson *et al.* 1987), as well as with case management methods adopted across many client groups (Challis and Davies 1986).

In distinction to these approaches, however, PCP emphasises three other characteristics. First, it aims to consider aspirations and capacities expressed by the service user or those speaking on his or her behalf, rather than needs and deficiencies. This emphasis on the authority of the service user's voice reflects dissatisfaction with the perceived failure of professionals to attend to what matters most to service users, the extent to which services are seen to constrain or impose goals (Crocker 1990; O'Brien and Lovett 1992) and the observation that services sometimes create artificial hurdles between goals in an inappropriate 'readiness model' (Wilcox and Bellamy 1987) or 'developmental continuum' (Taylor 1988).

Second, PCP attempts to include and mobilise the individual's family and wider social network, as well as to use resources from the system of statutory services. This partly reflects the special interest that family and friends have. Sanderson (2000) suggests that families in particular have a stake in the arrangements made to support an individual with learning disabilities in a way that service employees do not. Mobilising the service user's social network is also intended to deepen and broaden the range of resources available to help him or her. The social network is seen as a richer source of imagination, creativity and resources than the service system, especially in forming and maintaining social relationships, where learning disability services are seen as weak (Emerson and Hatton 1994).

The third distinctive characteristic is that PCP emphasises providing the support required to achieve goals, rather than limiting goals to what services typically can manage to achieve.

> Person centred planning assumes that people with disabilities are ready to do whatever they want as long as they are adequately supported. The 'readiness model' is replaced with the 'support model' which acknowledges that everyone needs support and some people need more support than others. (Sanderson 2000)

Taken together, these three characteristics are presented as making a fundamental break with previous methods of individual planning:

> It is not simply a collection of new techniques for planning to replace Individual Programme Planning. It is based on a completely different way of seeing and working with people with disabilities, which is fundamentally about sharing power and community inclusion. (Sanderson 2000)

ASSESSING THE POLICY INITIATIVE

There is now no serious alternative to the principle that services should be tailored to individual needs, circumstances and wants. The individualisation of service organisation over the last 30 years has been accompanied by the development of assessment and planning tools, from early work on goal planning (Houts and Scott 1975) through to care management (Challis and Davies 1986). However, it has also been accompanied by the investment of much greater resources in service provision and by new, smaller-scale services in the community (Mansell and Ericsson 1996). Greater individualisation in practice may, therefore, be the result of a number of different aspects of the great changes in service provision, acting alone or together. It may owe at least as much, for example, to changes in the attitudes of staff and the kinds of services provided as it does to particular methods of planning.

Assessment of the weight given to PCP in the 2001 White Paper *Valuing People* therefore requires an evaluation of the contribution made by planning systems as distinct from other changes in service organisation (i.e. answering the question 'are individual plans effective?'). If PCP is not likely to deliver the benefits required in terms of individualising services and driving their redevelopment, then its adoption as a central plank of the policy would be a problem. In particular, the diversion of large amounts of time, effort and money into switching from existing planning systems to PCP could not be justified if this turns out to be 'more of the same'.

The scale of the task

The first source of caution in assessing the emphasis given to PCP in the White Paper is the scale of the task involved. This is an extremely ambitious policy, and not just because of the number of people involved. The population of people with learning disabilities includes many individuals with very severe problems, which are likely to hinder or impede the development and maintenance of relationships with other people, making the maintenance of effective PCP difficult. For example, a study of adults in residential care (Mansell *et al.* 2002) found that 43 per cent had major communication difficulties, 63 per cent had impaired social interaction and 35 per cent had severe challenging behaviour. Each of these, alone and in combination with others, presents substantial difficulties. For example, there is evidence that staff often misjudge the receptive language ability of people with learning disabilities (Bradshaw 2001; McConkey, Morris and Purcell 1999; Purcell, Morris and McConkey 1999). Thus, in presenting and discussing options in the context of a PCP meeting, staff (and perhaps others too) risk failing to explain possible courses of action adequately. Similarly, the extent to which people with learning disabilities can understand choices and decisions is often limited and requires careful assessment (Arscott, Dagnan and Kroese 1999; Murphy and Clare 1995). The nature of the difficulties experienced by the individual service user may also interfere with PCP. For example, aggression or self-injurious behaviour often result in negative emotional consequences for staff (Emerson and Hatton 2000; Hastings 1995), which may make it more difficult to empathise with the individual or to identify feasible means to achieve their goals.

None of these characteristics is, in itself, insuperable, and individual case illustrations (e.g. O'Brien and Mount 1989) show that, irrespective of the level of learning disability or the nature of additional problems, people with learning disabilities can have close personal relationships; but the studies cited indicate the scale of the difficulty to be overcome.

Given the nature and extent of these problems it is not surprising that many people with learning disabilities are extremely socially isolated. Studies of people in residential settings, for example, often show low levels of contact from other staff and other residents, particularly for people with severe and profound learning disabilities (Emerson and Hatton 1994; Felce and Perry 1995; Mansell 1994). Cambridge *et al.* (2001) found that, on average, people living in the community 12 years after deinstitutionalisation had very limited social networks compared to the wider population. They found that only 19 per cent of members of these networks were unrelated to learning disability services. Robertson *et al.* (2001) found even smaller networks. Building the 'circle of support' around an individual to undertake is therefore likely to be difficult for many people in the White Paper target groups.

A third reservation about the scale of the task implied in the White Paper is the general difficulty in modern society of developing and sustaining relationships of the kind required. The language of PCP is the language of reciprocity, mutual interdependence and community. However, community in this sense is scarcer in reality than it is in rhetoric. As Bulmer (1987) points out, the most convincing general explanation of the nature of caring relationships is reciprocity. What sustains and nurtures helping relationships among people who are not kin is a sense of exchange and balance in the relationship. Here, people with very substantial disabilities face a particular problem, in that they may have great difficulty maintaining the sense of balance required in the relationship. Qureshi, Challis and Davies (1989) note the importance of payment to community care helpers as a way of enabling recipients of care to feel that this balance is maintained. This represents a further potential problem in the recruitment of effective circles of support.

Are individual plans effective?

As Kinsella (2000) points out, there is almost no evidence of the effectiveness of PCP compared to other approaches. What evidence there is largely comprises individual case studies referred to in the course of commentaries on the process and its desirability (e.g. Certo *et al.* 1997; Department of Health 2001a; Everson and Reid 1997; O'Brien and Mount 1989). A systematic review by Rudkin and Rowe (1999) found no statistically significant outcome differences with good statistical power for people receiving PCP.

Despite the lack of an evidence base, there are studies of other forms of individualised planning which share some characteristics with PCP. These include studies of individual programme plans in learning disability services, studies of care management arrangements and studies of the individualised planning process in special educational needs.

What these studies show, first, is that in practice individual planning only reaches a minority of service users. An inspection of day services by the British Social Services Inspectorate (1989) found that only 25 per cent of service users had an individual programme plan on file. Felce *et al.* (1998) report that during the implementation of the All-Wales Strategy for learning disability services the highest level of individual plan coverage achieved was only 33 per cent of service users. Problems in resourcing the level of individual planning required are also evident in special education – where despite a legal mandate, half of education authorities fail to achieve the 18-week target for production of a plan (Audit Commission 1998) – and in care management, where failure to hold effective reviews has been identified as a common problem area (Challis 1999).

Where individual plans are created, they are often found to be a paper exercise. The Social Services Inspectorate (1989) found evidence that plans were in case notes but not necessarily used. Radcliffe and Hegarty (2001) found that in two and three cases out of eight they studied in 1998 and 1999 individual plan goals were not translated into the daily programme of support to service users. Cambridge (1999) suggests that administrative interests predominate in care management assessment, with evidence of standard assessments that do not address the particular needs of people with learning disabilities (Challis 1999).

There is also evidence from several larger-scale evaluations that individual plans are not well-connected to the real lives of people using services. Shaddock and Bramston (1991) found serious deficiencies in the planning process in 50 plans drawn from group homes for people with developmental disabilities. Clients, relatives and advocates were often not present when goals were set. Long-term goals were often omitted. Typically, goals and objectives were not written in specific measurable terms, criteria were not stated, and the conditions under which the behaviour should occur were omitted. Cummins *et al.* (1994) found that 19 per cent of plans for 199 people had no review date and 30 per cent of meetings were not attended by any family, friends or advocates of the individual service user. In a later study, Cummins *et al.* (1996) analysed 163 plans from 11 community living support services. The average level of presentation was poor. Only 14 per cent offered any criterion for evaluating performance objectives, the average number of skill-building objectives was 3.25 per plan, and only 39 per cent of plans were current. Adams, Beadle-Brown and Mansell (submitted) compared 18 people who had functional individual programme plans with 18 who did not and found no difference between the groups in satisfaction, observed levels of engagement or records of participation in activity. Stancliffe, Hayden and Lakin (1999) evaluated plan objectives for 126 adults with mental retardation living in institutional or community settings and found no significant change in outcomes associated with having an objective. Miner and Bates (1997) found that participation in PCP increased the extent to which parents or guardians contributed to individual educational planning or transition planning meetings. These families perceived that meetings were more favourable and almost all rated PCP as valuable and effective, although there was no difference in their satisfaction with the meeting.

Thus, case studies suggest that PCP can be valuable and may change the perception of participants. There are no good-quality, systematic evaluations of PCP, but since PCP shares many characteristics with previous attempts at individual planning, evidence from these is relevant. This evidence suggests that when implemented on a large scale, there are problems with coverage, quality and outcomes. These findings should caution against believing that PCP will be any different. In order to achieve greater individualisation of service organisation and delivery, it is therefore important to analyse why earlier attempts at individual planning appear to have failed.

WHY DO INDIVIDUAL PLANS FAIL?

Resource constraints

A recurrent theme in reviews of care management is that an important factor shaping the operation of such individualised planning systems is the need for service organisations to control expenditure (Challis 1999). In the absence of effective financial information systems enabling devolved budgets, the freedom for care managers to design individually tailored arrangements is likely to be constrained. This appears to be achieved through the introduction of waiting lists, the use of standardised procedures for assessment (*prix fixe* rather than *à la carte*), the bureaucratisation of management processes and the reservation of funding decisions to higher-level managers removed from direct contact with service users.

An important factor in the British context may be that, unlike in the USA, individualised service plans are not legally mandated. The scope for redress if aspirations are ignored or subverted is therefore very limited. Even in British special education, where there is a legally enforceable right to a plan, delay and a restricted range of options appear to have been used to ration resources. Administrative culture may therefore be as important as legal entitlement in promoting meaningful individual planning.

If cost control intrudes in this way the implication is that simply changing the style of planning, from whatever went before to PCP, is unlikely to make any difference. It would be expected that if PCP became at all widespread, mechanisms would be developed to constrain it within financial limits. One particular risk that PCP presents in this respect is that it explicitly embraces the idea that informal care is important and possibly even preferable to formal service provision. Thus it opens up the possibility for service agencies to define activities that they would previously have funded as now the responsibility of the 'circle of support'. There is some evidence from the care management literature of emotional support and counselling not being provided even though identified as areas of need in their own right (Challis 1999), which might reflect rationing judgements that some kinds of services are not to be provided by the formal sector.

This suggests that the failure of individual planning might not primarily be due to lack of understanding or to the particular kind of planning approach used, but is instead a by-product of the need for public agencies to control their budgets. In this sense, failure may serve the true purpose of the organisations involved.

Implementation gap

A second feature evident in evaluation of individual plans is what might be called the *implementation gap* – the failure to carry through plans into practice. Although the evidence is limited because so few studies have addressed outcomes – real changes in the lives of the people with learning disabilities studied – there are sufficient grounds in the literature cited to be concerned that (or any other kind of individual planning) is largely a paper exercise.

The explanation for this implicit in the White Paper *Valuing People* is that there is insufficient understanding, so that the logical reform is thought to be more training in how to do . The alternative formulation given above is that lack of resources prevents implementation and undermines the motivation to take planning seriously. In addition, there is another aspect of individual planning which may help explain its limitations in practice; that is, the relationship between objective setting and the skills and daily practice of staff providing support.

There is extensive evidence that front-line staff working with people with learning disabilities, especially people with severe and profound learning disabilities, typically provide little in the way of facilitative assistance to support engagement in meaningful activity at home and in the community (Emerson and Hatton 1994; Perry and Felce 2003). In consequence, levels of engagement are low, with related evidence that people do not continue to develop and grow in competence in adult life (Cambridge *et al.* 2001) and have restricted social networks and relationships. Only a small proportion of these staff are trained (Ward 1999), and recent government initiatives acknowledge this and include attempts to increase training substantially (Department of Health 2001c, 2002). Therefore, if individual plan goals are developed which involve providing skilled support to the individual (for example, in accessing unfamiliar places and situations, or in coping with much higher levels of stress and demand) it is likely that staff will not be able to provide sufficiently skilled help for people with more complex needs.

Thus, where goals have resource implications – moving from a residential home to supported living, for example – expenditure constraints may prevent their achievement. Where they are concerned with changing individual experience without major new resources – such as helping a person with severely challenging behaviour to shop more independently – skill shortages among staff may do so. Both situations are likely to lead to individual planning becoming a paper exercise with little impact on real life. In a sense, staff working through these processes in services are once again in the grip of a 'readiness' model, not for the client but for the service: 'We are waiting until the person gets a new home/job/we get training/policy changes/we are reorganised.' In this situation, individualised planning becomes a kind of displacement activity, using staff energy, time and resources but not making any difference to people's lives.

Is a new kind of planning going to change this? Is pushing investment into training lots of people to make individual planning person-centred the best use of resources?

WHAT WOULD IT TAKE TO MAKE SERVICES MORE PERSON-CENTRED?

The implication of this analysis is that making British services more person-centred will not result from attempts to achieve the widespread introduction of a new model of individual planning. Instead, it directs attention to the way services are funded and to the skills of front-line staff.

Taking funding first, there are several ways, which are not mutually exclusive, in which to strengthen the hand of the individual service user against social services departments in determining the goals and implementation of any individual plan:

1. *Give PCP legal weight.*
   This might be based on legal entitlement to fair, humane and effective treatment based on a constitution or on human rights legislation. This would allow individual service users to challenge failure to provide services to help them achieve what they want and to test the decisions of public agencies in terms of their reasonableness. As British special education experience shows, legal entitlements are not everything; but in those countries where they exist there is evidence of them being used to secure improved services.
2. *Decouple funding decisions from individual planning.*
   This could be done by replacing local budgets managed to a fixed level, with social security entitlements based on assessed status. This would give service users with disabilities of a set degree an absolute entitlement to a particular level of funding; it would refocus individual planning arrangements in social services departments on the content of the plan and on helping people achieve better lives, instead of on rationing.
3. *Make more use of direct payments and user-controlled trusts/independent living trusts.*
   This is especially so for people with severe learning disabilities as well as those with more mild disabilities. This would potentially empower service users in achieving their individual plan, providing more security and consistency of service (in that, once agreed, it is harder

for a direct payment to be taken away or reduced in amount without evidence of mismanagement of the direct payment). However, for this to happen, local authorities need to be more open to the possibility of trust-managed direct payments.

4. *Use national policy to support achievement of personal goals.*
National policy could be used to set expectations that personal goals and plans would be resourced and achieved, instead of maintaining an equivocal stance that asserts on the one hand that person-centredness is a high priority but avoids, on the other, holding local social services departments to account for its delivery.

5. *Focus performance management on quality not quantity.*
Government could focus not on numbers of plans produced, but on the quality of the plans and the extent to which they are implemented. The focus of policy implementation and monitoring could shift from person centred *planning* to person-centred *action*. This would be likely to require a shift from a rationalist policy implementation framework, in which implementation is treated as a largely mechanical process, to focus on real effects in the lives of the people served and the development of expertise and creativity along the way.

Paying attention to quality – to person-centred action – directs attention to the quality of work of staff providing support and advice to people with learning disabilities and their families. Whatever national policy says, it is these staff who make it a reality or not. Here too there are several steps that could be taken to make services more person-centred.

1. *Focus training on action.*
Training in the goals of service provision could emphasise action that makes a tangible difference in the daily lives of people with learning disabilities as a priority, and distinguish this from action that is consistent with appropriate values but does not actually lead to change. This is likely to require a balance to be struck between relatively ordinary and more special activities. Ordinary, even mundane activities, which occur frequently and do not necessarily require great resources to change (but from which many people with learning disabilities are excluded through lack of appropriate staff support), may be important opportunities for personal growth, development and empowerment. The kind of dramatic, difficult, expensive activities which are often identified as important (because of the belief that they will transform expectations about individual people with learning disabilities) do not necessarily have much impact beyond the event itself.

2. *Focus training on facilitating change rather than planning.*
   Staff training could focus more on ways of facilitating real change for people with learning disabilities, instead of on individual planning systems. For staff with care management responsibilities, these would include brokerage skills. For those providing or managing direct support to individuals, these would be likely to include approaches such as active support (Felce, Jones and Lowe 2000) and positive behaviour support (Kincaid and Fox 2000). These approaches help staff develop skills to facilitate greater participation in activities and relationships by people with complex needs.
3. *Focus supervision on* real *change; not plans.*
   The supervision and monitoring of the quality of support provided by staff to the people they serve could focus on real changes in the everyday lives of people rather than on plans and planning.

These changes would be entirely consistent with the aspiration of proponents of PCP, that it should be a process of 'continual listening, and learning; focused on what is important to someone now, and for the future; and acting upon this in alliance with their family and friends' in which 'having meetings, involving the person and making the plan is not the outcome. The outcome is to help the person to get a better life on her own terms' (Sanderson 2000, p.4). They also reflect the concern of some (Black 2000) that making PCP a prescription in national policy is unlikely to produce the changes wanted in the lives of individual people with learning disabilities. As O'Brien and O'Brien (2000) point out:

> Agencies that want to benefit from person-centered planning often act as if person-centered planning were a sort of tool box of techniques which staff could be trained to use in workshops by studying protocols, hearing about ideas, and perhaps trying out a technique or even two for homework. Such context-free training no doubt teaches something, but we think it deprives learners of the kinds of social supports for inventive action that were available to the people who developed the first approaches to person-centered planning.

ACKNOWLEDGEMENTS

This chapter was developed from a paper published in 2004 in volume 17 of the *Journal of Applied Research in Intellectual Disabilities* entitled 'Person-centred planning or person-centred action? Policy and practice in intellectual disability services'.

REFERENCES

Accreditation Council on Services for Mentally Retarded and Other Developmentally Disabled Persons (1983) *Standards for Services for Developmentally Disabled Individuals.* Chicago: Joint Commission on Accreditation of Hospitals.

Adams, L., Beadle-Brown, J. and Mansell, J. (submitted) 'Individual planning: an exploration of the link between quality of plan and quality of life.'

Arscott, K., Dagnan, D. and Kroese, B.S. (1999) 'Assessing the ability of people with a learning disability to give informed consent to treatment.' *Psychological Medicine 29,* 6, 1367–1375.

Audit Commission (1998) *Getting in on the Act: A Review of Progress on Special Educational Needs.* London: Audit Commission.

Black, P. (2000) 'Why aren't person centred approaches and planning happening for as many people and as well as we would like?' www.doh.gov.uk/vpst/pcp.htm

Blunden, R. (1980) *Individual Plans for Mentally Handicapped People: A Procedural Guide.* Cardiff: Mental Handicap in Wales Applied Research Unit.

Bradshaw, J. (2001) 'Complexity of staff communication and reported level of understanding skills in adults with intellectual disability.' *Journal of Intellectual Disability Research 45,* 3, 233–243.

Brost, M., Johnson, T.Z., Wagner, L. and Deprey, R.K. (1982) *Getting to Know You: One Approach to Service Assessment and Planning for Individuals with Disabilities.* Madison: Wisconsin Coalition for Advocacy.

Bulmer, M. (1987) *The Social Basis of Community Care.* London: Allen and Unwin.

Cambridge, P. (1999) 'The state of care management in services for people with mental retardation in the UK.' In N. Bouras (ed) *Psychiatric and Behavioural Disorders in Developmental Disabilities and Mental Retardation* (pp.391–411). New York: Cambridge University Press.

Cambridge, P., Carpenter, J., Beecham, J., Hallam, A., Knapp, M., Forrester-Jones, R. and Tate, A. (2001) *Twelve Years On: The Outcomes and Costs of Community Care for People with Learning Disabilities and Mental Health Problems.* Canterbury: Tizard Centre, University of Kent at Canterbury.

Certo, N.J., Lee, M., Mautz, D., Markey, L., Toney, L., Toney, K. and Smalley, K.A. (1997) 'Facilitating natural supports: assisting Lisa to connect with her dreams.' *Developmental Disabilities Bulletin 25,* 1, 27–42.

Challis, D. (1999) 'Assessment and care management: developments since the Community Care Reforms.' In Royal Commission on Long Term Care (ed) *With Respect to Old Age: Research* (Vol. Cm 4192-II/3). London: The Stationery Office.

Challis, D. and Davies, B. (1986) *Case Management in Community Care.* Aldershot: Gower.

Crocker, T.M. (1990) 'Assessing client participation in mental handicap services: a pilot study.' *British Journal of Mental Subnormality 36,* 2, 98–107.

Cummins, R.A., Baxter, C., Hudson, A. and Jauernig, R. (1996) 'A model system for the evaluation of Individual Program Plans.' *Journal of Intellectual and Developmental Disability 21,* 1, 59–70.

Cummins, R.A., Jauernig, R., Baxter, C. and Hudson, A. (1994) 'A model system for the construction and evaluation of General Service Plans.' *Australia and New Zealand Journal of Developmental Disabilities 19,* 3, 221–231.

Department of Health (2001a) *Planning with People: Towards Person Centred Approaches; Guidance for Implementation Groups.* London: Department of Health.

Department of Health (2001b) *Valuing People: A New Strategy for Learning Disability for the 21st Century* (Cm 5086). London: The Stationery Office.

Department of Health (2001c) *Valuing People: A New Strategy for Learning Disability for the 21st Century: Implementation* (HSC 2001/016: LAC (2001) 23). London: Department of Health.

Department of Health (2002) *Care Homes for Younger Adults and Adult Placements: National Minimum Standards: Care Homes Regulations.* London: The Stationery Office.

Emerson, E., Barrett, S., Bell, C., Cummings, R., McCool, C., Toogood, A. and Mansell, J. (1987) *Developing Services for People with Severe Learning Difficulties and Challenging Behaviours.* Canterbury: Institute of Social and Applied Psychology.

Emerson, E. and Hatton, C. (1994) *Moving Out: Relocation from Hospital to Community.* London: Her Majesty's Stationery Office.

Emerson, E. and Hatton, C. (2000) 'Violence against social care workers supporting people with learning difficulties: a review.' Unpublished.

Everson, J.M. and Reid, D.H. (1997) 'Using person-centered planning to determine employment preferences among people with the most severe developmental disabilities.' *Journal of Vocational Rehabilitation 9*, 2, 99–108.

Felce, D., Grant, G., Todd, S., Ramcharan, P., Beyer, S., McGrath, M., Perry, J., Shearn, J., Kilsby, M. and Lowe, K. (1998) *Towards a Full Life: Researching Policy Innovation for People with Learning Disabilities.* Oxford: Butterworth-Heinemann.

Felce, D., Jones, E. and Lowe, K. (2000) 'Active support: planning daily activities and support for people with severe mental retardation.' In S. Holburn and P. Vietze (eds) *Person-Centered Planning: Research, Practice, and Future Directions.* Baltimore, MD: Paul H. Brookes.

Felce, D. and Perry, J. (1995) 'The extent of support for ordinary living provided in staffed housing: the relationship between staffing levels, resident characteristics, staff:resident interactions and resident activity patterns.' *Social Science and Medicine 40*, 6, 799–810.

Hastings, R.P. (1995) 'Understanding factors that influence staff responses to challenging behaviours: an exploratory interview study.' *Mental Handicap Research 8*, 4, 296–320.

Houts, P.S. and Scott, R.A. (1975) *Goal Planning with Developmentally Disabled Persons: Procedures for Developing an Individualized Client Plan.* Hershey, PA: Milton S. Hershey Medical Centre.

Jenkins, J., Felce, D., Toogood, A., Mansell, J. and de Kock, U. (1988) *Individual Programme Planning.* Kidderminster: British Institute of Mental Handicap.

Kincaid, D. and Fox, L. (2000) 'Person-centered planning and positive behavior support.' In S. Holburn and P. Vietze (eds) *Person-Centered Planning: Research, Practice, and Future Directions.* Baltimore, MD: Paul H. Brookes.

Kinsella, P. (2000) 'What are the barriers in relation to person-centred planning?' www.paradigm-uk.org/articlespcp.html.

Mansell, J. (1994) 'Specialized group homes for persons with severe or profound mental retardation and serious problem behaviour in England.' *Research in Developmental Disabilities 15*, 371–388.

Mansell, J., Ashman, B., Macdonald, S. and Beadle-Brown, J. (2002) 'Residential care in the community for adults with intellectual disabilities: needs, characteristics and services.' *Journal of Intellectual Disability Research 46*, 8, 625–633.

Mansell, J. and Ericsson, K. (eds) (1996) *Deinstitutionalization and Community Living: Intellectual Disability Services in Britain, Scandinavia and the USA*. London: Chapman and Hall.

McConkey, R., Morris, I. and Purcell, M. (1999) 'Communications between staff and adults with intellectual disabilities in naturally occurring settings.' *Journal of Intellectual Disability Research 43*, 3, 194–205.

Mencap (2002) *The Housing Timebomb: The Housing Crisis Facing People with a Learning Disability and their Older Parents.* London: Royal Society for Mentally Handicapped Children and Adults.

Miner, C.A. and Bates, P.E. (1997) 'The effect of person centered planning activities on the IEP/transition planning process.' *Education and Training in Mental Retardation and Developmental Disabilities 32*, 2, 105–112.

Murphy, G.H. and Clare, I.C.H. (1995) 'Adults' capacity to make decisions affecting the person: psychologists' contribution.' In R.H.C. Bull and D.C. Carson (eds) *Psychology in Legal Contexts.* Chichester: Wiley.

O'Brien, C.L. and O'Brien, J. (2000) 'The origins of person-centered planning: a community of practice perspective.' In S. Holburn and P. Vietze (eds) *Person-Centered Planning: Research, Practice, and Future Directions.* Baltimore, MD: Paul H. Brookes.

O'Brien, J. and Lovett, H. (1992) *Finding A Way Toward Everyday Lives: The Contribution of Person Centered Planning.* Harrisburg, PA: Pennsylvania Office of Mental Retardation.

O'Brien, J. and Mount, B. (1989) 'Telling new stories: the search for capacity among people with severe handicaps.' In L. Meyer, C. Peck and L. Brown (eds) *Critical Issues in the Lives of People with Severe Disabilities.* Baltimore, MD: Paul H. Brookes.

Perry, J. and Felce, D. (2003) 'Quality of life outcomes for people with intellectual disabilities living in staffed community housing services: a stratified random sample of statutory, voluntary and private agency provision.' *Journal of Applied Research in Intellectual Disabilities 16*, 1, 11–28.

Purcell, M., Morris, I. and McConkey, R. (1999) 'Staff perceptions of the communicative competence of adult persons with intellectual disabilities.' *British Journal of Developmental Disabilities 45*, 88, 16–25.

Qureshi, H., Challis, D. and Davies, B. (1989) *Helpers in Case-Managed Community Care.* Aldershot: Gower.

Radcliffe, R. and Hegarty, J.R. (2001) 'An audit approach to evaluating individual planning.' *British Journal of Developmental Disabilities 47*, 93, 87–97.

Robertson, J., Emerson, E., Gregory, N., Hatton, C., Kessissoglou, S., Hallam, A. and Linehan, C. (2001) 'Social networks of people with mental retardation in residential settings.' *Mental Retardation 39*, 3, 201–214.

Rudkin, A. and Rowe, D. (1999) 'A systematic review of the evidence base for lifestyle planning in adults with learning disabilities: implications for other disabled populations.' *Clinical Rehabilitation 13*, 5, 363–372.

Sanderson, H. (2000) 'Person-centred planning: key features and approaches.' www.doh.gov.uk/vpst/pcp.htm

Shaddock, A.J. and Bramston, P. (1991) 'Individual service plans: the policy–practice gap.' *Australia and New Zealand Journal of Developmental Disabilities 17*, 1, 73–80.

Social Services Inspectorate (1989) *Inspection of Day Services for People with a Mental Handicap.* London: Department of Health.

Stancliffe, R.J., Hayden, M.F. and Lakin, K.C. (1999) 'Effectiveness of challenging behavior IHP objectives in residential settings: a longitudinal study.' *Mental Retardation 37*, 6, 482–493.

Taylor, S.J. (1988) 'Caught in the continuum: a critical analysis of the principle of the least restrictive environment.' *Journal of the Association for Persons with Severe Handicaps 13*, 1, 41–53.

Ward, F. (1999) *Modernising the Social Care Workforce – The First National Training Strategy for England: Supplementary Report on Learning Disability.* Leeds: Training Organisation for the Personal Social Services.

Wilcox, B. and Bellamy, G.T. (1987) *A Comprehensive Guide to the Activities Catalog: An Alternative Curriculum for Youth and Adults with Severe Disabilities.* Baltimore, MD: Paul H. Brookes.

CHAPTER 3

Relationships between Care Management and Person Centred Planning

Simon Duffy and Helen Sanderson

INTRODUCTION

This chapter provides a framework within which it is possible to review the role of care management in terms of the outcomes it is expected to achieve, the process by which it works and the particular tasks it requires. It is important to recognise that many different professionals, not just those named as care managers, carry out the care management role. In particular specialist and community teams frequently function as care managers and the term 'care manager' as it is used in this chapter refers to anybody who has the responsibilities that we will go on to outline.

The critical theme of this chapter is that care managers must work in a way that supports, rather than hinders, the self-determination of people with learning difficulties. This is not because self-determination is the only ethical principle that matters; but it is because human services struggle to respect that principle. We will explore how the care manager can develop a more equal relationship with people with learning difficulties, their families and other allies. The care manager must both enable the individual and their allies to take more control of their own lives while also supporting them to make effective use of other services, professionals and wider community resources. This means working intelligently to make the best use of the available resources, including the energy of the individual, his or her community and other services. One example of this new style of working is provided by the way in which Paul and his family have been supported by a local authority.

In this chapter we analyse the role of care manager into two distinct parts and offer a conceptual model that will, we hope, help care managers and statutory authorities reflect on the complex nature of care management. It is also hoped that this will provide guidance both on how care managers should make use of the techniques of person centred planning (PCP) and how best to interpret their role.

Case study: Paul

As a teenager Paul was sent away to a residential school hundreds of miles from his home; that service was not ideal and his family were keen that he should return home. Now this local authority has had significant experience of person centred planning (PCP) and was committed to the principle that decisions should be made by the person or by those closest to the person. Instead of commissioning a service for Paul in the ordinary way, they helped Paul, and his family, to lead the development of an alternative support service.

Initially the family and Paul were given the opportunity to develop a PCP, and a care manager trained in Essential Lifestyle Planning developed a plan with Paul. The family together then decided upon the kind of support service they wanted. Paul was to move back home, but to his own house close to his family. He would get an individually tailored package of support and his brother would work as his team leader. The family were told that they could spend up to £70,000 per year on his support (this being approximately 60 per cent of the cost of the segregated service he was using at that time). Equipped with this knowledge the family interviewed service providers but finally decided to manage the service themselves. Paul now lives in a house he was able to buy himself and has support from his family and a small, dedicated support team, led by his brother. The arrangement has worked well for all concerned and while the care manager has a critical role in supporting, monitoring and reviewing the service, most work is carried out by Paul or by people close to him. The care manager played a vital role in this story, but also a minimal role. Once she had helped formulate the initial plan the family's confidence grew and they began to take increased responsibility. The result is a support service that has enabled a young man to return home, share in the life of his family and begin his own life in his own community.

THE TWO FUNCTIONS OF CARE MANAGEMENT

The role of the care manager is complex. There is no single model of best practice; instead there are many local interpretations of how to 'do' care management. The term 'care manager' itself is not even accepted in all parts of the UK. The work of the care manager is multifaceted, touching on every aspect of human services, and his or her situation is often fraught. The care manager works to fixed budgets in a bureaucratic system, but he or she is subject to fluctuating political priorities and the rising expectations of individuals and families. However, amidst all of this, it is still possible to identify two roles that are typically assigned to care managers:

1. *Support co-ordination role:* helping people get the help they need by organising paid or unpaid support.
2. *Resource allocation role:* allocating 'community care' resources to people who are deemed to need them.

These two roles, while clearly linked, are distinct and in practice they can even be separated from each other. For instance the Futures For Young Adults project in Victoria, Australia, assigns resources using an objective points system and a computer software program. Help is then organised by an independent advocate who supports individuals and families to use the resources allocated to them. The people who sort out how much money the person will receive can therefore be different from the people who co-ordinate support. Nevertheless, at present, these two functions are usually combined to some degree in the care manager's role.

PROCESS: DIFFERENT STYLES OF ASSESSMENT

The means by which a care manager is to fulfil these two functions is by carrying out an assessment of need. The assessment informs the support the individual will receive from human services. However, there are radically different ways of doing an assessment and Gerry Smale (1993) has offered a useful analysis of these different approaches.

Questioning model

In the questioning model the care manager asks questions to determine what the person needs. The questions reflect what the professional sees as important according to his or her particular expertise and understanding of 'need'. The person's disability and its impact on his or her life is typically the focus of the questions. This approach assumes that professional knowledge provides the critical authority for the care manager's work and this authority is exercised as a professional judgement about the individual's needs.

Procedural model

The second possible approach is the procedural model; in this model the critical authority for the care manager's work is the system of services and resources that are available for the disabled person. Instead of exercising professional judgement the care manager has a set of forms to complete to determine the person's eligibility for these services. The professional's expertise is used to accurately complete the forms and determine action. The care manager is effectively an agent of the statutory authority, operating with limited discretion to ensure the objectivity of the decisions that are made, offering statutory authorities a seemingly fair and efficient way of rationing and allocating resources.

Exchange model

In the exchange model it is assumed that the person is the expert in his or her life and problems, and that professional expertise lies in helping to create a shared understanding of the person and his or her situation, negotiating, problem solving and co-designing solutions. Gerry Smale states:

> it is assumed that all people are expert in their own problems and that there is no reason to assume that the worker will or should ever know more about people and their problems than they do themselves, and certainly not before they do. (Smale *et al.* 1993)

Both the questioning and procedural models of care management are highly unattractive. Both models radically limit the ability of individuals to take control of their own lives; moreover both models fail to respect the genuine and positive contribution that care managers can make. It is only the exchange model that offers an attractive account of the process of care management.

However, there are strong structural reasons that encourage the prevalence of both the questioning and procedural approaches. One reason is that, historically, services have been under the control of experts and professionals, to whom the community granted power over disabled people (see Duffy's account of the Professional Gift Model in Duffy 1996). This assumption encourages the view that only professionals can evaluate what is appropriate for the person and it encourages the questioning approach. A second reason is that valuable human services have become fixed into a series of slots, which need to be rationed out. This rationing requires clear criteria to be applied by an objective professional and encourages the procedural approach. In fact these two models are in conflict with each other and care managers can be torn between these two contrasting interpretations of how they should fulfil their purpose.

However, the questioning and procedural models are being challenged, both by care managers and by the people they serve. The paternalist assumptions of the past are being replaced by an increased understanding that people have rights, including a right to self-determination. Services are no longer seen as an unmitigated good, to be parcelled out by benevolent professionals. Instead individuals, families and professionals are recognising that they must work in the spirit of the exchange model, by collaboration. This shift in assumptions has been reflected in a number of practical changes; two of the most important, for our purposes, are PCP and individualised funding.

PCP

PCP is an approach to planning and decision-making that supports individuals, in partnership with others, to think through their needs, identify their goals and to set out to achieve those goals (see Sanderson *et al.* 1997). The techniques of PCP are designed to help people move beyond planning systems that are constrained by professional assumptions of need and are limited in their practical application to a world of service options. PCP provides a holistic and human approach to planning, within which decisions about the help people need and how best to deliver that help are led by the person him- or herself.

Individualised funding

Individualised funding is a resource allocation system that assigns money to an individual and enables the individual to have control over how these resources are used to provide support. At present only a fraction of existing resources are managed in this way, but direct payments and the Independent Living Fund (ILF) have enabled some disabled people to take advantage of individualised funding.

The assumption that drives the rest of this chapter is that both of these approaches are correct; we should encourage and develop PCP and we must promote individualised funding. Together, these two measures will better enable care managers to work to the exchange model.

TASKS: THE FIVE GEAR MODEL

We start with an account of how care managers can best fulfil both of their roles with a focus on the support co-ordination role. At first it might seem that the ideal alternative to the paternalist assumption that the professional knows best is to deny that the professional care manager has anything to offer, for the care manager is a stranger in the life of the individual and brings with him or her no special knowledge of the individual or of his or her community. However, even if the care manager is not always the *best* person to determine what is right this does not mean that he or she should have *no* role in determining what is right.

There are at least two clear reasons why care managers should continue to have a critical role to play in planning and organising the support people need.

First, there are many people who live in conditions that make it imperative that somebody organises some help, and yet there is nobody to take on that role (see Margaret's case study).

Case study: Margaret

Margaret is a lady who used to live in a mental handicap hospital. She was 60 years old and there was no family contact and no records of any other family members. Margaret was clearly unhappy living in hospital and she was not well liked by the nursing staff within the hospital. She was isolated and unable to communicate her desires directly by speech. In that situation it was entirely appropriate that the care manager developed an initial plan, based on the little known about Margaret's needs, in order to help Margaret move on. As supporters were recruited for Margaret who genuinely liked her and came to understand her better, the role of the care manager could become increasingly facilitative, less directly involved in Margaret's life. However, the care manager played a critical part in helping Margaret escape unacceptable circumstances.

Second, the care manager does have a unique contribution to make. While the individual and his or her allies may have the most accurate picture of what he or she needs, there are other things to consider and care managers are in a good position to make the following contributions:

- *Systems knowledge.* Care managers are well positioned to help the individual navigate the human service system itself: the rules, policies and procedures, the various service options and the systems of advocacy, complaint and conciliation. The care manager is in the ideal position to deliver this information.
- *Planning skills.* Good planning takes skill, and while care managers may not be the only people with the necessary skills, these skills are central to the care manager's job, enabling him or her to facilitate good decision-making by the individual and those close to the individual.
- *Community knowledge.* Good support does not just involve using professional services, it also involves using community resources: relationships and friendships; employers; associations and groups;

leisure and ordinary community facilities and many other aspects of ordinary life. Again, care managers will not be the only people who know about these resources, but care managers may have their own knowledge of the community.

- *Individual insight.* While each of us may be a relative expert about our own needs and while the people close to us may know us better than the people who are more distant there is always room for individual insight. Sometimes someone different can see something different. Knowledge of the self and knowledge of our needs is always imperfect and there is no reason why even a stranger cannot contribute his of her own insights (see the analysis of need provided by the CAROMA Window in Burton and Kagan with Clements 1995).

Consequently, we need a model of how support co-ordination should work that is sophisticated enough to recognise both the different starting points for planning and decision-making, and the range of skills and expertise that is required for good planning. It is to meet this need that we would propose the following: the Five Gear Model of Care Management.

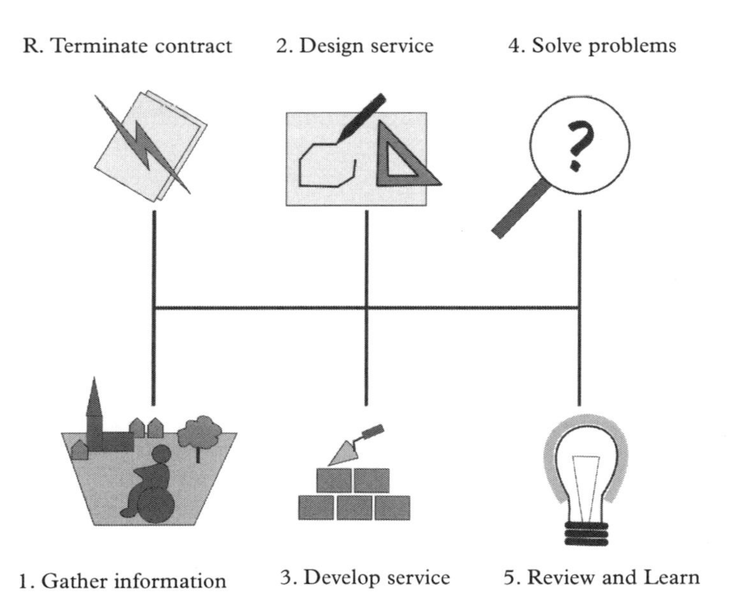

Figure 3.1 Five Gear Model of Care Management

This model sets out a number of different interventions that care managers can make to suit best the different contexts in which they work. The idea that there are different gears (or modes of intervention) between which the care manager must move arose from the need to acknowledge the different circumstances in which people live and the assumption that the best intervention will be the lightest, or least taxing, intervention necessary to achieve what is necessary. A car needs a first gear in order to overcome its inertia and to get the car moving; but in first gear a car is at its least efficient and it uses a lot of energy to go a small distance. However, for all its inefficiency, first gear is essential. As the car speed increases to move and as the road becomes easier then the car can climb through the gears, becoming increasingly efficient and getting much further for less effort.

The value of this model is twofold. First, it aims to represent the complexity and sophistication of the role of the care manager. The work of the care manager varies depending upon the circumstances of the person served and the extent to which the planning process is under way. The care manager's role shifts as the planning process matures, moving through the following stages:

1. reaching an initial understanding
2. agreeing goals
3. making use of available resources
4. implementing change
5. reviewing, learning and amending.

Moreover the care manager will, therefore, need to carry out different tasks in order to suit the different stages of the planning process.

Second, this model also aims to reflect the different circumstances within which people operate. Margaret's circumstances were radically impoverished. She had nobody to care about her or to advocate for her and it was only after a service provider was introduced to her that she could begin to form alliances and friendships. Other people are luckier. Unlike Margaret, Paul had an empowering network of friends and family. Working with Paul effectively means respecting this network, but it also means that much of the necessary work needed to improve Paul's situation could be left to others. The role of the care manager was minimal and is presently restricted to monitoring and supporting Paul and his family to reflect on the lessons they are learning. This story represents an ideal situation, where the individual's circumstances enable the care manager to operate effectively with only minimal interference in the life of the individual. In terms of this model Margaret's situation was akin to starting a car on an upward slope, requiring a lot of energy in first gear to ensure progress. Paul's situation was akin to starting a car on a downward slope, where quick progress can be made through the gears.

First gear: reach initial understanding

When there is a need to work out what an individual needs and there is no one else available to do this job effectively then the care manager must try to clarify with the individual hir or her fundamental needs and preferences, who needs to be involved in decision-making and how that process will be managed. This first gear requires real engagement with the individual and those close to him or her and is clearly more effective where care managers have developed the questioning skills used in person centred planning.

If the individual has many allies, like Paul, then this process may only require the care manager to judge whether the plans seem an authentic expression of the individual's needs. However, many people, like Margaret, will lack such allies. Clearly this implies a strategic imperative for human services to avoid crises and build in support before major service interventions are necessary.

Second gear: agree goals

When there is some clarity about who the individual is and what the fundamental issues are then the care manager can begin the process of developing a service design – that is, working out what he or she needs to keep safe and to begin the process of developing a better life.

Clearly where there are services or people close to the individual then they are likely to do a much better job of ensuring that a good service design is developed; yet frequently such people are absent and it is only after initial service design work has begun that appropriate providers or supporters are identified.

Third gear: use available resources

After the initial service design the service needs to be developed; this means dealing with all the compromises, problems and opportunities that reality brings to the process. This is an essential part of the process of really helping the individual take responsibility for his or her life and moving beyond dreaming and planning; this process should build capacity within the team and the individual.

Ideally the care manager should be able to stand back, offering support and encouragement; however, in reality, the care manager often has to solve specific problems, deal with certain organisations or renegotiate on behalf of the individual.

Fourth gear: implement change

Even when a service has been developed it is sometimes the case that unforeseen problems occur or that the individual continues to act in ways that could be harmful to him- or herself or others.

Again it is best if the individual and his or her allies can resolve these problems; however, it is often the case that the support and guidance of the care manager is required and frequently there is an essential element of accountability to the care manager for any serious issues that may arise.

Fifth gear: review, learn and amend

Ideally every care manager, once a service has been developed, can simply check out that the service is operating well and in accordance with the individual's wishes and agreed specifications. If this is the only role that care managers had to carry out it is likely that there would only be a few care managers required and care managers would be able to interfere with people's lives to the absolute minimum necessary. In reality care managers must spend much of their time operating in the lower gears.

Reverse: end arrangements

Often it is possible to manage change by moving down through the gears for a period in order to ensure that significant change can be managed with the least possible disruption to the individual's life and community. Unfortunately there are also times when there needs to be more radical change – change that can take the care manager right back to first gear and the whole business of developing a service from scratch. In these situations care managers need to act to terminate arrangements while salvaging whatever might be useful to the individual in the future. As the model suggests, contract termination (reverse) is only safely done after the process of change has been brought to a halt, ideally after moving down through the gears:

- by trying to help supporters to change their practice
- by trying to reorganise or renegotiate resources
- by redesigning the basic assumptions of the service or
- by trying to begin again the process of trying to understand the individual's needs.

On this analysis care managers must embrace PCP; but they must not dominate the process. PCP offers care managers a range of tools that will enable them to do their job better and in a way that is more facilitative. In particular, at each stage of the planning process, there are useful techniques that can apply (see Table 3.1).

To this list could be added many other techniques from within and from without the canon of PCP. Mastering these techniques provides care managers with a flexible repertoire of facilitative questions by which they can help individuals achieve the maximum possible control over the process of support co-ordination and help them achieve the most appropriate support.

Table 3.1 The value of person centred planning techniques

Stages in planning process	Elements of person centred planning
Reach initial understanding	Mapping personal history (from MAPS*) Catching the dream (from PATH*) Discovering what is important to the person (from Essential Lifestyle Planning) Mapping how to support individual successfully (from Essential Lifestyle Planning) Communication charts (from Essential Lifestyle Planning) Mapping gifts (from MAPS)
Agree goals	Define vision for change (from Personal Futures Planning) Design a positive week (from Personal Futures Planning) What is working/not working (from Essential Lifestyle Planning)
Use available resources	Define obstacles and opportunities (from Personal Futures Planning) Mapping relationships, community and other features of individual's life (from Personal Futures Planning)
Implement change	Action planning (from Personal Futures Planning) Backwards planning (from PATH)
Review, learn and amend	What's working and not working (from Essential Lifestyle Planning) Learning Log (from Essential Lifestyle Planning)

* MAPS and PATH are styles of PCP

However, as we have already indicated, this model also implies that the job of care managers will become easier and more efficient if individuals are empowered to take control; that is, not just empowered by the techniques of planning but empowered by their situation in the community. This means that care managers will benefit if they can shift responsibility from themselves to those closer to the individual or those with the relevant skills. From the care manager's perspective this could be described as delegation, although in fact it is better described as subsidiarity: the principle that it is wrong to remove from someone the responsibility for a decision, unless genuinely necessary. This does not just mean enabling individuals to make their own choices; it also means supporting any other process that makes individuals more able to make decisions or leaves decisions to those with the relevant expertise. An example of this approach could be given for each stage of the planning process (see Table 3.2).

Table 3.2 Subsidiarity strategies

Objective	Delegation or subsidiarity strategy
Reach initial understanding	Enable a family to develop their own plan of support
Agree goals	Expect a service provider to develop the necessary service design
Use available resources	Encourage people to make use of natural community resources or their own personal networks
Implement change	Take on the minimum necessary tasks; leave most tasks to those closest to the action
Review, learn and amend	Enable the individual to monitor and review his or her own service

Again, these practical empowerment strategies are only examples; they will not always be possible and other better strategies will suit different situations. However, mastery of these techniques will certainly enhance the planning skills of the care manager and hence better enable them to fulfil their role as support co-ordinators.

THE CHALLENGE OF RESOURCE ALLOCATION

So far we have argued that support co-ordination will benefit from the use of PCP, particularly if that is done in a way that is sensitive to the different stages of planning and the need to manage interventions carefully in a way that maximises individual empowerment. Now we must review the second function: resource allocation.

In fact there is good reason to believe that the two functions of care management are in significant tension, largely because the resource allocation role undermines the spirit of equal exchange and partnership required for good planning. In general the majority of resources used to pay for human services are not allocated in accordance with the objective needs of the individual; instead resource allocation is driven by the need to solve crises. You are more likely to get more resources allocated to you if:

- you lack any unpaid or natural support systems
- your situation is dangerous or attracting negative attention from other citizens
- you have put pressure on officers or politicians to get what you want.

Resource allocation is proportionate to critical needs, rather than objective needs. Not only does this fact have perverse long-term effects (poorly designed services and poor use of natural supports), it also damages the relationship between the care manager and the individual, for when resource allocation depends on the care manager's perception of the individual's critical needs then planning becomes confused with bargaining.

In planning we try to identify constraints and then decide how to manage them positively. In bargaining we try to get the best deal we can. Given the implicit criteria (critical needs) used for allocating resources and given the care manager's role in resource allocation it is difficult for both sides to avoid bargaining instead of planning. Rather than trying to reach a true understanding of what is available and what is possible the care manager is under pressure to ration limited resources by offering as little as possible; at the same time the individual has an incentive to maximise needs and minimise any natural supports that he or she may have. This distorts planning by misrepresentting the picture of needs and disguising the resources available to meet those needs.

The ideal solution for this problem would be to change the principles used to ration resources. If resources were allocated in accordance with an objective measure of need then these perverse incentives that distort the relationship between the care manager and the individual would end. This is not impossible, for Disability Living Allowance (DLA) is already allocated by a set of objective measures. Moreover when an individual is injured and receives damages to compensate for a disability the courts are quite capable of measuring a disability, governed by principles of natural justice.

However unlikely it is that these rules will change there is still much that a care manager can do to limit the damage inherent in the present system. One response is to avoid bargaining by allocating resources (by whatever principle) as early as possible. If the care manager sets out what is on offer in a way that enables people to have faith that those resources will not be removed if natural or other resources are added to the package then it is much more likely that effective planning can be carried out.

Second, while it may not always be possible to enable people to use direct payments there are a range of possible resources that may enable individuals or families to both exercise more control and enjoy more flexible and responsive services. While the resource situation is still not totally flexible there has been an increased shift away from inflexible service slots. In fact there are two dimensions to this increased flexibility.

1. *Improved customer authority.*
   Increasingly it is possible to enable people to have more control over their own services. At its most extreme this may mean enabling people to purchase their own support services with a direct payment. However, there are also other options between that and offering someone no choice or control:

   - offering a choice of providers
   - using a provider who uses an Individual Service Fund in which the individual's service money can be kept and which can be used by agreement with the individual[1]
   - providing people with tokens they can exchange for services.[2]

2. *Improved service flexibility.*
   In addition to offering people more control over services it is also possible to offer more flexibility in the service they receive. If it is not possible to offer money then it is still possible to offer flexibility in one or more of the following ways:

   - the times that support is provided
   - the location where support is offered
   - who provides the support
   - how support is provided and the policies used.

One local authority that has piloted this approach is North Lanarkshire Council, Scotland. North Lanarkshire launched a pilot project to encourage the families of people with significant learning difficulties to take more responsibility for planning and managing their own support services. Robert's case study is an example of how this project can work.

Although this model of work is in its early days it seems to offer a coherent antidote to the failings of the present system and offers a way in which PCP can be made central to the role of the care manager without the care manager's role becoming impossibly onerous and incoherent. Care managers will be more able to play this role effectively if the resource allocation role is clarified. Ideally it would operate more objectively and would be carried out at the beginning of the planning process. Allocating resources after planning has been completed inflates costs and leads to less effective community support solutions.

In fact this analysis of the relationship between support co-ordination and resource allocation is suggestive of an extension to the Five Gear Model of Care Management. We might see resources as the fuel that drives the car. In order to start the planning process it is best to allocate a fair level of resources first, before planning gets under way. In the same way it is best to start a car in neutral, the ignition process injects fuel into the engine and only then do we put the car in first gear.

Case study: Robert

Robert lives at home with his mum and dad and they are all happy for that to continue; but the whole family wished to give Robert more independence inside and outside the home. The care manager approached the family and told them about the project and described how money could be provided to pay for additional support as long as there was an appropriate support plan. The care manager also indicated how much money would be available (£30,000 per year, of which £20,000 would be available from the ILF). The care manager went on to set out the key elements of the required support plan and gave the family the choice of how to write the support plan: the care manager offered to support the planning directly herself, offered them a source of independent support and also offered them the chance to do the planning themselves. The family decided to write the support plan themselves. One week later the care manager returned and received the support plan that the family had developed together over their Sunday lunch. She was delighted at the quality of the plan, which she acknowledged would have taken her many weeks to complete.

CONCLUSION

Care managers fulfil a useful role in co-ordinating services to disabled people and other people who need support. They should work in a spirit of equal exchange and partnership using the techniques of PCP. However, the care manager will need to work intelligently, doing the least possible and enabling others to take a lead where they can. Moreover, in order to best fulfil this role it is necessary for care managers to manage their second role as resource allocators. Where possible they should try to allocate resources as early as they can in the planning process and try to offer those resources in ways that give the individual

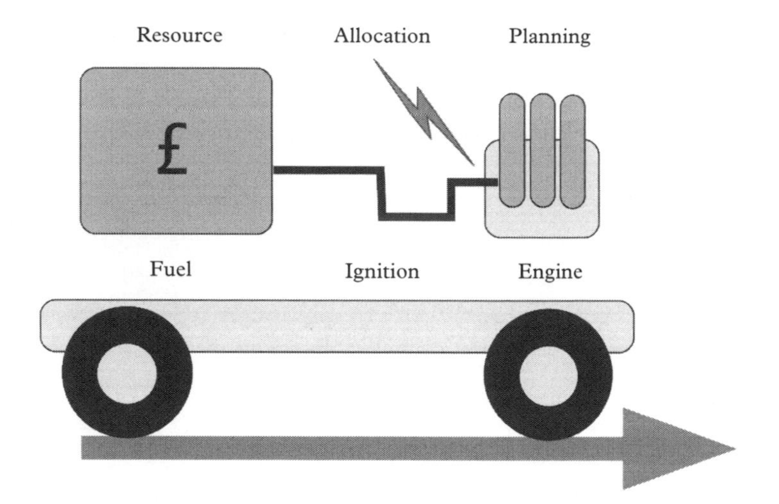

Figure 3.2 Resource allocation

control over how they will be used and the maximum degree of flexibility. Figure 3.2 offers one possible metaphor for this development of the care management role. The early allocation of resources acts as the injection of fuel into the planning process.

Of course this discussion raises wider issues, for it is not just care managers who have an impact on the self-determination of disabled people. Strategies could be pursued to equip the community better to develop its own skill. For example:

- training in planning could be provided to individuals, families and other citizens
- written guidance could be made available
- independent sources of advice and support could be developed, e.g. service brokers, personal assistant advisers, Independent Living centres etc.

Care managers sit at an important point between human services and the wider community. How they manage relationships with those they serve and fellow professionals within human services has an enormous impact. No one approach provides the answer; instead care managers must change the approach and energy they take to reflect both the individual's situation and the different stages of the planning process. Sometimes a care manager must take the lead to push things forward. Sometimes the care manager will need to stand back and let others take the lead. It is hoped that this chapter offers a framework for reflecting on the varied options confronting care managers in their work.

NOTES

1 For example, this approach has been used extensively by Inclusion Glasgow, a service provider based in Scotland.
2 For example, this approach is used as a fundamental component of service delivery by Dane County, Wisconsin, in the USA.

REFERENCES

Burton, M. and Kagan, C. with Clements, P. (1995) *Social Skills for People with Learning Disabilities.* London: Chapman and Hall.

Duffy, S. (1996) *Unlocking the Imagination.* London: Choice Press.

Sanderson, H., Kennedy, J., Ritchie, P. and Goodwin, G. (1997) *People, Plans and Possibilities.* Edinburgh: SHS.

Smale, G., Tuson, G., Biehal, N. and March, P. (1993) *Empowerment, Assessment, Care Management and the Skilled Worker.* London: HMSO.

CHAPTER 4

Managing the Tensions between the Interests of Organisations and Service Users

Tony Osgood

INTRODUCTION

> We have historically been more efficient in providing people for services than services for people... (O'Brien and Lovett 1992, p.9)

The context to arguments over the organisational implementation of person centred planning (PCP) and action is the lives of people using services and there are examples in this chapter illustrating why person centred planning and action are vital to underpin changes in power and power relationships between services and service users.

As person centred planning has gained an increasingly high profile in the UK, many organisations are awash with person-centred language. *Valuing People* (Department of Health 2001) places PCP centre stage in service delivery for people with learning disabilities. The implementation guidance (Department of Health 2002) suggests there are two elements – PCP and person-centred approaches – meaning that services, in their systems and practice, should be responsive to individuals. However, are learning disability services *en masse* able to implement such innovation meaningfully, particularly when PCP ideologies fundamentally challenge conventional systems and traditional thinking? Moreover, PCP has been considered 'mindful', in that it requires openness to new ideas and perspectives, and involves creating new ways of doing and being. This compares to the relative mindlessness of old rigid ways of thinking and acting, precluding new events, and operating from a single perspective. The question 'what happens when a radical mindful concept such as PCP is thrown into the mindless mainstream?' (O'Brien, O'Brien and Mount 1997) needs to be asked. Barbara's case study illustrates this process. There is clearly a risk that services will unwittingly debase person centred planning. This chapter identifies major potential obstacles for larger organisations when implementing PCP and will argue that this family of approaches is primarily about people, rather than organisations.

Case study: Barbara

Barbara has a 'bad' reputation. People coming into the house she shares with four men are warned, 'She'll have you'. In her bedroom her clothes are locked away and her bedroom door is locked. She loves clothes, but access is restricted, controlled by staff with controlling paradigms (e.g. 'This is a challenging behaviour unit, you know!'). Barbara has learned to urinate in order to get a change of clothes. She spends hours in a dressing gown. 'She doesn't win,' staff say. 'Don't worry, we're covered, it's in the care plan.' Staff shout at her. Recently, the provider of the service changed the name of their recording system. Barbara no longer has an Individual Service Plan – as the format has altered slightly it is now called a PCP. The content, however, remains largely unchanged.

IMPLEMENTING PCP

The recommendation to generalise PCP without clarity about how to turn person centred *planning* into person-centred *action* in large service systems is potentially problematic, as PCP is an idiographic qualitative process. Large disability services in the UK are in the main nomothetic quantitative systems, dealing with conceptions of groups of people as homogenous classifications (O'Brien 2002). Person centred planning originated from the voluntary commitment of people toward a fellow human, and we need to consider if and how organisations can legislate for ways in which poorly paid employees are to empower service users. Services focusing on their own needs, such as implementing PCP in line with *Valuing People*, may be tempted to adopt a wholesale model of planning. This simply demonstrates a lack of understanding about the individual approach required by PCP and its emphasis on creative collaboration and the challenging of boundaries around both practice and thinking.

According to Allard (1996), the themes of person centred planning are reasonably clear:

- Listening to the focus person or their representatives.
- Identifying the person's preferences and core values.
- Addressing the very real issues that disability presents.
- Developing a vision of a desirable future.
- Mobilising community resources.

How might large providers respond?

PCP developed within 'communities of practices', rather than formal 'institutionalised' organisations such as NHS trusts or social services departments, and in a culture different from that prevailing in services in the UK. We are faced with the challenge of generalising bespoke tailored provisions to large services familiar only with providing off-the-peg solutions. Learning disability service organisations often function by viewing service users as a population – a homogenous whole or collection of people with defining deficits requiring professional intervention. PCP, on the other hand, focuses on people, gifts and community (O'Brien and Lovett 1992).

QUALITY VS. QUANTITY?

The requirement on services to produce so many plans by such-and-such a date may possibly encourage a greater emphasis on planning rather than outcomes, encouraging organisations to focus on the breadth rather than the quality of implementation. The greater the number of plans, the higher the kudos of achieving a quantitative target. Fewer, higher quality plans leading to better outcomes for individuals may not attract the same kudos. Plans are easier to deliver and complete than person-centred action and improvements in quality of life. It is easier to complete a plan than change how organisations and those who work in them operate. Rather than measuring the number of plans started or completed, the emphasis needs to be switched to the number and types of goals set in plans, and their achievement. We need also to appreciate the complexity and quality of many of these goals; if we are obliged to produce numbers, perhaps we should measure how many people are happier as a result of their plans, or perhaps how many new friendships people have developed, even what new skills have been learnt and what new attributes have been acquired. Counting the number of people with plans is easier than establishing the quality of PCP and the actions which follow. There is also the thorny issue of rationing of scarce resources. There is a sense of thinking where 'better everyone get a little' (namely a plan), than 'a few get a lot' (namely achieving the goals). Services may rightly be concerned with equality and equity in coverage, but this brings with it the risk that PCP becomes just another service tool – a sure way to disenfranchise users.

ISSUES FOR ORGANISATIONS

Changing the language, not the action

Changing organisational appearance is relatively easy (Praill and Baldwin 1988) and adherence to PCP is something any individual or organisation is able to claim. Existing planning formats are being modified to incorporate the language of PCP and person-centredness. Some organisations are issuing pro-forma person-centred plans, with staff and service users, where able, simply filling in the gaps. Yet such practice is not what was intended when trying to give the individual a real voice, leading to wider questions about who judges the quality of PCP and with what credentials. Standard definitions and criteria of what does and does not constitute PCP may simply lead to unthinking compliance, rather than innovation in practice and user involvement and quality outcomes for people. One possibility is that organisations may soon be found to adopt the language and appearance of person-centredness without the action inherently demanded by PCP.

> Although valuable, planning is not sufficient. There must be distinct assistance that can be made available to implement the plans. Without the commitment of resources and personal effort, the planning process can end up as little more than a vacuous gesture. (Dunlap and Fox 1996, p.44)

If services focus on changing language without changing actions, relationships, finances, functions and structures, PCP is likely to go the way of other innovations, lost in a mire of organisational cognitive dissonance and a battleground of professional interests. 'New names and phrases always run the risk of becoming spiffy euphemisms for "business as usual"' (Lovett 1996, p.xiii).

Reflecting on ideology and its impact

The generalisation of PCP is fraught with dangers that may 'discredit' the family of approaches that constitute it (O'Brien and Lovett 1992). For example, experience suggests normalisation ideology has often been poorly applied (Emerson 1992; Mansell *et al.* 1987; Tyne 1992; Wolfensberger 1983). 'Like other efforts for social change, person-centered planning has been used and misused, complicated and simplified, lengthened and shortened, trivialized, legalized and lionized' (O'Brien and O'Brien 2000, p.2). As Lovett noted, nothing named remains unchanged (Lovett 1996). To establish whether PCP is improving things for people and changing organisations, it is essential to gather qualitative and quantitative information. Both research approaches have their benefits and deficits, but when combined, such 'data-stories' can help us reflect, learn and distribute the myriad ways of listening and doing (Holburn and Vietze 2002).

Existing services have often failed to wholly learn the lessons of past innovations, as the quality of life of many people with learning disabilities using some services remains some distance from what experience and research, as well as values, suggest might be achieved. Without a clear understanding of why previous value and practice initiatives have failed to be implemented or maintained effectively, services are likely to poorly apply, support and maintain the paradigm-challenging themes underpinning PCP, diluting its aspirations and ultimately leading to it being discredited. Larger organisations are likely to resist the changes in thinking and functioning required by PCP and may seek to adopt superficial aspects of the person-centred movement, by focusing on plans, not action (Carnaby 1997, 1999).

For example, if organisations have really adopted normalisation principles, or the Five Accomplishments (O'Brien 1987a), we can ask why so many people are living and working in (and are arguably brutalised by) such controlling and institutionalised regimes, in ecologies and with barren lifestyles few of us would choose to inhabit (Durand 1990; Risley 1996). Ericsson and Mansell (1996) suggest 'the poorest community services appear no better...than the institutions they were designed to replace' (p.15), partly due to 'unclear goals and lack of direction' with 'little guidance on interpretation of...principles' (Mansell 1996, p.55) in services where 'the home leader...becomes an administrator' (p.56). Mansell notes 'it is as if the hard lessons learned in the institutional scandals of the 1960s have been forgotten'. The reality seems to be, regardless of what mission statements may proclaim, that 'serviceland' (Sanderson 2002) is often inefficient and wasteful (Emerson 2001), not only in resources, but in putting values into action (Allen 1999; Kinsella 2000; Wolfensberger 1980). 'Much of what is being done represents no real change in practice. It is business as usual masquerading as being person centred' (Smull 1996, p.1).

The risk of 'service-led' vs. 'person-led' services

Services seem doomed to repeat the mistakes of failing or poor application of past innovations because people who create, commission, manage, work in and impose service models may not consistently or clearly have learnt from experience why individualisation has failed in the past. Larger human service organisations often gravitate toward promoting centralised and generalised systems of working. PCP is a dynamic *process* for individuals, challenging traditional roles and responses to the needs and hopes of people using services. The general 'rolling out' of person-centred approaches, without insight from examination of implementation difficulties with previous innovations or understanding why maintenance of quality is problematic, simply raises the probability of failure and the repeat of historical mistakes.

Case study: Del

Del wears arm splints because a decade ago he hurt himself by trying to swallow his hand (no one tried to work out why, they just wanted to stop him). People know if you spend time with him he often doesn't hurt himself, 'sometimes for whole shifts'. Splints are still used as there are not enough staff. The solution – arm splints – offers the potential for resolving fiscal dilemmas, as much as for avoiding behaviour problems. It is more economical for the service in resource terms and easier for staff in terms of competence to rely on splints than alternative approaches. Again, it needs to be stated that Del wears splints even though the service know if you do things with Del he tends not to put his hand in his mouth. He has a pro-forma PCP, with standardised sections, completed by nurses and support workers, but it's difficult to recognise Del as anything other than a collection of medical and behavioural problems.

At a strategy meeting in a local authority, people were enthusiastic, but when the question of where to begin implementing PCP was raised, answers included that there was a need for 'more resources', 'more care managers', 'more training' and so on. All these things are important, but all focus on the needs of the organisation, rather than users. Senior managers sought a single model to roll out across the whole authority, at the cheapest price. They wanted, above all, to control the process and to minimise the organisational risks, eliminating ambiguity and retaining organisational control, but in the process stifling innovation. There were few suggestions about listening to what people currently failed by services were already saying and few suggested looking at where (and why) person-centred approaches have been successful – for example, smaller organisations, with flatter management structures, where change is implemented in smaller steps, with the organisation slowly learning and growing in responsiveness.

Person-centred paradigms are often ambiguous for organisations, as they highlight tensions between the individual and the organisation and create uncertainties for managers. PCP arose in a different culture, from a *real* disappointment with conventional approaches, growing at the angry chaotic creative community edges of no or poor traditional service options and provisions. PCP consequently demands flexibility of resources and roles, and creates ambiguity compared to current practices.

There is a real danger that service-led implementation of PCP will not affect organisational functioning as larger organisations are usually bureaucratic and often have established or acknowledged why current claimed practice paradigms fail to be fully implemented or maintained. The NHS case study provides an example of this. It is consequently difficult for staff to implement person-centred approaches when they are poorly paid, often not valued, and receive poor guidance and training on implementation. Few organisations are staff orientated and in most the voice of service users is less evident than the voice of staff.

Case study: The NHS campus

Imagine a campus with four bungalows, next to a special needs school. It stands on an old hospital site. The bungalows house between five and seven people and all have one respite bed. This means that there are a lot of people, all with learning disabilities and complex health needs, in one place. The bungalows are called homes but are classified as a hospital in law. This means little food is prepared in the bungalows, with most meals arriving from another hospital some 15 miles away. As food is ordered in advance, you cannot change your mind about what food you want to eat the next day and, anyway, most of the wheelchair users living in the bungalows tend not to be able to use the kitchen areas due to their poor design (even though the bungalows are 'purpose built'!). In 2003 the commissioners decided to try out Essential Lifestyle Planning (ELP) with 12 service users. They felt this would challenge practice and perhaps identify who might be able to move into different settings, such as supported living and smaller community group homes. Many were trained in ELP facilitation (all being employed by the NHS), consuming significant resources. The outcome for one individual was that he is woken with a radio alarm, rather than staff with medication, and most of the 12 plans have not resulted in any meaningful changes or outcomes. Some of the campus staff apparently opposed the planning and the commissioner has now called in an external organisation to take over the planning, at further cost, without identifying or doing anything to address the culture that stopped ELPs from being completed or actioned in the first place.

Quality of life and the management of risk

Management often seems uninterested in the quality of life of service users, seemingly focusing on financial security and uniformity in creating certainty and control. Acknowledging individual variation among 'consumers' creates uncertainty and ambiguity, and muddies the clear water for administrators.

Organisations have been obliged to focus on budgets as a primary function, with quality outcomes secondary. When presenting their results, organisations display turnover, potency, efficacy, and penurious management systems, not the life stories of 'users'. This is simply because these are the normative standards by which services are judged. However, standards, structures and criteria need to acknowledge that people with learning disabilities are not a homogenous whole (Felce and Emerson 2001; Felce *et al.* 1999; Hatton *et al.* 1995; Schreibman 2000), and that each person has his or her own preferences, which come before the organisation's interests.

When managing risk, organisations focus on protecting themselves from liability, yet in relative terms there are few legal consequences for managers and executives whose services fail to deliver a quality of life for users so commonly claimed in brochures and their mission or value statements. Compare this to the consequences of financial overspend, and the pressures and distortions on services are apparent. What are the benefits of promoting independence for organisations when income depends on disability and why promote PCP when this may increase uncertainty and thus risk? The voiceless remain, at the dawn of the new century, hidden way behind the balance sheets and organisational audits, lost in powerful ideologies (Tyne 1992). Organisations fudge 'user' and quality outcomes, and it is salutary to remember: 'The way a service works before intervention is...functional for someone' (Mansell, McGill and Emerson 1994, p.76). 'The failure of change to match rhetoric' (Felce 1991, p.286) is partially accounted for by services not being explicitly designed to achieve defined service user outcomes. Services 'evolved in a...haphazard way...[not] as a response to a specific rationale' (Praill and Baldwin 1988, p.3). O'Brien suggests we need to acknowledge our failings and ignorance in providing services for people with learning disabilities:

> We promise to prevent, we promise to cure, we promise to rehabilitate, we promise to make independence as if it were a Chevrolet. And our promises have been fruitful, up to a point. If we are to move beyond that point we need the courage and the grace to learn the lessons of our collective ignorance and fallibility. There is much to learn in close attention to our errors and failings as we work to share and improve the lives of people with handicaps. (O'Brien 1987b, p.24)

We need to redefine success and quality not simply in terms of the numbers of people 'served' by having a plan, or financial outcomes, but by including the outcomes for people and such success criteria need to be developed in conjunction with a focus on the person. However, this also implies each individual's definition of success might be different, leaving plenty of room for dilemma and ambiguity, although it seems likely that some common themes may emerge.

The dominance of administrative procedures

Management in services seems to be becoming increasingly administration-focused, although an obvious response is that one cannot lead from an office. Nor can one write person-centred policies or plans from ivory towers. To begin to apply some degree of person-centred thinking, leaders not managers are needed. Leaders are dynamic, responsive to the ambiguity arising from person-centred work and involve people with different views to invent creative solutions. They also aid teams to create unique solutions for individuals. Conversely, administrators would perhaps try to avoid such ambiguous creativity, simply reaching for policy statements (O'Brien 1987b). The underpinning approach of PCP and action, as well as its tools, demands that we commit to people, not time-limited cases. Services will need to reconceptualise their roles and reorganise. Emerson recently noted 'evidence suggests many approaches to intervention may either need to be sustained over considerable time or require permanent changes in interaction between people and those that support them' (Emerson 2001, p.148); so, maintaining gains and achieving broader lifestyle outcomes needs sustained support: 'Interventions need to be seen as an ongoing process rather than a time limited episode of treatment' (Emerson 2001, p.148).

Those responsible for funding Martin's care, and commissioning the plan, might wish to consider Michael Smull's view:

> Learning how people want to live and then doing nothing with the information is a form of abuse. A good plan not only clarifies what each individual wants but creates the perception that those who participated in the planning will do something about it. Planning should only occur where there is commitment to implement. (Smull 2000a, p.75)

Commissioning people to do the plan without enabling them to follow through is simply not sufficient in terms of social validity, as Martin's case study demonstrates. It allows commissioners to say that they have started person centred planning, without changing anything. Thus commissioners endanger the credibility of PCP itself.

CONCLUDING COMMENTS

Services are never enough to meet people's needs (O'Brien 1987a), yet disability services and professionals are striding into the future claiming to adopt PCP. Many have voiced the fear of the debasement of PCP and the obstacles to implementation are clearly acknowledged (Holburn and Vietze 1999; Kinsella 2000; O'Brien, O'Brien and Mount 1997). It is encouraging that outcomes of PCP are being examined (Hagner, Helm and Butterworth 1996; Holburn *et al.* 2000), and though the potential 'fad-trap' of the initial burst of enthusiasm followed by a steady decline in direction and development is worrying, it is not unique to person-centred innovations.

Case study: Martin

Martin lived at home with his mother and his sister. He was largely cared for by his mother who, as she grew older, found it more difficult to care for him. Martin and his family were offered respite care in a residential home where, eventually, Martin asked to go and live, and he was able to do more of the things he loved. He continued to stay with his mother for weekends and other visits. After a time, structures, staff and regulations changed within the home and Martin's lifestyle changed. He became increasingly unhappy with his situation and expressed this by becoming physically and verbally aggressive towards other people. Unfortunately, this became a pattern in Martin's life and the rhythm of his life was changed. Things he loved were taken away, people didn't listen to him or realise how important his lifestyle was to him and he lost respect. His sexuality, dress, language and preferences were also lost and Martin ended up with a severe reputation. *He* became a problem, with the people who did not listen to him not subject to such categorisation.

At around about the fourth move, a community nurse who Martin liked was asked to come and help discuss with him how he would like his life to be. They discussed the problems of finding his ideal place to live and what that ideal place might be like. The community nurse felt that a new way of looking at the issues Martin faced should be used at the next planning meeting. Stakeholders were invited and the information that Martin and the nurse had gathered over the previous few weeks was used to develop a PATH.[1] This clearly stated what Martin wanted out of life, namely a bungalow, a couple of people to live with, a girlfriend, a particular local radio, time, space to be who he was and dress as he wished, and support when he needed it. The stakeholders present agreed to the plan and, by planning, promises were implied. It was decided that this was the way forward for planning Martin's care. Since this meeting, however, Martin has moved a further three times and is still waiting for his ideal place to live, as he was promised, with the move following the plan being the antithesis of his dream. His behaviour deteriorated again and although Martin still holds on to his PATH, hopes and dreams, they haven't changed much, as no one in authority has followed through on promises they made to him.

For many decades now professionals have tried to control services and systems and we have not maintained or generalised that many good results, making PCP a welcome challenge to service and clinical control. Services wanting to facilitate person-centred practice will need to learn and not condemn, surrender power and professional interest, and listen to the sometimes challenging and humbling experiences of service users (Iles 2003), as illustrated by Fred's case study. Such listening implies a conversation and a partnership but currently many services are ironically designated, as for many users they do not serve, they subjugate.

Recommending person centred planning for everyone illustrates, I would suggest, how poorly it is understood by those in control of policy. Rather than the wholesale adoption of approved planning methods across services, service leaders would do well in listening to the advice of the originators of PCP and action, and the experience of people charged with introducing it – start small, learn, respond, change and grow (Butkins *et al.* 2002; O'Brien and Lovett 1992; Sanderson 2002; Smull 1998, 2000b; Smull and Lakin 2002). It is perhaps salutary to listen to the person credited with helping to develop Essential Lifestyle Plans:

> Person centred planning should be done with everyone only where there is the willingness to make the investments and changes necessary...we should not make the promise unless we believe we can keep it. (Smull 1996, p.3)

A graphical analogy provided by O'Brien and Lovett suggests PCP might be conceptualised as circular or oval (adaptable), whereas service systems are square and rigid, sometimes triangular (O'Brien and Lovett 1992). Larger organisations adopting PCP approaches without radically changing how they think and act may simply be attempting to literally square the circle. Soon, in the United Kingdom, it is probable that a thousand squares will be claiming to be spherical.

Case study: Fred

Fred asks staff about what's happening. He asks this frequently and it can get tiresome for staff. But there are no schedules, prompts, landmarks or ways of Fred knowing, and staff are reluctant to tell Fred about the few plans there are in case he 'becomes obsessed' – or rather in case he knows. The other day a senior support worker got fed up with Fred asking if he could go out in the bus the next day, and she said, 'You know what we always say, Fred, wait and see what tomorrow brings.' Fred looked at the senior support worker, and said, 'But tomorrow never comes.'

NOTE

1 PATH (Planning Alternative Tomorrows with Hope) is a tool which can be used in person-centred planning. Using the focus person's dreams as a starting point, a PATH is used to help plan the steps necessary to achieve those dreams.

REFERENCES

Allen, D. (1999) 'Success and failure in community placements for people with learning disabilities and challenging behaviour: an analysis of key variables.' *Journal of Mental Health 8*, 3, 307–320.

Allard, M.A. (1996) 'Supported living policies and programmes in the USA.' In J. Mansell and K. Ericsson (eds) *Deinstitutionalization and Community Living: Intellectual Disability Services in Britain, Scandinavia and the USA.* London: Chapman and Hall.

Butkins, S., Rotholz, D.A., Lacy, K.K., Abery, B. and Elkin, S. (2002) 'Implementing person-centred planning on a statewide basis: leadership, training and satisfaction issues.' In S. Holburn and P.M. Vietze (eds) *Person-Centred Planning: Research, Practice and Future Directions.* Baltimore, MD: Paul H. Brookes.

Carnaby, S. (1997) '"What do you think?": a qualitative approach to evaluating individual planning services.' *Journal of Disability Research 41,* 225–231.

Carnaby, S. (1999) 'Individual programme planning: where is the "Individual"?' *Tizard Learning Disability Review 4,* 3, 4–9.

Department of Health (2001) *Valuing People: A New Strategy for Learning Disability for the 21st Century* (Cm 5086). London: HMSO.

Department of Health (2002) *Valuing People: A New Strategy for the 21st Century: Towards Person-Centred Approaches: Planning with People: Guidance for Implementation.* London: Department of Health.

Dunlap, G. and Fox, L. (1996) 'Early intervention and serious problem behaviours: a comprehensive approach.' In L.K. Koegel, R.L. Koegel and G. Dunlap (eds) *Positive Behavioural Support: Including People with Difficult Behaviour in the Community.* Baltimore, MD: Paul H. Brookes.

Durand, V.M. (1990) *Severe Behaviour Problems: A Functional Communication Training Approach.* New York: Guilford Press.

Emerson, E. (1992) 'What is normalisation?' In H. Brown and H. Smith (eds) *Normalisation: A Reader for the Nineties.* London: Routledge.

Emerson, E. (2001) *Challenging Behaviour: Analysis and Intervention in People with Severe Intellectual Disabilities.* Cambridge: Cambridge University Press.

Ericsson, K. and Mansell, J. (1996) 'Introduction: towards deinstitutionalisation.' In J. Mansell and K. Ericsson (eds) *Deinstitutionalisation and Community Living: Intellectual Disability Services in Britain, Scandinavia and the USA.* London: Chapman and Hall.

Felce, D. (1991) 'Using behavioural principles in the development of effective housing services for adults with severe or profound mental handicap.' In B. Remington (ed) *The Challenge of Severe Mental Handicap: A Behaviour Analytic Approach.* Chichester: John Wiley and Sons.

Felce, D. and Emerson, E. (2001) 'Overview: community living.' *Mental Retardation and Developmental Disabilities Research Reviews 7,* 73–74.

Felce, D., Lowe, K., Perry, J., Jones, E., Baxter, H. and Bowley, C. (1999) 'The quality of residential and day services for adults with intellectual disabilities in eight local authorities in England: objective data gained in support of a social services inspectorate inspection.' *Journal of Applied Research in Intellectual Disabilities 12*, 4, 273–293.

Hagner, D., Helm, D.T. and Butterworth, J. (1996) "This is your meeting": a qualitative study of person centred planning.' *Mental Retardation 10*, 3, 353–363.

Hatton, C., Emerson, E., Robertson, J., Henderson, D. and Cooper, J. (1995) 'The quality and costs of residential services for adults with multiple disabilities: a comparative evaluation.' *Research in Developmental Disabilities 16*, 6, 439–460.

Holburn, S., Jacobson, J., Vietze, P., Schwartz, A. and Sersen, E. (2000) 'Quantifying the process and outcomes of person centred planning.' *American Journal on Mental Retardation 105*, 402–416.

Holburn, S. and Vietze, P. (1999) 'Acknowledging the barriers to person centred planning.' *Mental Retardation 37*, 2, 117–124.

Holburn, S. and Vietze, P.M. (2002) *Person-Centred Planning: Research, Practice and Future Directions.* Baltimore, MD: Paul H. Brookes.

Iles, I.K. (2003) 'Becoming a learning organisation: a precondition for person centred services to people with learning difficulties.' *Journal of Learning Disabilities 7*, 1, 65–77.

Kinsella, P. (2000) *What are the Barriers in Relation to Person Centred Planning?* York: Joseph Rowntree Foundation.

Lovett, H. (1996) *Learning to Listen: Positive Approaches and People with Difficult Behaviour.* Baltimore: Paul H. Brookes.

Mansell, J. (1996) 'Issues in community services in Britain.' In J. Mansell and K. Ericsson (eds) *Deinstitutionalization and Community Living: Intellectual Disability Services in Britain, Scandinavia and the USA.* London: Chapman and Hall.

Mansell, J., Felce, D., Jenkins, J., de Kock, U. and Toogood, S. (1987) *Developing Staffed Housing for People with Mental Handicaps.* Tunbridge Wells: Costello.

Mansell, J., McGill, P. and Emerson, E. (1994) 'Conceptualising service provision.' In E. Emerson, P. McGill and J. Mansell (eds) *Severe Learning Disabilities and Challenging Behaviour: Designing High-quality Services.* London: Chapman and Hall.

O'Brien, J. (1987a) 'A guide to lifestyle planning: using the *Activities Catalog* to integrate services and natural support systems.' In B. Wilcox and G.T. Bellamy (eds) *A Comprehensive Guide to the Activities Catalog: An Alternative Curriculum for Youth and Adults with Severe Disabilities.* Baltimore, MD: Paul H. Brookes.

O'Brien, J. (1987b) *Embracing Ignorance, Error, and Fallibility: Competencies for Leadership of Effective Sevices.* Lithonia, GA: Responsive Systems Association.

O'Brien, J. (2002) 'Numbers and faces. The ethics of person centred planning.' In S. Holburn and P.M. Vietze (eds) *Person-Centred Planning: Research, Practice and Future Directions* (pp.399–414). Baltimore, MD: Paul H. Brookes.

O'Brien, J. and Lovett, H. (1992) *Find A Way Toward Everyday Lives: The Contribution of Person Centred Planning.* Harrisburg, PA: Pennsylvania Office of Mental Retardation.

O'Brien, J. and O'Brien, C.L. (2000) *The Origins of Person Centred Planning: A Community of Practice Perspective.* Responsive Systems Associates.

O'Brien, J., O'Brien, C.L. and Mount, B. (1997) 'Person centred planning has arrived...or has it?' *Mental Retardation 35*, 480–484.

Praill, T. and Baldwin, S. (1988) 'Beyond hero-innovation: real change in unreal systems.' *Behavioural Psychotherapy 16*, 1–14.

Risley, T. (1996) 'Get a life! Positive behavioural intervention for challenging behaviour through life arrangement and life coaching.' In L.K. Koegel, R.L. Koegel and G. Dunlap (eds) *Positive Behavioural Support: Including People with Difficult Behaviour in the Community.* Baltimore, MD: Paul H. Brookes.

Sanderson, H. (2002) 'A plan is not enough: exploring the development of person centred teams.' In C.S. Holburn and P.M. Vietze (eds) *Person-Centered Planning: Research, Practice and Future Directions* (pp.97–126). Baltimore, MD: Paul H. Brookes.

Schreibman, L. (2000) 'Intensive behavioural/psycho-educational treatments for autism: research needs and future direction.' *Journal of Autism and Developmental Disorders 30*, 5, 373–378.

Smull, M. (1996) *Person Centred Planning: Should We Do It with Everyone?* College Park, Maryland: Support Development Associates.

Smull, M. (1998) 'A plan is not an outcome.' *Impact 11*, 2, 17–27.

Smull, M. (2000a) 'After the plan.' In J. O'Brien and C.L. O'Brien (eds) *A Little Book About Person Centred Planning* (2nd printing). Toronto: Inclusion Press.

Smull, M. (2000b) 'Think before you plan.' In J. O'Brien and C.L. O'Brien (eds) *A Little Book About Person Centred Planning* (2nd printing). Toronto: Inclusion Press.

Smull, M. and Lakin, K.C. (2002) 'Public policy and person centred planning.' In S. Holburn and P.M. Vietze (eds) *Person-Centred Planning: Research, Practice and Future Directions* (pp.379–398). Baltimore, MD: Paul H. Brookes.

Tyne, A. (1992) 'Normalisation: from theory to practice.' In H. Brown and H. Smith (eds) *Normalisation: A Reader for the Nineties.* London: Routledge.

Wolfensberger, W. (1980) 'The definition of normalization: update, problems, disagreements and misunderstandings.' In R.J. Flynn and K.E. Nitsch (eds) *Normalization, Social Integration and Community Services.* Baltimore, MD: Pro-Ed.

Wolfensberger, W. (1983) 'Social role valorization: a proposed new term for the principle of normalization.' *Mental Retardation 21*, 234–239.

Part 2

CHAPTER 5

Promoting Empowerment

Your Life Can Change If You Want It To

Doris Clark, Robert Garland and Val Williams

Doris: Years ago, social workers and professionals used to say to me, 'You can't have dreams like that.' But I am living proof – and I would say, 'Don't let people put you off, because your dreams can come true.'

Robert: That's where circles are so powerful; there are so many people getting together and supporting each other as well as supporting you.

HOW WE WROTE THIS CHAPTER

We are three different people, who have written this chapter together, with the idea of telling our true stories about person centred planning. These are the questions we were asking: What does it mean to us, and what do we think of it? Two of us (Doris and Robert) are people who have circles of support[1] around them, but who also do a lot of work in supporting other people. Val is a non-disabled researcher, who supports people with learning disabilities to do research, and outside her work she is also involved in two circles.

We wrote this chapter by working together to support each other. Val had been asked to find some people who might like to talk about their experiences of person centred planning, and she happened to meet up with an old friend, Doris. We went out for a meal together, and decided on some questions that could get us thinking about person centred planning. Then we met again, and Doris answered all the questions from her own life experience. We agreed we would like to have some different experiences in the chapter as well, so Doris arranged to meet with Robert, to interview him about his life. Robert then became a co-author. In addition, a fourth friend, Matthew, got involved, whose planning has been far from person-centred. He agreed to talk about some of his experiences, and was happy for Val to write about them in this chapter.

We have tried to work together on making decisions about how this chapter will look. While Val has put the words down on paper, both Doris and Robert talked about their ideas and opinions, as well as their lives, on the tape. We wanted to talk about some of the problems, as well as the good things, and so we have thought about other people we know, or about people we try to support. We hope the chapter will give readers some idea of the differences in people's lives, as well as the things that we feel are important about person centred planning.

Much of this chapter is written from the tape, and so Doris's, Robert's and Matthew's words should be more or less as they were spoken. Other parts of it were written by Val and checked out with Robert and Doris. Our general rule was only to use words that *we* could all understand. We hope that, in reading this chapter, you will be able to hear us talking!

WHAT'S ALL THIS PLANNING ABOUT?

We are going to start with a conversation between Doris and Val.

Val: What does the word 'planning' mean to you, Doris?

Doris: People have got to plan their life, to reach where they want to go. If you don't plan, you can't expect to get anywhere.

Val: Well, that sounds good, but I am not sure that I plan everything in my life. And I think I know lots of people who don't plan things at all. For instance, I know lots of people who are doing jobs that have nothing to do with the things they set out to do when they were young. A lot seems to happen by chance.

Perhaps the answer lies in how easy or difficult your life is. A parent of a disabled child recently said to Val:

> For you and me, and for my other non-disabled children, life is easy. Things seem to fall into our lap. But for my disabled son, every step has to be fought for. That is why he needs person centred planning.

Of course the world is not simply divided into people who need person centred planning and those who do not. Everyone does have problems at some points in their life, and may need assistance with planning their next step. When we do need that help, we turn naturally to our friends and family, and so we may not realise that we are getting natural support. However, for the most part, we may be quite happy to get on with our jobs and our lives, taking some decisions, but leaving a lot to chance.

It is no different for people who have learning disabilities. They too have good and bad times (for further life stories, see Atkinson *et al.* 2000; Goodley 2000; Souza with Ramcharan 1997). However, many people with learning disabilities feel that their chances in life are not equal to other people's, and that life has treated them unfairly. Person centred planning is a tool to help them fight back, as Simone Aspis puts it (Aspis 2000). It is not just about support services, as our life stories will show. We think person centred planning and circles go naturally together, and so in this chapter we will talk about how our support circles have helped us to plan our lives.

In fact, people with learning disabilities aren't short of plans. They have loads of plans, but the trouble is that they are imposed on them. And they aren't told the reason why. So the important word is 'person-centred' not planning. So often, the professionals assume that people only have needs and problems, and they don't see that we have our own talents and dreams and want to choose our own route to get there.

We are now going to tell two very different stories of people with learning disabilities, which will show some of the differences that person centred planning can make.

DORIS'S STORY

When I was a child, I was always told things that I had to do – like I had to go to boarding school, then to long-stay hospital. When I grew up, it didn't change. I was still told to do things, like go and live in a group home. I was never consulted about where I was going to be put. I was just told I had to go to that place, and I had to like it or lump it.

Boarding school was a real dump, and I said, 'You know where you can stick it.' I said that to my social worker, and she didn't know what to say. When I was 16, I was leaving boarding school. Nobody had told me where I was going to next, so I decided I wasn't going to move from Temple Meads Station in Bristol, until they told me. I kept on asking where I was being taken to, but they never told me. I was told, 'Wait until you get there.'

So when I look back now, I did have confidence to speak up for myself when I was young. The problem was that I was not listened to properly.

How did my circle start?

About ten years ago, I was in a crisis. I had broken a bone, and I knew someone called Jane through People First[2]. She told me there was going to be a Circles conference, and it was a gathering event. And they celebrate the good things there, as well as tackling the bad things. That was how it started. I found people who really cared for me, through circles, and they made me feel included. It took time to get to know people, but I met people through gatherings and events.

Once I knew about circles, I thought I would like to have one. I kept on asking for a circle of support around me, because I was in a crisis. I got to know Ruth through gatherings and events, and when I wanted a circle, Ruth said she would do it. And if I hadn't had that circle, it would have taken me even longer to get back on my feet.

In my circle, I have done person centred planning. That includes a relationship map to see who's in my life. It's important to me to have people in my life who are friends and volunteers. Ruth was just a volunteer for me, and all the people in my circle were new people that I was meeting. Before that, the people in my life had all been paid people. It used to just be paid people who made decisions for me. Now people care who I am as a person, and respect me, and it's better to have people who love and care for you. It's better now, because I can say when I need something, and it's not just other people telling me.

Inside my circle

How does my circle work? At first I chose to meet in pubs and restaurants. I wanted to get out and go to places.

My circle was just a small group of two or three people to begin with. I was the focus person. As I got to know people, it built up. But you've got to give people time to commit themselves. And people do come and go out of your life.

Being in the centre means being consulted and asked, but it also means having more people in my life to help me to do what I want. It's also important to me to have unpaid, not just paid people.

In my meetings, they focused on what I wanted. Ruth was my facilitator, and she helped me. I spoke first, and I said why I had invited them to be in my circle. I said I was lonely and isolated, and I didn't care about my appearance and how I looked. We chatted about it, and how I could get people to respect who I am. Ruth was there to make sure the meeting went OK, and people had their say. And she came back to me each time, and asked if what people were saying was true. So that made me feel I was included and I was in control.

Sometimes it was hurtful. People told me a few home truths, but I took it on board. Things like getting my flat up together. People had always told me that, but then just dumped me and left me to get on with it. But the people in my circle respected me and valued me, and so I responded to them. I wanted to look tidy and respectable to go to conferences. I felt included, not excluded.

My dreams

My original dream was to travel abroad. The dreams came right at the beginning. People cannot tell you that you can't do things – the people in my circle said it can come true, if you work at it. A lot of people don't know what they want, but I went on a course called Partners in Policymaking.[3] That really helped me to change, and it gave me ideas too. It's important to know what you want in the beginning, but people can help you to get to that stage too.

Once I was in the course, and Jenny called me out of the meeting and I said, 'Is there anything wrong?' and she said, 'Would you like to go to Portugal?' and I said, 'You're joking, aren't you? I haven't got a passport', and she said she'd help me get a passport and the forms. I felt shocked, stunned, and couldn't believe it. I was so excited. But it did happen – I made it to Portugal.

After that, my dream was to go to America, and I was just helping out again on the Partners in Policymaking course. Jenny called me out and said, 'One of your dreams is coming true. Somebody wants to speak to you on the phone. How would you like to go to Washington DC to speak to the President's Committee on Mental Retardation?' I was speechless. But then I said, 'Yes please.' It was always one of my dreams.

Then a conference came up the following year in Seattle, and I went there too. I spoke to 1600 people at the conference.

Years ago, social workers and professionals used to say to me, 'You can't have dreams like that.' But I am living proof. I have been to those places, and I would say, 'Don't let people put you off, because your dreams can come true.' My life has completely changed since person centred planning.

Comment

Doris has turned her life around completely, and is a strong advocate for circles and person centred planning. Readers can find out more about her life in a book she has recently published (Clark 2001). Published life stories are often of people who have been strong and overcome barriers (see also Goodley 2000; Walmsley and Downer 1997). However, we know that there are many people who have not been fortunate enough to change their lives. So now we will tell the story given to us by someone we are calling here Matthew.

MATTHEW'S STORY

Matthew first looked back at some of the places he had lived in the past, and compared them with where he is now.

The places I have lived

At one time, I used to live in a hostel. It was a horrible area. People were always swearing and were a bit rude out in the street. When I was in the bus queue one time, the other people there pushed. And the bus driver said, 'This person was before you.'

It was horrible in the hostel, because the other people living there didn't speak. I had to go out on my own, to get my medication or to go to the dentist. One time, I went to the dentist with another resident, because she didn't fancy going on her own. She was scared, so I sat with her. That was great – I thought I was doing well. But when I got back, the staff person said, 'She could have gone on her own. You shouldn't have done that.' That was putting me down. I thought I was doing something really brilliant, but they thought she was a baby because she wouldn't go on her own.

I moved from the hostel to Oaklands because I wanted better staff. Some of the staff were nice when I first went, but then they all left. I got fed up, because you know I can't walk very well. I was getting the support from the day centre, and all those people I know well who could help me onto the bus to get home. But once I got home, no one would come out to the bus to help me get off. The coach driver used to drop me, but the staff never came out. It was nice in the hostel at the beginning; the only person I didn't like was the manager. But when you look back, all of the staff who were any good have gone now.

Some of the other residents had dreadful problems, and they were difficult to live with. I didn't get a choice; I just moved in there. My social worker decided it. I didn't think much of that.

So now I've had another move, right out of the city I lived in. It's much better here. For instance we all sit together of a night-time, and we talk a little bit. And when it's finished, they go to bed. We had our supper, and we sat in the lounge last night, all of us – having a laugh and having a joke. You wouldn't get that at the hostel. I can get on with the staff and the residents in this house. It's like team work. So life here does have its good points, but I didn't know about them when I came. I hadn't met people here. It all happened by chance.

Planning my life

I did move to a better place in the end, but how have all these moves happened?

When I wanted to leave the hostel, my social worker got involved to help me. Then he left, and I had another social worker. But the house wouldn't help me. Luckily, the deputy manager at the day centre got involved. They all got together with me, and that was great. I didn't like living there. I didn't like the staff, and I didn't like the residents.

When I wanted to leave the second place, then I had problems again. They told me I had to move away from the city I lived in. I didn't have any choice. The social worker said, 'The trouble is, you can't walk.' So she found me this place. There weren't any places in the city, so I ended up down here.

It is not that good, because my sister lives a long way away, so I don't see much of my family here. Where I lived before, I could go to college, and spend time with my friends. That is what I miss. My family asked me to go and see them, but I can't, because by the time I get over there, it would be time to come home again.

At first it felt horrible moving out here. I remembered my old friends. When it is nice weather, I wish I was back where I used to live. It was nice sitting out in the garden at the day centre. But when I moved here, they told me I can't go to the day centre. The daft thing is, I can go to college, but I can't go to a training centre, because I am too old. Does that sound a bit silly to you?

So I only kept in touch with one person from where I used to live.

Do I have dreams?

Have I had a good deal out of my life? Sometimes. For instance, I have got a guitar, but it's not very good. I got someone to come down and help me buy it. I asked him nicely, and he came down to the shop with me, and we got one. If you want people to do things for you, you need to be nice to them. I always say to the member of staff, 'Are you busy?' or 'Are you doing anything important? Can I ask you something please?' Then I tell her what I want, and she says, 'I will think about it.'

I also got my dream to go back to Scotland. If you have done People First for a long time, then you have made friends. And you can get the gift of the gab. Then you can get round people.

Living with other people that you haven't chosen

The staff sometimes say to me, 'What would you like to do tomorrow?' I am not a nasty person, sometimes I go along with them, and do what the others want to do. There is give and take. What annoys me, I like to go out – I don't *mind* going out with other people, but I don't like it when they take a long, long time. I am sitting there with my hat and coat on, and I do get a bit fed up and impatient. I want to go, and I want to go now. They take so long to make up their minds whether they are coming or not. You say, 'Are you coming?' And they say, 'I don't know.' And they stand and look at you. For God's sake! So I say, 'Let's go, we can't wait any longer.'

You can choose your friends; you can choose your key worker. I can't have a social worker, because there aren't many – that doesn't matter. But you can't choose the people you've got to live with. Isn't it about time they had a bloody law out, to say you can choose who you would like to live with? You've just got to put up with people. If you don't like them, you've got to lump them.

I'm not sure anything will ever change. You've got to go along with the social worker. If I could have a choice, that would be great, but it is never going to come up like that. How can people have different choices? They say, 'You can't live by yourself, because you can't walk and you can't do your own cooking.' It is horrible, isn't it? That's why I've got to live in a residential home. I've complained to people, but the trouble is that I can't walk. That's why I've had no choices.

WHAT CAN WE TELL FROM LOOKING AT DORIS'S AND MATTHEW'S STORIES?

The stories above are from two different people, and many readers may feel that we are looking here at two people with 'different needs'. However, their experiences do not just seem to relate to their own needs. They have very similar personalities in some ways, but have had very different types of support and encouragement to plan their lives. We sat down to look at the two stories side by side, and found some of the things that were important to us.

The first thing is the importance of friendships. Matthew seemed to be very lonely, while Doris was happy to find friends she could trust and who really cared for her. Doris's planning and support were tied up with friendship, which was very important to her, as friends are unpaid. Matthew's planning, however, was done entirely by social workers and professional staff, who kept leaving and changing jobs. Of course, you can't avoid that. People do come and go out of your life, both social services staff and people in circles. But on the whole, a circle of support will give people more permanent friends that they can trust.

Another related point was that the support which Doris got was something far more ongoing, something that carried on helping her through her problems, and also giving her opportunities as they arose. Planning cannot be done and dusted, and then put away, as it was for Matthew, who does not even have a social worker now.

The people who did help Matthew plan his moves were of course part of the social care system, and so could only see within that system. That was why they had such difficulty finding exactly the right residential home for Matthew, and why he had to move out of the city where he had always lived. The social worker could only see Matthew's needs, and not his personality and interests. It was the level of his needs that led to the situation where he felt he had no choices. Person centred planning, by contrast, should help people to think creatively, and to find ways of living that are *not* just part of the social care system.

The most important things affecting quality of life for Matthew were the staff, and the fact that he could not choose the people he lived with. He also wanted friends of his own. It is interesting to hear the interaction between himself and his staff. He is always trying to please them, because he considers that they have power over his life. Doris was helped to make choices, to live on her own, and to get the support she needed. Her relationships with people that help her are quite different from Matthew's, and again, we can perhaps trace this back to Doris's circle. She was assisted to be in charge, and that was the important thing for her.

Finally, both Doris and Matthew did have dreams, and both of those involved travel. Additionally, they were both involved with People First, which is very important in all this. Matthew said that People First had given him the 'gift of the gab'. For Doris, however, People First gave her a way to join in and change things for others. People First can have both sides to it. If people have got their own self-advocacy, that is good, because then they can stand up for others. But it is also about empowerment, and helps individuals work together and get what they want.

We have probably written enough by now to show that person centred planning can make a real difference in people's lives. It means friendships, enjoyment, trust, caring and having a life. But we'd like to tell one more story, as we hope it will show in some more detail how person centred planning has changed Robert's life.

ROBERT'S STORY

Early years

I was born in Cardiff in 1953, and fortunately I had wonderful loving parents and good neighbours, but when I was little my co-ordination wasn't very good, and I sometimes had difficulty concentrating on things, and I did panic a bit more than most children. The doctor wasn't at all helpful, he just decided I would always be a cabbage, and he told my parents. But they were wonderful, and refused to accept what he said. I was placed in a mainstream nursery, where I was quite happy. I did much the same as any child – I played with the paints and the crayons and kicked a ball around.

But I do remember one of the teachers that I overheard, saying I was backward. I didn't really know what that meant, but I knew it meant something not very good.

I went to a mainstream school when I was five, but to be honest I didn't get much help from my teachers. I was very slow writing, and I got behind the rest of the class. To be honest, the teachers were very impatient with me, and they didn't think I had much in the way of ability. When I was seven, against my wishes, the professionals decided that I should go to a special day school. My education was a complete mess. I went round one special school after another, and I had a nervous breakdown when I was 13, which meant I spent some time away at a psychiatric hospital in Oxford.

It made me feel very isolated. I was very lonely and depressed, and felt different and inferior. I had very few real friends, and I was segregated. I just didn't do any of the things that teenagers do. My younger lady friends wouldn't believe it now, but I hardly met girls in those days, which didn't help. I had very little encouragement and few opportunities. I just didn't have a normal childhood or teenage years at all.

Some of my teachers were very good, as were lots of people in my church. I did have a psychiatrist who was a lovely lady, and she tried awfully hard, but I think she was trapped a bit within the system.

After I left school

I went to college after I left school, but had no real support, and so then had another nervous breakdown. Anyway, I spent some time in an industrial therapy unit at a psychiatric hospital. The work wasn't good, and naturally it wasn't a very happy place. But with my mum's help, I started to make friends of my own age at youth clubs, and I went to a classical music society and made friends there. So I was developing interests. And I was very busy in my church, and had friends there. Ever since my late teens I've had close friends. They've all supported me and advocated for me when needed.

My mum gave me a lot of help. One of her friends worked in the Spastics Society centre and introduced me to it. But the work was very repetitive and we didn't have choice. Also the centre was segregated. All the staff were able-bodied, and all the trainees were disabled. Although the staff were very kind in some ways, we weren't listened to. I did pick up a few skills, and we had a trainees' magazine, and somebody chose me to edit it. Anyway, I then worked in the Spastics Society office for a few years, answering telephone enquiries, doing bits of research, drafting letters, using a word processor. Doing all the office things. It was better than the day centre.

Then after that I went on an employment training course, when of all things I got the award for the best all-round trainee that year, and that was a real boost, and gave me lots of confidence and self-esteem.

How did my circle start?

My poor dad had died of cancer when I was away at boarding school at 16 or 17. My mum was marvellous to me, but the time came when I needed to move away. So I lived with a couple of carers for a few years, but it all proved a bit much for them and their marriage broke up. When I first started the circle, I was still living there, so my circle's been going for about ten years now. And it's helped me with all my moves, and it's helped me with other things too.

The circle was started by Gill, the vicar's wife from my church. She had started to form circles, and had been to Bristol and was sold on the idea. She took me over to a conference in Bristol, where I met Doris for the first time. Anyway, we then got our circle going, and before the first meeting we made up a list of my friends, who I wanted to invite to my circle.

The first meeting wasn't very good, because some of them wanted the circle to be formal and have agendas and so on, but Gill and I wanted it to be very relaxed. But afterwards, we got them to do it the way I wanted, and we had a meeting in Gill's house. She cooked a lovely meal, and my friends who didn't know each other too well before all became firm friends with each other by the end of the evening. It went from strength to strength. The circle advocated for me when I wanted to move on, first to another carer, and then to a flat.

My dreams

When I was young, I suppose I just had the normal dreams about getting a decent job, and getting married, and possibly getting a few qualifications and making friends, and having a bit more of a social life, and going off on holidays. Nothing wild, just all the normal things really.

Once I got my circle, we made up a list of my dreams, and we decided that I wanted to live in my flat, have more control of my money, go on more holidays, have more friends, hopefully have a girlfriend and settle down. And to a large extent, I have done all those things. That's where circles are so powerful; there are so many people getting together and supporting each other as well as supporting you.

The circle really made a difference with my social workers as well. My social workers weren't at all convinced, you know, when I had to move out of my first carer's place. The circle persuaded them that I needed to move. Afterwards, my circle helped me to settle down with my new carer and helped her to understand my abilities and character. After a few years I decided I wanted to move on and get a flat of my own, and my circle helped me get my flat in Barry Island, a small seaside town just outside Cardiff. It is a lovely little place.

Inside my circle

How does my circle work out? Normally, there is some business to talk about so we discuss that at the beginning, then we relax and have a drink or a pot of tea or whatever, and have a good natter and a bit of fun. And actually, apart from the fact that they are there to support me, we find out if the people in the circle want any support, and then they can support each other, or I can support them. So we all work together – we often have meetings in a pub, when we want to be more relaxed. And we sometimes go to my favourite place in Cardiff, called the Peppermint Lounge. It's a dark secret! It's a studenty café, very near the university. But Doris pulls my leg, because there are a lot of attractive young ladies, and I make friends with a different group of them each year. But it is very relaxed and informal. They play popular music in the background, but not too noisy. The staff are very friendly, everyone chats to everyone else, you've got a good selection of food, and you can have alcoholic drinks if you want. So we go there sometimes for an informal evening together and a bit of a laugh. I have been wondering if we can have a bit of a picnic on the cliff top in Barry this summer.

A whole group of my friends come to the meetings and a couple of people from work. Not my social worker, but my boss in Mencap where I was working as a volunteer, she came along. My colleague in Circles, Simon, he often comes to meetings. But lots of them are friends from the church; a couple of them are friends from other places. My former carer is still very involved. His children have come to the Peppermint Lounge with us once or twice, and Gill has got two teenage children now; they were about ten and six when we first started. But now they are teenagers and they join in with us, and it's a good group of friends. Not everyone can manage to make every meeting, but normally we manage to get about five or six of us together at least.

Gill was the person who set things up and got things going. She is very good at getting people together, and getting things organised, and is very good at helping me run the meetings, and getting everyone, myself included, back to the point.

Being the focus person

At first I did feel just a little bit nervous about people discussing my life, but people do it very delicately and very sensitively. Once I got into it, I felt fine. I feel very relaxed about it now, because we are all friends, and we can all say whatever we like, without anyone getting upset. It took me one or two meetings before I got completely used to it. But once you do, I find there is no problem. And if there's anything that's off-limits, I can say so.

I don't need much encouragement to have my say, but they do encourage me if we get too sidetracked. They give me a gentle poke under the table if I am talking too much – in a figure of speech. It's just to make sure that the focus of the meeting comes back to me, and what I want to talk about. If anyone is talking too much or getting off the subject, Gill is normally the one who calls us all to order, and gets it going.

Once, for instance, we had a meeting about my flat. There was a choice of two flats, one of which was quite near the Peppermint Lounge. A nice area, but a little bit boisterous. So we decided I needed to live somewhere quieter, which is more of a settled community, and the area I am living in is very friendly and very supportive. We discussed it all round, and we discussed all my worries and fears about moving in. I felt very good about that, and much happier by the end.

Achieving my dreams

Lots of things have happened from my circle. I have had lots of support with moving into my flats. Gill and I have been on a couple of pilgrimages with the church, to Walsingham. And we go off in the evenings to the local pubs, and let our hair down a bit. They helped me set up a trust fund, with the sale of Mum's house, after she died. My brother set up a trust fund in my name, and if I want to access money for anything, say if I am going on a holiday, I will have a talk with them and we talk about me accessing a couple of hundred for the holiday. They've helped me over various little crises in my life, and they have advised me over voluntary work, when my voluntary placements have dried up.

So I've got lots of things, but most of all, I have got the love and support and friendship of my friends. We sort out my problems together. And I like to support Gill too. Because poor Gill is a very busy lady, and she has been very exhausted at times, and I have tried to support her over that. So we support each other mutually. I think I've got lots more confidence in dealing with people, and more understanding of people.

I have achieved most of my dreams. I live on my own with support. My circle has advocated for me to get more support from social services. I have got two ladies who come in during the week now, and help me with cleaning the flat and so on. I have achieved more control over my money, and I've now got a wider range of friends, which was very important to me. I go on a wider range of holidays, and I'm hoping to go on a cricketing holiday soon.

I went up to a cricket match, a one-day international up at the Oval, with my friend Andy from Circles, and we had a really wonderful day. The London coach used to coach my county, Glamorgan, and I knew him well. And as it turned out, I knew quite a few of our county players, because I meet them after play at the pub. The England coach popped out of the dressing room to discuss something with the umpires, and on his way back, Andy met him, and he asked if I could have the England players' autographs, and he got them to sign a little miniature bat, which I have got in my house.

What person centred planning means to me

Person centred planning means empowering people to make decisions over their lives. Things being done in an informal way, not the rigid way that social services have done things. People having control over the whole process, and sorting things out the way they want to, where they want to. You can have person centred planning meetings anywhere. Normally it's in my house, you know, in the flat, or sometimes in Gill's house, but sometimes in the café or the pub. And other people sometimes meet on the beach, or on a picnic in the woods. Wherever they feel relaxed and comfortable. Basically, it's about the focus person having control over things, and being listened to and being respected. And being able to plan things in the way they want to, and at the pace they want to, and having their needs and capabilities taken into account. People really work to their own agenda, and not the ones that social workers have sat down and done without much consultation with them.

A plan can mean lots of things. It can mean something very definite like a PATH.[4] I have got my own path, so that's got a definite set of aims and objectives there, and I have achieved a lot of the dreams on it. But it can mean something much more informal, like getting together and deciding what you need to do next. It can mean anything, according to what you need to do and achieve, and what sort of problems you need to sort out and how you are going to go about it.

SUMMING UP

We hope you have enjoyed reading about Robert's life story. We think that his story illustrates how complex people's lives are. No one can just come in and plan someone's life, and change things overnight. Robert did a great deal for himself, and his circle just fitted in at the right moment to give him an extra boost. There seems to be a big theme in this chapter about 'new thinking' and 'old thinking'. Most of the negatives happen by people being stuck in the old thinking. Person centred planning, as Doris and Robert both feel, is the new way, and it's about treating people as people first, not as their disability.

The focus person has to be at the centre of it, and they have to be listened to. They have to be discussing the problems that they want to, and focus on their wishes and their dreams. That's one absolute rule, and everything else can be changed to fit in with that.

Supporting each other

Looking at Robert's and Doris's stories, compared with Matthew's, one of the main differences seems to be the quality of the relationships that you can get in a circle. Hearing Robert's tales of life in Cardiff cafés, for instance, many readers may feel that they want to take part in his circle! Not only does it give Robert the chance to have something 'person-centred', but others in the circle also seem to get support, friendship and fun. When one member of Robert's circle was ill, they all went round and visited her and tried to do things for her. How many social workers or key workers could say they had support or friendship from case meetings they go to?

Another aspect that Robert was also very clear about was informality. Although his circle had started to try and be rather formal, he felt that he did not need an agenda. The place also makes a difference. Social services often have meetings in really unfriendly, drab offices, and very impersonal places. It makes people far more relaxed if they are in somewhere they choose. You can break things up if you want to have a bit of fun in the middle of it and have a dance, or play a game, and relax.

Getting out of the system traps

Robert used a very interesting phrase, 'trapped in the system', in his story. Afterwards, we had this conversation.

Val: I thought that was an interesting phrase – trapped in the system. What did you mean by that?

Doris: It means it's what the social worker wants, and not what the person wants.

Robert: But the focus person can also get trapped in that thinking sometimes.

Val: Yes, people often feel that others have to make decisions for them.

Robert: That means they are not in control of their lives.

Getting out of the system means, then, first building up one's confidence. As Doris later said, 'We've all got gifts in us, and it's really important to know that your voice is valued and wanted.' Planning is not just about identifying needs, but also about valuing and respecting what people have to offer.

Working together

Planning one's life within a circle of friends, of course, is fine if one doesn't need any formal support from services. The problems can start when social services do not recognise the circle's aims and intentions, and communication can become very difficult. However, Robert was clear that he wanted members of his circle to be included in his social services planning meetings. 'At first my social worker was very reluctant to accept that, but we said – we are not trying to fight them, we are trying to work in partnership with them, and we're not in opposition to the social services, we are trying to work together.' At that point, Robert had a crisis, as he had to move and had nowhere to go. The circle, in fact, helped social services to find good solutions.

There seem to be two ways that professionals can get involved in the sort of circles that Doris and Robert both have. One way is to actually take part, but for this, Doris is quite clear, they have to take their professional hat off, and to be there because they really care about the person. In practice, this may well mean they have to turn up in the evening, in their own time. Many social workers quite deliberately decide not to do this, since they want to keep the professional boundary. The other way open to them, however, is simply to set up a way of communicating with a person's circle. The two sets of interests are then kept separate, but the business of the circle and the decisions arising out of it can be fed into the person's care plan. This is what happened when members of Robert's circle actually went to his social services planning meetings. As he says, people want to have support from social services, but they need social services to work together with their circles.

Who is in control?

Our stories of person centred planning show that it is different from social services planning. If a social worker tried to do it, it wouldn't be the same. You can't develop person centred planning and stay in control. People don't seem to realise that there are two different things here.

We're no longer isolated, and we are in control of our lives, with self-confidence and fulfilment. This is the positive side, not the negative side. So many people put us down on the negative side, but we're saying no – the way our lives are changing now is on the positive side. It has helped us to fulfil our potential and achieve our dreams.

NOTES

1 A circle of support, sometimes called a circle of friends, is a group of people who meet together on a regular basis to help somebody accomplish their personal goals in life (see www.circlesnetwork.org.uk)
2 People First is the name chosen by many people with learning disabilities for their own self-advocacy organisations
3 Partners in Policymaking is a training course for adults with learning disabilities, as well as parents of children with learning difficulties. You can find out more on www.circlesnetwork.org.uk/partners_in_policymaking.htm
4 PATH (Planning Alternative Tomorrows with Hope) is a tool that can be used in PCP. Using the focus person's dreams as a starting point, a PATH is used to help plan the steps necessary to achieve those dreams.

REFERENCES

Aspis, S. (2000) 'Fighting back.' In D. Attkinson, M. McCarthy, J. Walmsley, M. Cooper, S. Rolph, P. Barette *et al.* (eds) *Good Times, Bad Times: Women with Learning Difficulties Telling Their Stories.* Kidderminster: BILD Publications.

Atkinson, D., McCarthy, M., Walmsley, J., Cooper, M., Rolph, S., Barette, P. *et al.* (eds) (2000) *Good Times, Bad Times: Women with Learning Difficulties Telling Their Stories.* Kidderminster: BILD Publications.

Clark, D. (2001) *Living Our Lives: Doris.* Nottingham: DfES Publications.

Goodley, D. (2000) *Self Advocacy in the Lives of People with Learning Difficulties.* Buckingham: Open University Press.

Souza, A. with Ramcharan, P. (1997) 'Everything you ever wanted to know about Down's syndrome, but never bothered to ask.' In P. Ramcharan, G. Roberts, G. Grant and J. Borland (eds) *Empowerment in Everyday Life: Learning Disability.* London: Jessica Kingsley Publishers.

Walmsley, J. and Downer, J. (1997) 'Shouting the loudest: self-advocacy, power and diversity.' In P. Ramcharan, G. Roberts, G. Grant and J. Borland (eds) *Empowerment in Everyday Life.* London: Jessica Kingsley Publishers.

CHAPTER 6

Involving Young People with Learning Disabilities Leaving School in Planning for the Future

Steven Carnaby and Patricia Lewis

BACKGROUND

The ways in which as individuals we approach the process of leaving childhood and facing the uncertainties of adult life may take a variety of forms. Our thinking may be piecemeal, developing ideas and hypotheses about our future through a process of trial and error as we encounter and assimilate new experiences and opportunities. Indeed, the richness and variety of what is encountered both in childhood and during the 'transition' phase is likely to have considerable bearing on the conclusions that we draw and the plans that we make. Throughout childhood we are asked by those around us – teachers, family members and friends – 'What do you want to be when you grow up?' Our responses change and develop as we grow older, but it is likely that in our teenage years our thinking and concentration sharpen and become more focused, with the realisation that adult life is imminent. The factors influencing our decisions about adult life are varied and a potentially complex mix of individual beliefs derived from personal, familial, cultural and societal values and attitudes (Coleman 1979).

When the individual concerned has a learning disability, the adult world may appear even more daunting and overwhelming – both to the young person and to his or her family and friends acting as support at this important time. Influences and forces known to shape the lives of young people *without* disabilities – such as peer groups (Salmon 1979) and the media (Barbera 2004) – may leave young people with learning disabilities feeling confused and bewildered as to what is expected of them because of difficulties in understanding or inconsistencies in the delivery of messages or information.

Valuing People (Department of Health 2001) suggests that:

> Young disabled people have the right to the same opportunities in education, training or employment as other young people. The Government recognises it is important to make sure that care and support continues as they move into adulthood.

The emphasis on the continuation of care and support is central to government policy. This chapter argues that there is more chance of success if careful planning is adopted before, during and after the transition phase of the young person's life. Crucially, this planning needs to place the young person and his or her supporters at the very heart of the individual development process.

TRANSITION AND YOUNG PEOPLE WITH LEARNING DISABILITIES

According to *Valuing People* (Department of Health 2001) there are about 1.7 million children with special educational needs in Britain, of whom around 250,000 have statements of Special Educational Need (SEN). *Valuing People* outlines a range of problems and obstacles currently preventing young people with disabilities and their families from participating in society. One area highlighted is the transition from special school to adult services, and this is supported by research that suggests the need for careful planning at this important time (Hanley-Maxwell, Whitney-Thomas and Mayfield Pogoloff 1995; Orlowska 1995).

A number of key pieces of legislation are relevant to the way in which this transition process is conducted, namely the Disabled Persons Act (HMSO 1986), the Education Act (HMSO 1993) and associated Code of Practice (revised 2001 and enforced 2002) and the NHS and Community Care Act (Department of Health 1990). The resulting consensus is that, ideally, various agencies and systems (e.g. health, social services, housing, employment, further education and leisure) co-ordinate to provide cohesive services, while the revised SEN Code of Practice emphasises the need for children with disabilities to be involved in decisions about their education.

However, there is evidence of late of poorly co-ordinated transition for students with challenging behaviour (Orlowska and Rye 1996), with Madden (1991) reporting that there can be limited evidence for coherent, creative transition planning for students with severe learning disabilities. As Griffiths (1994, p.16) points out:

> Those who live and work with [young people with severe learning disabilities] must also make a transition in terms of their own thinking and in their perception and treatment of the young people...this is a relatively new concept for those involved with young people with significant learning disabilities.

Russell (1995) lists some of the challenges of transition planning, including the development of continuity in assessment, review and programme planning in order to prepare for a valued and productive adult life. She stresses the need for a positive approach to transition that encourages and supports students and parents in assessment and planning. Indeed, research suggests that transition is likely to be more successful if those concerned are able to contribute meaningfully, have a degree of control over the transition and have support readily available during the process itself (Collins 1994; Kobasa, Madd and Kahn 1982; Lynggaard 2002)

INDIVIDUALISED PLANNING AND TRANSITION REVIEW MEETINGS

The practice of individual programme planning, under various names, is commonly justified on the basis that it secures well co-ordinated services that are highly individualised and drive forward client development through assessmment, goal setting and review (Blunden, Evans and Humphreys 1987). Available evidence suggests that there is a lack of clarity as to the nature of effective planning (Greasley 1995). Studies at the systems level raise concerns about the ways in which individual planning processes operate (e.g. Sutcliffe and Simons 1993) and the assumptions made (Carnaby 1997a; de Kock *et al.* 1985). In addition, there can be a tendency to set 'service-related' rather than 'service-user-related' goals (O'Brien and Lovett 1992), inadequate involvement and consultation of service users in the process (Carnaby 1997b; Crocker 1990) and a bias towards focusing on the person's needs rather than strengths (e.g. Wilcox and Bellamy 1987).

The Connexions Service has significant potential for supporting an individualised approach to transition planning, which may ease what can be a difficult journey into adult services (see *Valuing People*, Department of Health 2001). In turn, placing young people at the centre of transition planning lays the foundation for person centred planning (PCP), now set to form the main framework for service provision within adult services. Individual planning for young people with learning disabilities usually takes place at a transition review meeting (TRM), making it both an essential forum for interagency co-operation and an opportunity for involving young people and their families in planning their future. However, it is essential that any planning process ensures the meaningful involvement of the young person (and his or her supporters) in ways that are personally relevant and person-centred.

REVIEWING LEVELS OF INVOLVEMENT OF YOUNG PEOPLE IN THE PLANNING PROCESS: A CASE STUDY

With national legislation, policy and practice guidance increasingly emphasising the educational as well as the ethical and psychological importance of person-centred transition planning, staff at the Shepherd School in Nottingham decided that it would be useful to reflect on the ways in which transition was currently being conducted. Of central importance was the extent to which young people themselves were enabled and supported to influence and/or control the events and outcomes of this significant phase in their lives.

A two-phase study was designed, aimed initially to determine the *extent* to which young people with learning disabilities were involved in the transition process, and then make recommendations for enhancing their involvement. The second phase assessed ways in which the school had addressed issues raised during the first phase. The Shepherd School is an inner-city special school for children and young people with learning disabilities. The level of disability observed at the school ranges from mild to profound learning disability. A total of 160 students were attending the school at the beginning of the study, decreasing to 120 by its completion. There were two main phases to the study, which took place over a four-year period.

Phase 1

A sample of 15 young people with a range of learning disabilities (ages ranging between 16 and 18) and their families participated in the study. The students were all in transition and scheduled to attend a TRM. Consent was obtained from the students and their families to conduct participant observation during the meetings. Half were observed with the intention of noting important themes arising and general trends in the decision-making process, while a detailed record of interaction between participants was made at the remaining eight meetings.

Observation focused on the frequency of interaction between participants, with attention paid to who initiated the interaction, who was being addressed and whether or not the interaction involved or excluded the young person. Inclusion was defined as communication (verbal and/or non-verbal) directed towards or initiated by the young person with learning disabilities. Exclusion in this context referred to interaction between members of a meeting other than the young person with learning disabilities, and which consisted of discussion about that young person in some way, for example, 'talking over their heads'.

This method has been employed and reported elsewhere in research looking at the exclusion of adults with learning disabilities in their individual planning meetings (Carnaby 1997a, 1999). Fictional examples of interaction are represented below to clarify the method.

Interaction including the student (Mary)

Teacher:	Mary, what do you like doing at school?
Mary (or supporter):	Drawing

Interaction excluding the student

Teacher:	What do you think she'd like to do when she leaves school?
Parent:	She likes drawing a lot.

Interaction excluding the student and then referring back

Teacher:	What do you think she'd like to do when she leaves school?
Parent:	She likes drawing a lot – don't you, Mary?

There was also an 'other' category of interaction. This included discussion that might have been relevant but which was not addressed to the student and conversation that had no relevance to the meeting's agenda. An example of this type of interaction follows:

'Other' interaction

Teacher:	How are things?
Other professional:	Well, my manager's on leave this week; it's been so busy.

Of the eight meetings which were recorded using this method:

- five were held for students able to speak for themselves (*Category 1: mild learning disabilities*)
- two for students who need more support with communication (*Category 2: moderate to more severe learning disabilities*)

- one for a student who needs others to speak on his or her behalf (*Category 3: profound and multiple disabilities*).

Phase 2

Results from Phase 1 of the study were reported to the school in the form of recommendations for improving practice and enhancing student and family involvement. Key staff were then allocated the task of reviewing and implementing these recommendations. Phase 2 of the study was conducted four years after completing Phase 1, to assess ways in which practice in conducting the TRM programme had progressed. A total of 12 students (ages ranging from 16 to 18) and their families gave their consent to participation in Phase 2, with participant observation of TRMs taking place using the same methodology as described for Phase 1. All qualitative data gathered is reported here as a review of the main issues and themes observed.

Findings from the study: Phase 1

Inclusion and exclusion of young people with learning disabilities in transition review meetings

Recorded interaction was divided into that which *included* and that which *excluded* the student. Table 6.1 shows these findings as percentages of total interaction during the meetings, with the students grouped according to their support needs.

The findings suggest that students able to speak for themselves (Category 1) were actively involved in their meetings for at least half of the time – in some

Table 6.1 Inclusion and exclusion of students with learning disabilities from discussion taking place in TRMs

Category of student ability	Average percentage of time spent in discussion style			
	including student	excluding student	excluding student, then discussion referred back	other
1	66.6%	16.3%	0.7%	14.6%
2	12.2%	32.3%	0.0%	55.7%
3	3.8%	33.4%	0.0%–	62.8%

cases, between 70 and 80 per cent of the time. Students needing moderate levels of support (Category 2) attended meetings that tended to exclude (32.3%) rather than include them (12.2%), and also consisted of a large proportion of discussion not directly relevant to the student's transition process (55.7%). The meeting held for the student represented in Category 3, who has profound and multiple disabilities, consisted of discussion mainly about issues outside the student's transition process (62.8%) with a third of the meeting spent in discussion that excluded the student.

It would appear that students in the sample who do not communicate in conventional ways (Categories 2 and 3) were not participating in their transition meetings as fully as those students able to speak for themselves.

Issues and themes arising in transition meetings held in Phase 1

Format

There were no written agendas for meetings, although all involved a teacher encouraging the student and/or his or her family to talk about the activities currently enjoyed at school. This preceded an outline of local service options and any new activities identified during the meeting. A large sheet of paper on the wall, completed by teachers and/or students themselves, served as a pictorial record of activities identified, decisions made, tasks set and people confirmed as supporters of the young person for helping achieve the various goals.

Location

All 15 meetings observed during Phase 1 were held in the school staff room. It is unclear whether students and/or families were given a choice of meeting place.

Timing

All meetings were held during school hours, causing potential difficulties for parents and carers and for students needing to miss favourite activities.

Duration

The majority of meetings lasted an hour, which seemed manageable for most of the students, although one meeting lasted for over two hours.

Range of participants

School staff (the Deputy and Head of Upper School) attended all meetings. In addition a range of other people attended – usually one or both parents of the student, and various combinations of the Disabled Persons Act worker, careers officer (usually for more able students), school nurse and educational psychologist. Professionals usually considerably outnumbered students and their families.

In only one meeting was an 'advocate' present, a class teacher who had known the student for only three weeks. Friends of students were not present.

Prior contact between the student and other participants

For some of the meetings, a significant degree of previous communication and collaboration between professionals had occurred, helping to ensure that informed, appropriate choices could be offered to the student and his or her family. For others, it appeared that it was the first time that the student's situation had been thought about individually in any great detail, and the sense was that the meeting became a focus for the professionals to define the ways in which they would be working together.

Structure

All meetings adopted a pathway approach, although in practice this was not always clearly used, with several meetings beginning with a discussion of the student's medical needs, or almost immediate discussion of the day centres that students would attend. This was often at the expense of discussing current activities and preferences. With the exception of medical files brought by the nurse, there was no evidence of files being brought into meetings or of agendas being used to guide the structure of the meeting. There was little or no reference to previous objectives set during the student's school career. The impression was that the transition review meetings were not fully based in the pre-existing context of future planning. In this way the meetings departed from the conventional planning process which tends to build on strengths and needs profiles on an ongoing basis.

Contribution of the student

Options available to the student were recorded in words and drawings on a wall poster and, where appropriate, students were encouraged to identify and record their preferred activities themselves. This approach was less appropriate for students with physical disabilities and/or sensory impairments, or those with severe cognitive disabilities.

Contribution of parents

Some parents came to meetings relatively well informed, with networks of people whom they could call on for support and information, were actively supporting their son or daughter in a range of out-of-school activities and intended to continue to do so. Other parents and relatives found it was more difficult to get involved and some had little prior information about services. Some had limited expectations of their son or daughter or did not want to consider certain options such as work experience.

Thinking about the future

Some of the concepts used in meetings to encourage students to think about what they wanted were complex and potentially confusing. Many students with learning disabilities, particularly those with more severe disabilities, found abstract concepts involving time difficult to manage.

The final year at school

Discussion about the final year included visits to service options for students and their families. Beyond this, the degree to which meetings concentrated on using the final year as a bridge towards the future varied. Some students were offered suggested extra days at college while they were still at school, opportunities to practise various tasks such as sandwich making or the chance to learn to use buses independently. This would expose them to a broad range of activities and perhaps new people, an important part of making the break from school. For students with severe or profound disabilities, the final year appeared to be occupied more with waiting to move to a day centre, with little planned development and the school 'weaning off' their initial input into day centre placements.

Post-school options

Meetings focused largely on formal service structures such as day centres and college places. Students' current preferences for activities were ascertained where possible but less attention was given to people changing their minds or disliking, in the future, something that they currently liked. College places were considered for students with mild learning disabilities, although by the end of some meetings it was often unclear what the student might be doing at college. No prospectuses were available for people to look at.

There was generally less attention given to what the future might hold for students post-college. Supported employment opportunities were scarce and the option of living outside the family home was only touched on briefly. Day centre places were considered automatically for students with severe or profound disabilities and there appeared to be little discussion of what would happen once the students attended day centres. Mention by professionals of 'detailed individual programmes' at day centres sounded positive but it was unclear if students with multiple disabilities would receive these in practice.

At some meetings a lot of time was spent discussing transport. This was seen to be a major issue and restricted the choice of options if parents were unable to support a student in reaching a pick-up point for a service out of his or her immediate catchment area.

Friendships

All students were invited to join the Old Students' Association, and some were heading to services where they already knew other people. The potential for greater attention to friendships existed – both old and new – and to the benefits these brought for students.

Health care

Where health issues were key to the student's future choices, discussion of health care took up substantial parts of the meeting. These discussions were sometimes very negative, seemed almost to replace discussion of student development and tended to exclude students themselves.

Careers advice

The careers officer only attended some meetings, usually those held with students with mild learning disabilities.

Results from Phase 2

The findings from Phase 1 of the study were reported to the professionals and parents involved, with a list of recommendations focusing on the themes described above. The overall recommendation was that increased student involvement is likely to arise from individualisation of the planning process, using formats and materials that are meaningful to the young person, with the style of the meeting being developed according to his or her abilities, interests and skills.

Inclusion and exclusion of young people with learning disabilities in transition review meetings

A radical change in policy resulted in students across all levels of disability being involved in meetings for at least 80 per cent of the time. This was largely due to the recognition that not all students find the traditional meeting format meaningful. For those not able to participate by speaking for themselves, 'meetings' were held in familiar environments, such as the classroom. Students were supported to show a video of themselves participating in their favourite activities, or objects of reference, symbols, photographs and drawings were used to illustrate how they spend their time at school and the activities they enjoy most. Evidence from research involving people with learning disabilities through individualised communication (Cambridge and Forrester-Jones 2003) indicates that such techniques can increase participation and choice-making. From these presentations, participants were able to draw conclusions about what the student liked and disliked. There was very little discussion above the individual's head, a stark contrast to practice observed during Phase 1 of the study.

Most importantly, considerable time and effort was spent with the person and his or her family *before* the meeting. In some cases, a year's worth of work led to impressive portfolios that acted as summaries of gathered information about the young person's life. This provided an insight into how individuals spent their time and a holistic picture of their life from their perspective. Such approaches are likely to increase autonomy and help develop self-esteem, as school and other agency structures are encouraged to work from this material, rather than fitting students into a traditional format for discussing the future.

For students able to speak for themselves – generally those with mild or moderate learning disabilities – meetings were held in a specially designed meeting or 'family' room, an environment in which all students are encouraged to spend time for a range of activities throughout their school career. The meeting format consisted of a wall plan, which placed the student's name in the middle and participants' names around the outside. Discussion centred on asking the student what he or she would like to do, and who might be best placed to help achieve goals that were set. Once again, the contrast here was striking, in that not only were students excluded from discussion to a lesser extent but, as importantly, were given the chance to practise what they wanted to say using role play and other skill-building activities. In this way, the TRM was demystified and became empowering.

Summary of changes in practice aimed at increasing student involvement in the planning process

A general review of practice relating to TRMs, leading to the allocation of specialist staff working with students in their final years at the school, has established a number of areas of development.

Ensuring that discussion is always meaningful to the student

Student participation is now central to activity, with visual aids such as videos and individualised communication through photographs, objects of reference, scrapbooks and other personalised documents used to structure the student's contribution. Participation was not only individualised for each student – for example, by providing prompts such as computer-generated symbols or laminated photographs of key people relevant to the imminent discussion – but was practised during role-play sessions facilitated by staff allocated to the transition process. This preparation helped students feel more confident and more informed about what was expected of them during the TRM and also helped ensure that discussion began with, and continued to focus on, the young person's perspective. For students with profound disabilities, the contribution is likely to be the presentation of video or photographs showing preferred activities or examples from the student's portfolio of work recently completed. In such cases, school staff are able to share with the individual's family and professionals the results of work which attempted to assess the young person's expressive skills and how his or her views are best sought.

Discussion of health issues

Issues concerning the student's health are discussed at a separate meeting, which takes place before the meeting attended by the young person. Key outcomes and recommendations can then be fed back clearly and in an appropriate format to maximise understanding. Health issues are therefore acknowledged as part of the TRM, but are discussed in inclusive ways and within the context of the young person's strengths and achievements across his or her life. This approach is particularly important where a young person's health has previously been seen to prevent him or her from accessing community facilities or activities or where a health issue has often been the first attribute noted by others around that young person.

Timing of meetings

TRMs are now scheduled to meet parent and carer needs wherever possible, although clearly the school needs to work within a range of given constraints. As importantly, the aim is to plan meetings to avoid clashes with activities or classes that the young person particularly enjoys. Again, the research to inform this is carried out by the allocated transition staff.

Contact with outside professionals prior to the TRM

Contact and the building of a working relationship with the student is now actively encouraged wherever possible, but continues to require attention and monitoring. Transition staff at the school work with the young person during the final year to establish the role and identity of attending professionals and, wherever possible, arrange informal meetings between the young person and each professional to foster familiarity – particularly important in the case of the Disabled Persons Act worker. It is no longer considered acceptable for students at the school to enter the room for their TRM without having met the participants beforehand on at least one occasion.

The role of friendships during transition

Some students participating in Phase 2 of the study invited their friends to the meeting, while others mentioned previous students they had known and who were now working in various settings that were discussed by other participants in the room. Meetings were therefore more likely to discuss the experience of friends and other students, giving the key student a 'flavour' of a particular setting. However, where it was felt that students were making a choice about a particular option simply because their friends were going there, this was considered inappropriate. Friendships and relationships are seen as an important topic for discussion, as students are encouraged to think about their social networks and how they might seek support during the time ahead, but not sole determinants of service options.

The TRM as the first occasion where the student's future is discussed

Considerable effort is made to provide students with a clear focus towards the end of their school career. Students write letters to colleges enquiring about courses and visit a range of settings and options to discover what is available for themselves. Work is gathered into a portfolio recording these activities, all of it written from the student's perspective, enabling the student to enter the TRM with a concrete account of the choices that have been considered and the opportunities that have been explored.

In line with mainstream education, there is a real sense of helping students adjust to the challenges of adulthood not only in practical terms, but also in a psychological sense. The physical environment has been modified for this age group (with an internet café and common room), encouraging an approach towards the students from staff and towards each other that recognises their maturity and the need to develop a sense of responsibility.

In practice these changes appear to have led to marked improvements in the quality of the transition process for students leaving the school, although the process itself is still considered to be evolving.

Future development proposals include the following:

- The possibility of facilitating workshops for parents where transition is discussed both in terms of the immediate events but also within the context of adult life for people with learning disabilities. Presentations from relevant professionals and representatives from adult learning disability services and more informal discussions from other parents of young people with learning disabilities who have already experienced the transition process are all possible themes and methods.
- Clarifying the role of careers advice within the transition process and encouraging contact between the careers officer and the student and his or her family well in advance of the meeting to discuss the options available – or at least to make informal introductions.
- Establishing a 'buddy' system, where students visiting employment and further education settings make contact with ex-students already working in these settings and spending time talking about what happens.

- When students visit the options available to them, it might be useful to make video recordings and take photographs in order to capture and recall some of the experience of being there. Such records can enable discussion with staff on their return to school about how the student had perceived the setting and help avoid situations where students are merely visiting settings and forgetting the purpose of the visit – namely to decide whether they would like to be there on a long-term basis.

CONCLUDING COMMENTS

The case study reported here highlights a range of issues concerned with the transition of young people from school to adult services, of which the involvement of students in the process has been central. It is apparent that significant energy and planning needs to be allocated to support young people with learning disabilities during their transition to adult services. The changes in practice outlined here aim to enhance the quality of student and family involvement as an important focus for services. It is also suggested that greater co-ordination between schools and adult services could lead to more effective provision. If this co-ordination initially focuses around service planning, it is likely to result in greater choice and flexibility for service users with more profound disabilities, as well as for those able to assert their needs in standard ways.

ACKNOWLEDGEMENTS

This chapter is based on an adapted version of a research paper that first appeared in the *British Journal of Special Education, 30*, 4 (2003).

The research and suggestions for good practice reported in this chapter were developed with support and guidance from David Stewart, Di Martin, Angela Mallett and John Naylor, all from Shepherd School, Nottingham.

REFERENCES

Barbera, V. (2004) *Media Influences on Adolescents.* http://inside.bard.edu/academic/specialproj/darling/transition/group210/vicpage2.html

Blunden, R., Evans, G. and Humphreys, S. (1987) *Planning with Individuals: An Outline Guide.* Cardiff: The Mental Handicap in Wales Applied Research Unit, St. David's Hospital.

Cambridge, P. and Forrester-Jones, R. (2003) 'Using individualised communication for interviewing people with intellectual disability: a case study of user centred research.' *Journal of Intellectual and Developmental Disability 28*, 1, 5–23.

Carnaby, S. (1997a) 'A comparative approach to evaluating individual planning for people with learning disabilities.' *Disability and Society 12*, 3, 381–394.

Carnaby, S. (1997b) '"What do *you* think?": A qualitative approach to individual planning for people with learning disabilities.' *Journal of Intellectual Disability Research 41*, 3, 225–231.

Carnaby, S. (1999) *Designs for Living: A Comparative Approach to Normalisation for the New Millennium.* Aldershot: Ashgate Press.

Coleman, J.C. (1979) 'Current views of the adolescent process.' In J.C. Coleman (ed) *The School Years.* London: Methuen.

Collins, J. (1994) *Still to be Settled: Strategies for the Resettlement of People from Mental Handicap Hospitals.* London: Values into Action.

Crocker, T. (1990) 'Assessing client participation in mental handicap services: a pilot study.' *British Journal of Mental Subnormality 36*, 98–107.

de Kock, U., Saxby, H., Felce, D., Thomas, M. and Jenkins, J. (1985) *Individual Planning for Severely and Profoundly Mentally Handicapped Adults in a Community-Based Service.* Southampton: Health Care Evaluation Research Team.

Department of Health (1990) *NHS and Community Care Act.* London: HMSO.

Department of Health (2001) *Valuing People: A New Strategy for Learning Disability for the 21st Century.* London: HMSO.

Greasley, P. (1995) 'Individual planning with adults who have learning difficulties: key issues – key sources.' *Disability and Society 10*, 3, 353–367.

Griffiths, M. (1994) *Transition to Adulthood: The Role of Education for Young People with Severe Learning Difficulties.* London: David Fulton Publishers.

Hanley-Maxwell, C., Whitney-Thomas, J. and Mayfield Pogoloff, S. (1995) 'The second shock: a qualitative study of parents' perspectives and needs during their child's transition from school to adult life.' *Journal of the Association for Persons with Severe Handicaps 20*, 1, 3–15.

HMSO (1986) *Disabled Persons (Services, Consultation and Representation) Act.* London: HMSO.

HMSO (1993) *Education Act.* London: HMSO.

Kobasa, S.C., Madd, S.R. and Kahn, S. (1982) 'Hardness and health: a prospective study.' *Journal of Personality and Social Psychology 42*, 168–177.

Lynggaard, H. (2002) 'Issues across the life path: managing change, transition and loss.' In S. Carnaby (ed) *Learning Disability Today.* Brighton: Pavilion Publishing.

Madden, P. (1991) 'On the threshold of change.' *Community Care,* 2 December, 22–23.

O'Brien, J. and Lovett, H. (1992) *Finding a Way Toward Everyday Lives: The Contribution of Person Centred Planning.* Harrisburg, PA: Pennsylvania Office of Mental Retardation.

Orlowska, D. (1995) 'Parental participation in issues concerning their sons and daughters with learning disabilities.' *Disability and Society 10*, 4, 437–456.

Orlowska, O. and Rye, L. (1996) *Students with Learning Disabilities and Challenging Behaviour Leaving Special Residential Schools: A Pilot Study* (end of grant report for the Mental Health Foundation). Canterbury: Tizard Centre, University of Kent at Canterbury/Hastings and Rother NHS Trust.

Russell, P. (1995) 'The transition plan.' In *Schools Special Education Needs Policies Pack.* London: Council for Disabled Children/SENJIT/Institute of Education, University of London.

Salmon, P. (1979) 'The role of the peer group.' In J.C. Coleman (ed) *The School Years.* London: Methuen.

Sutcliffe, J. and Simons, K. (1993) *Self-Advocacy and Adults with Learning Difficulties: Contexts and Debates.* Leicester: National Institute of Continuing Education.

Wilcox, B. and Bellamy, G.T. (1987) *A Comprehensive Guide to the Activities Catalogue: An Alternative Curriculum for Youth and Adults with Severe Disabilities.* Baltimore, MD: Paul H. Brookes.

CHAPTER 7

Total Communication, Person Centred Planning and Person-Centred Services

David Dick and Karin Purvis

> In an uncertain world, where all we know for sure is that nothing is sure, we are going to need organisations that are continually reviewing themselves, reinventing themselves, reinvigorating themselves. These are learning organisations, ones with the learning habit. Without the habit of learning, they will not dream the dream, let alone have any hope of managing it. (Handy 1985)

INTRODUCTION

This chapter outlines some of our first steps in trying to become a more person-centred organisation. Being a person-centred organisation also means being a learning organisation, namely one that proactively listens to those who use the service, learns from this listening and adapts its behaviour in response to this learning.

In Somerset we are in the process of trying to create a culture and environment that supports and enhances the use of person centred planning (PCP) and other person-centred approaches within our directly provided services. The chapter will outline some of the procedures we are putting in place to support this, concluding with a case study to demonstrate how we are starting to action this.

BACKGROUND

It is our belief that PCP cannot be successful unless there are wider processes that encourage services and support to be delivered in a person-centred manner. Without these processes, plans may be made, but it will be very hard for them to be implemented appropriately.

When Somerset produced its PCP framework for the Valuing People Support Team, the framework undertook to concentrate at least as strongly on person-centred approaches as on person centred planning. By doing this, we could enhance person-centred approaches for all people accommodated within the service and/or receiving day or work preparation services. This means that the PCP framework will positively affect the majority of service users.

Key driving factors to enhance person-centred approaches for Somerset have been the following initiatives.

Valuing People

The principles of rights, independence, choice and inclusion are fundamental to the implementation of *Valuing People* (Department of Health 2001b). Objective 3 of *Valuing People* states:

> Enabling People To Have More Control Over Their Own Lives: To enable people with learning disabilities to have as much choice and control as possible over their lives through advocacy and a person centred approach to planning the services they need. (Department of Health 2001b, p.26).

National Care Standards

The National Care Standards (Department of Health 2001a) focus on informing and consulting with residents, namely:

> Standard 7: Staff respect service users' right to make decisions... (p.18)

> Standard 8: The registered manager ensures that service users are offered opportunities to participate in the day to day running of the home and to contribute to the development and review of policies, procedures and services. (Department of Health 2001a, p.19)

Both these initiatives consequently require services to work in more person-centred ways by enhancing the control service users have over the services they receive. This has resulted in an unprecedented demand being placed on the communication skills of people with learning disabilities. If services are to become more person-centred, enhancing choice and control for people with learning disabilities, appropriate communication support must become an inherent part of all services offered to and taken up by people with learning disabilities. Such communication support cannot be effective if it is only delivered as a specific activity, as it needs to be an integral part of people's daily lives.

OVERVIEW OF SERVICES IN SOMERSET

Somerset County Council Social Services Department is unusual in that it directly provides the majority of accommodation and day services for adults with a learning disability in the county. It supports approximately 1500 service users and provides accommodation and support through residential or supported housing services for about 700 people, as well as providing day services and work preparation services for approximately 1000. Somerset offers an integrated service for adults with learning disabilities through a pooled health and social services budget, and singly managed co-located health and social services community teams. There is a long tradition of multidisciplinary support for directly provided services, particularly since the completion of the Somerset mental handicap hospital closure programme in 1993.

This style of service holds obvious potential dangers for developing a centralised and aggregate approach to service delivery. However, it also offers the opportunity and capacity of implementing clear and consistent policies for enhancing user choice and control throughout the service.

THE NEED FOR COMMUNICATION SUPPORT IN SOMERSET

Empowerment through supporting the communication needs of people with a learning disability has been a long-held goal within adult learning disability services in Somerset. Speech and language therapists work to a consultative model. Those who know service users best – usually their support staff – provide day-to-day communication support. This has been achieved through the development of Somerset Total Communication (Jones 2000a; Purvis 1996).

Specialist speech and language therapists for adults with learning disabilities developed Somerset Total Communication in the 1990s to provide consistent staff training and local resources (e.g. symbols) to support them in their work (Jones 2000b), an initiative which received national recognition. Individualised communication within the total communication framework was also successfully employed at various localities across the county to facilitate user participation in a national research programme on the long-term outcomes and costs of community care (Cambridge and Forrester-Jones 2003).

In 2002 Somerset Total Communication was reconfigured as a multi-agency organisation to co-ordinate and support the use of specialist communication techniques for children and adults with a communication disability in the county. It aims to achieve this by developing a co-ordinated approach and addressing the key issues of management support, staff training, networking and resources across all partner agencies. In the long term, this cradle-to-grave approach to communication is likely to further enhance the empowerment of people with learning disabilities through the development of a 'language' which crosses all agencies, and is common throughout an individual's life.

In spite of the Somerset Total Communication approach and the excellent multidisciplinary working relationships between speech and language therapists and service providers, communication support was still not always functional. Signs, symbols, photographs and objects of reference were present, but not necessarily being used to provide service users with information or to support informed choice-making. The Somerset 'joint personal annual review system' had been redesigned and made more accessible using simplified language and symbols to encourage service user involvement. However, this accessible version of the review documentation was not used throughout the county. In the majority of instances, the use of accessible information in enabling people to be actively involved in planning their future seemed to be an activity that just happened on an annual basis. Supporting and involving service users to make simple choices and decisions about their lives was not always an inherent part of service delivery. As service users were not involved in making simple everyday choices it was much more difficult for them to make complex and abstract choices and decisions about their lives. It is hard to make proactive choices if you are lacking in confidence and have not experienced the power and responsibility of making choices for yourself.

There are also tendencies for services to set up systems that limit choice and control. It is easier to provide all residents with the same meal at a set time. Risk management rules often restrict people's control of their own money. Staff rotas tend to be set without any reference to service user preferences. When staff were questioned about enhancing choice and control for service users it was often hard for them to move on from the very basic areas of choice of clothing or drinks. This was even more so when the issues involved staff having to give up substantial amounts of power or control themselves – service users selecting staff, choosing who gave them support, controlling the telephone, managing their own money or medication, for example.

We wanted to hand over more control over such issues and to achieve this we required clear expectations for staff over areas where more choices for service users and clear support for staff in offering these choices were required – ensuring that new choices were offered in appropriate ways, the ability of service users to make choices was developed and the competence of staff to communicate appropriately with service users was enhanced. Over time, speech and language therapists and social services' managers had started to address these issues of developing more functional communication support through a system which is now called the 'communication development plan' (Purvis and Butler 2003).

In Somerset, the communication development plan became one of the major processes for ensuring that the wider environment supported person-centred approaches. It is of prime importance in addressing issues concerning choice and control and the development of staff skills, values and attitudes.

COMMUNICATION DEVELOPMENT PLANNING

The purpose of the communication development plan is to:

- identify areas of good practice and strategies to extend them
- identify obstacles to good practice and strategies to overcome them
- identify and set standards for staff training
- identify and set standards for supporting communication
- ensure communication support is appropriate, relevant and achievable
- set standards, targets and timescales for communication action for individuals and environments
- define and agree areas of responsibility
- agree monitoring systems
- show effectiveness and quality of communication support.

The communication development plan comprises three levels.

1. *Strategic*
   An overarching framework of principles and priorities to ensure national policy requirements are met. Priorities were set through using the 'Deciding Together' audit tool (Aitchison *et al.* 2001). There is one strategic plan for Somerset.
2. *Locality*
   A local framework for implementing principles and priorities agreed at strategic level. There are four locality plans in Somerset.
3. *Team*
   A framework to provide an environment which reflects and supports functional communication for the service users in that environment. Underpinning this are the communication strategies and targets for the individual service users supported by the team.

   Each residential/supported living/day service/work preparation service and community team in Somerset has a team communication development plan and there are currently approximately 60 such plans in Somerset.

Each level has recording sheets for the following areas:

- choice and control (choice-making, service user involvement, accessible information)
- staff training and support
- prioritisation.

The standards become more personalised and specific as the process moves from the strategic to team levels. This means that communication support can be planned to meet the needs of the individual service user and the environments in which he or she lives. As support is targeted it is more effective, resulting in increased motivation and ownership of the communication environment for the service user and staff.

Table 7.1 provides an outline example of the goals and action points for the different levels in staff training. In addition, timescales and responsibility for action will be recorded.

Table 7.1 Communication development plan: staff training

Training level	Goals and action points
Strategic communication development plan	• Identify staff development and support needs in light of departmental priorities • Identify strategic training standards • Evaluation of communication training
Locality communication development plan	• Agree locality training programme • Identify local standards • Plan release of staff
Team communication development plan	• Identify training to meet the needs of the team • Identify named staff to receive training, and date to be achieved • Evidence that skills acquired are put into action

SUPPORTING PERSON-CENTRED SERVICES

The next section of this chapter outlines the range of processes established to support person-centred services, and the outcomes hoped to be delivered through this approach (summarised in Figure 7.1). The central ring (A) refers to the deliverable outcomes for the individual service user. The three outer rings (B, C and D) refer to the processes that support the deliverables at a team, locality and strategic level respectively. These are in turn affected by external influences, such as government policy.

It will be shown that the communication development plan is the keystone of our processes supporting the delivery of person-centred services. It is, however, only one of a wide range of initiatives being used to this end.

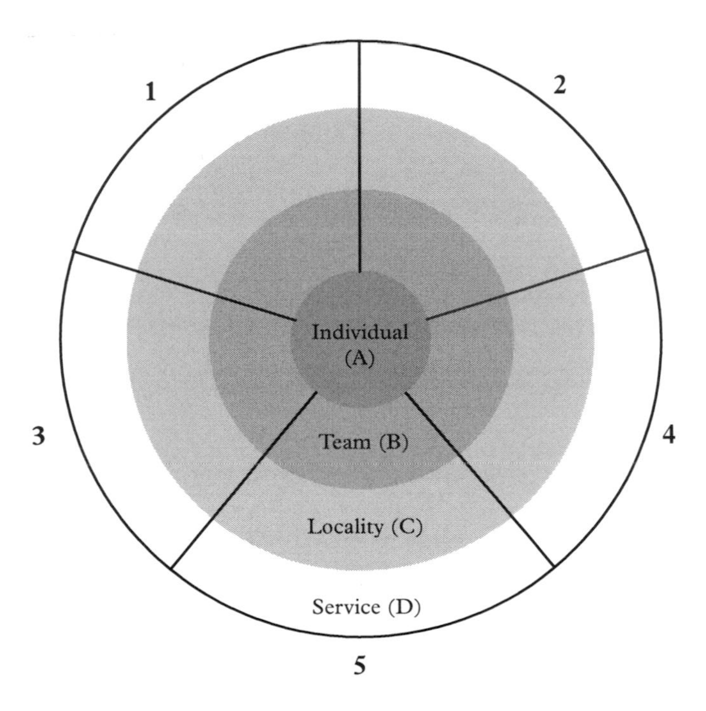

Figure 7.1 Range of processes supporting person-centred services.Key: 1 = choice and control; 2 = staff skills, values and attitudes; 3 = person centred planning, assessment and review process; 4 = partnership working; 5 = quality assurance

The key themes for supporting PCP have been divided into the following areas:

- choice and control
- staff skills, values and attitudes
- PCP, assessment and review process
- partnership working
- quality assurance.

These themes are presented in Table 7.2, identifying some of the barriers to effective service delivery, and how the communication development plan and other approaches attempt to overcome these barriers at strategic, locality and team levels.

The following case study demonstrates how these processes are being implemented. For each of the five areas illustrated in Table 7.2, we give examples of how the processes at the strategic, locality and team levels are resulting in deliverable outcomes for the service user.

Case study: John

John is a 42-year-old man, who has lived in residential and supported living for ten years. Prior to this, John lived in mental handicap hospitals since childhood. John has attended a traditional day centre for 20 years. He attends the day centre for four days per week.

John has significant difficulties with communication:

- He understands sentences containing three or four information-carrying words, provided he is familiar with the concepts. If John cannot understand what is being said, he tends to follow non-verbal cues. This means that John often agrees to things that he may not fully understand or want to do. At times, John becomes anxious, confused and angry when he is not able to understand.
- John is lacking in confidence and compliant – he follows the staff lead, and rarely takes the initiative.
- John finds it very hard to make choices. He is able to choose what he wants to drink. When John goes out for a meal, he always eats the same thing. John finds any kind of change difficult and prefers things that are familiar (people, places, activities, routines).
- John communicates through speech. At times, this can be unclear. John's expressive language is at a higher level than his ability to understand. This means that people often think John understands more than he does. John does not like to sign, although he doesn't mind if people sign to him. John enjoys looking at photographs and recognises some symbols.

Table 7.2 Key themes for supporting PCP, their potential barriers and strategies for overcoming them at strategic, locality and team levels

Key themes for supporting PCP	Barriers	Supporting processes at the strategic level	Supporting processes at the locality level	Supporting processes at the team level	Deliverable outcomes for the service user
Choice and control	Staff attitudes Staff reluctance to give up personal control Defensive organisational culture Statutory requirements Lack of skills in appropriate communication support Lack of skills in supporting choice and control Compliance/ confidence Life experience	The Somerset communication strategy sets out priorities from the 'Deciding Together' audit The strategic communication development plan incorporates these priorities into action plans PCP framework	The locality communication development plan translates strategic priorities into local action	The team communication development plan in which teams plan how service users will be supported to gain more choice and control The team communication development plan addressing team strategies for improving levels of engagement Evidence of the above	Individual communication strategy which addresses choice and control issues for the service user Person-centred care and support plan incorporating choice-making and service user involvement Opportunities to expand life experiences and make choices Support in choice-making at an appropriate level

	Assumptions made about choice and control Lack of information available in appropriate formats				Accessible information tailored to the individual for use in life and service planning
Staff skills, values and attitudes	Traditional attitudes towards people with learning disabilities Traditional ways of working Staff wanting to protect service users Staff are often reluctant to take risks Concerns about resources – involving service users is more staff intensive	Somerset training strategy, PCP training, communication training, national vocational qualification training Staff supervision and appraisal structure Clear policies and expectations of staff through management guidelines and the communication development plan	Local delivery of training in: • PCP • communication Managers' supervision and appraisal Local ownership of guidelines Training targets set through the communication development plan	Staff training in communication support, personalised to meet the needs of the team Staff training in PCP and other person-centred approaches Implementation of skills acquired Staff supervision and appraisal	More appropriate care and support Empowerment and opportunities to make choices as a matter of course

Continued on next page

Table 7.2 (continued)

Key themes for supporting PCP	Barriers	Supporting processes at the strategic level	Supporting processes at the locality level	Supporting processes at the team level	Deliverable outcome for the service user
Staff skills, values and attitudes cont.	Lack of knowledge and skills in person-centred approaches Lack of knowledge and skills in communication techniques	Risk management strategy Consultation with staff Training targets set through the communication development plan		Staff contribute to the team communication development plan Training targets set through the communication development plan	
PCP, assessment and review process	Not everyone having a named care manager Care managers lacking skills in PCP Inaccessible information Assessments and reviews that do not involve the service user sufficiently Service users lacking confidence and being compliant	PCP framework Reframing community care assessments and reviews so they are more person-centred Management targets Developing accessible communication resources through communication development plans	Training care managers in person centred planning skills Development of communication resources through the communication development plans Training care staff in involving the service user and using new assessment and review formats	Systems to support service user involvement in reviews Care managers to outline a strategy for including the service user Development of team communication resources through the communication development plans	Personalised communication strategy for the individual service user Meaningful involvement in planning/review processes Adaptation of 'community care assessments' to include relationships/places mapping and aspirations

					Holistic plans that include the non-statutory services Information in appropriate formats
Partnership working	Conflicting policies and priorities between agencies (e.g. children and adults) Reluctance to cross the traditional boundaries between services Reluctance of 'mainstream' services to offer services to people with learning disabilities Mainstream services feeling unskilled	Targets for strategic partnerships with health, social services, independent providers, colleges, employers, housing and leisure agencies, advocacy services, Mencap etc. in the service plan PCP implementation group Partnership board and working groups	Interagency partnerships and training for partner agencies Identified lead officers for different partnerships Priorities within locality service plans	Identifying and supporting individual community links through team service plan Providing appropriate support for the individual	Opportunities to try new activities Accessing community resources A 'seamless' service
	Other barriers to accessing services – physical, information, attitudinal, policy Inappropriate services being offered				

Continued on next page

Table 7.2 (continued)

Key themes for supporting PCP	Barriers	Supporting processes at the strategic level	Supporting processes at the locality level	Supporting processes at the team level	Deliverable outcomes for the service user
Quality assurance	Consultation only seen as a response to specific issues (e.g. not integral to all aspects of service delivery) Lack of clarity about desired outcomes Low levels of criticism by service users due to confidence/compliance Difficulty in consulting service users with severe communication impairment	Service user satisfaction survey (questionnaire using simple language and total communication) BILD Life Experiences Checklist (Ager 1998) measuring quality of life outcomes for *all* service users Accessible complaints system Management targets through 'balanced scorecard'	Annual service plan includes strategies to achieve policy targets Department-led local service user consultations Service user consultations led by non-statutory agencies	Monthly report between the team leader and senior manager Use of BILD Life Experiences Checklist at every review Service user satisfaction survey at reviews	Service users express levels of satisfaction Service users are enabled to complain Equitable outcomes for people with different support needs

Supporting John

Choice and control

Strategic

- It is policy for service users to be involved in staff selection.
- It is policy for every person to be supported to make choices in their life.

Locality

- Staff have increased the range of activity choices available by making local links with community providers such as college and swimming.
- John has done a training course on choosing staff at his local college.

Team

- The staff team are supporting a group of service users to help choose new staff coming to work in the service.
- The staff team has highlighted choice of food as a priority idea for increasing choice. They are developing accessible information about this. They are identifying opportunities for offering more choice.
- John's care and support plan indicates how he makes choices. In addition it includes how John communicates when he is happy or unhappy with something. Staff involved John in writing his care and support plan.

Outcomes for service user

- John has had a detailed communication assessment by a speech and language therapist. The assessment report highlights John's strengths as well as aspects of communication that he finds difficult. John has a communication strategy that outlines methods of communicating with him and alternative ways of presenting information to him (e.g. simple language, familiar symbols and photographs).
- Prior to his review John is being helped to talk about his life. Relationships and places maps are being developed using photographs. John is making a scrapbook about what he likes and doesn't like.
- John's house uses photographic rota boards to give people information. Staff support John to use this, so that he can begin to be more independent in finding out what is happening. Later John may learn to choose which staff he would like to support him on each shift.

- In addition, John has a symbol timetable outlining his programme. When things change, John has a special symbol timetable, telling him what is different.
- John is being supported to expand his choices. Before he goes out for a meal, staff show him photographs of different foods, so that he can be helped to choose.
- John has chosen staff who now support him on a daily basis.

Staff skills, values and attitudes

Strategic

- The communication development plan sets targets for staff training in communication skills.
- The PCP framework sets targets for staff training in PCP and different approaches.

Locality

- Training in PCP and person-centred approaches is being offered in the locality. Locality targets have been set.
- Local speech and language therapists offer communication training as outlined in the communication development plan.

Team

- Staff team supporting John have all had total communication training.
- John's house has a communication development plan highlighting choices that are on offer and choices that John specifically is offered.
- Staff values and attitudes are assessed using the national occupational standards in supervision and staff appraisal. Evidence is used to support national vocational qualifications.

Outcomes for service user

- John has two key workers whom he trusts. His key workers talk to him about what he would like to do, and support him to go to new places and experience new activities.
- John has a say over what happens in his home, and in his locality.

Person centred planning, assessment and review process

Strategic

- Basic standards for service user involvement in reviews are set out in the communication development plan.
- After John's review the information from the review is put together in a way John can understand, following a format developed centrally as part of the communication development plan.

Locality

- John's care manager has been trained in person centred planning, person-centred approaches and communication in order to involve John fully. John's community care assessment includes information on his communication, and how he can be supported to be involved.

Team

- Before his review John's key workers at home and the day centre spend time with him, talking about what he does and what he would like to do. They use photographs and symbols to help John.

Outcomes for service user

- This information is put together in a way John can understand, using photographs, symbols and pictures. If he wants, John can go to his review and take this information to help him talk about his life. If John does not want to go to his review or does not want to talk in his review, staff can present John's information on his behalf.

Partnership working

Strategic

- The department has set a target for the number of activities accessed in the community as part of the annual service plan.
- The service plan requires lead workers in key areas of partnership working.

Locality

- John's confidence in experiencing activities outside the day centre has grown. He has chosen to start going to a skittles session run by the local leisure centre. Staff from the leisure centre have had total communication training arranged by the local leisure lead officer and are becoming more experienced at communicating with John.

Team

- Levels of community presence for all residents in John's household are being measured using the BILD Life Experiences Checklist. Staff use this to identify and address inequalities in service delivery within the service.

Outcomes for service user

- John is doing more things in the community than he used to.

Quality assurance

Strategic

- It is policy that at the time of people's reviews they are assisted to complete the BILD Life Experiences Checklist and service user satisfaction survey.

Locality

- The locality in which John lives has a communication development plan. This sets and monitors standards for staff training, service user involvement and working with partnership agencies. This is reviewed twice a year, and fed back to more senior managers. In John's locality targets are set for the number of satisfaction surveys to be completed. Information derived is used for service planning.

Team

- The speech and language therapist reviews the team communication development plan every six months. The team leader has to provide evidence of how choice-making and service user involvement and consultation are being supported. The speech and language therapist reports this review back to the senior managers.

Outcomes for service user

- John is involved in more activities where he expresses his views about services and his life.
- John is encouraged to complete a satisfaction survey as part of the preparation for his review. Issues arising are addressed with John.

THE FUTURE

A wide range of initiatives are happening, which aim to shift the power balance within the organisation, so we can become better at listening, learning and responding to the users of the service. The initiatives are summarised as:

- the extension of the communication development plan to better address issues of choice and control
- implementation of the BILD Life Experiences Checklist in order to monitor real outcomes for people
- setting clear targets through 'balanced scorecard' and service planning
- educating staff in PCP and person-centred approaches through the PCP framework.

The real mark of success will be whether staff see these as fitting together rather than competing with each other. More importantly, over time, we should have a noticeable improvement in outcomes for service users, as measured by the Life Experiences Checklist and the service user satisfaction survey. Doubtless we will need to keep listening and learning if we are to be successful in our attempts to become a more person-centred organisation.

REFERENCES

Ager, A. (1998) *The BILD Life Experiences Checklist.* Plymouth: British Institute of Learning Disabilities.

Aitchison, J., Greig, R., Hersov, E., Perez, W. and Towell, D. (2001) *Deciding Together: Working with People with Learning Disabilities to Plan Services and Support.* London: Institute for Applied Health and Social Policy.

Cambridge, P. and Forrester-Jones, R. (2003) 'Using individualised communication for interviewing people with intellectual disability: a case study of user centred research.' *Journal of Intellectual and Developmental Disability 28*, 1, 5–23.

Department of Health (2001a) *Care Homes for Younger Adults and Adult Placements. National Minimum Standards. Care Home Regulations.* London: Department of Health.

Department of Health (2001b) *Valuing People: A New Strategy for Learning Disability for the 21st Century.* London: Department of Health.

Handy, C. (1985) *The Age of Unreason.* London: Arrow Books.

Jones, J. (2000a) *Communication and Choices. Everyday Lives, Everyday Choices.* London: The Foundation for People with Learning Disabilities, The Mental Health Foundation.

Jones, J. (2000b) 'A total communication approach towards meeting the communication needs of people with learning disabilities.' *Tizard Learning Disability Review 5*, 1, 20–26.

Purvis, K. (1996) 'An Evaluation of the Implementation of Somerset Total Communication.' Unpublished research project. Avalon Somerset NHS Trust.

Purvis, K. and Butler, S. (2003) 'Communication development plan; inter agency working.' *Bulletin.* London: Royal College of Speech and Language Therapists.

CHAPTER 8

The Role of Communication in Person Centred Planning

Working with People with Complex Needs

Jill Bradshaw

INTRODUCTION

This chapter outlines the important considerations for supporting communication and facilitating user involvement for people with a learning disability, with particular reference to people with complex needs. The current issues are explored through the use of examples and information from services themselves.

The chapter therefore aims to provide some useful information on current practice and to highlight the amount of investment required to involve people with complex needs in person centred planning (PCP). Where barriers to involvement exist, examples of how these can be addressed are discussed. Yet it is also important to recognise the limits to involvement that some of these difficulties impose.

Choice and control are key elements of person centred planning, as outlined in *Valuing People* (Department of Health 2001) and communication is central to effective involvement in PCP (Bradshaw and Carnaby 2002; Grove and McIntosh 2002). Communication difficulties undoubtedly create potential barriers to ascertaining service user views and wishes, coupled with potential additional barriers present because of the nature of the learning disability. Examples of the latter include the attitudes of others and the person's life experiences. There is certainly evidence that people with complex needs are less likely to have access to involvement in the process of planning for their futures (Edge 2001).

THE PREVALENCE OF ADDITIONAL NEEDS AMONG PEOPLE WITH LEARNING DISABILITIES

It is estimated that around 40 per cent of people with learning disabilities have a moderate or severe hearing loss (Yeates 1995) and that a similar proportion experience visual loss (Foundation for People with Learning Disabilities 2001). At the same time it has been recognised that these needs may go unrecognised or unmet (Purcell, Morris and McConkey1999). Additional physical disabilities are present for 20 to 30 per cent of people with learning disabilities (McLaren and Bryson 1987) and in 42 per cent of people with severe learning disabilities (McLean, Brady and McLean 1996).

Studies of challenging behaviour estimate prevalence figures of between 5 and 15 per cent of people with learning disabilities (Emerson *et al.* 2001). Dementia is also being increasingly recognised as people with learning disabilities live longer and Alzheimer's disease has been shown to be a particular issue for people with Down's Syndrome (The Foundation for People with Learning Disabilities 2001). Autistic spectrum disorders are thought to occur in about 20 per 10,000 children with learning disabilities and additional mental health needs are also more likely among people with learning disabilities (The Foundation for People with Learning Disabilities 2001).

Bradley and Darbyshire (1993) note that the impact of these additional disabilities may be difficult to quantify. Where there are additional complex needs such as those created by the presence of additional sensory impairments, challenging behaviour, physical disabilities or mental health difficulties, the combined effect can pose severe constraints on involvement, necessitating service providers to devote resources to developing and evaluating creative solutions.

ACCESS TO INFORMATION

In order to make the process of person centred planning more accessible to people with learning disabilities, Grove and McIntosh (2002) highlight the importance of considering the method or combination of methods most useful for each individual and ways of giving the service user control and ownership over the information. They further suggest that this may involve using pictures, photographs and symbols to present written information (see case studies) or the use of communication passports (Millar and Caldwell 1997). These provide an overview of important information about the person – for example, key things you will need to know about the person, the way you need to communicate and support him or her and so on. In addition, methods may involve signed communication, gestures, objects (e.g. memory boxes which contain items that can be used to aid communication, objects of reference used as cues to events (see Park 1997)) and videos.

Acting Up are using multimedia profiling to increase the accessibility of information to service users. This profile is a computer-based catalogue of information, including stills, video, sound, graphics and text, that is central to that individual – for example, activities, personal history, interests, likes and dislikes. The individual is then able to share this information with other people (e.g. to contribute to person centred planning, reviews, staff training, provide reports of issues and support needs etc.) (See Acting Up online – www.acting-up.org.uk/actup.htm) Similarly, The Big Tree multimedia and learning disability research project (see www.uel.ac.uk/thebigtree and www.thebigtree.org) are using multimedia profiling in innovative projects involving people with learning disabilities, such as in transition between school and adult services.

Acting Up stress the importance of involving the person at all stages of the process, such as illustrated in the case of Sally, who was initially consulted about the most appropriate use of communication methods (see the case studies later in this chapter). However, in practice, this does not always occur. In some situations, communication seems to be considered at the point where the plan has already been produced, as those involved recognise the need to make information accessible to the service user. The pros and cons of this can be seen in the example of Michael (see case studies), where the request to make the finished PCP document more accessible to him led to the eventual realisation that he could (and should) be involved in the whole process.

There is also a need to acknowledge that people with little or no intentional communication will be dependent on skilled advocates and that the use of additional means of communication will not automatically enable the involvement of the person with severe communication needs. The use of advocacy services is illustrated in the cases of Sally and Craig (see case studies).

MAKING CHOICES

Grove and McIntosh (2002) describe a 'choice-making cycle', highlighting that the most useful opportunities to make choices between different experiences are when the person is involved in a situation where real choices are being offered, rather than discussing choices in abstract (see Figure 8.1).

Some of these issues around choice-making can be seen in the case of Craig where the process has focused on making concrete changes that the person will be able to view and will therefore be meaningful to that person. In doing this over time, the person is able to increase their involvement in decision-making,

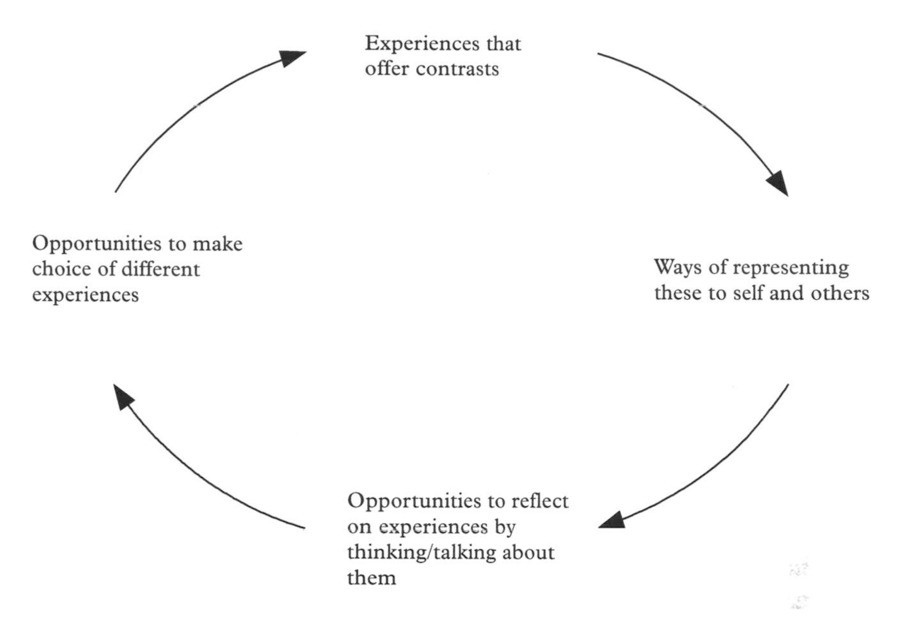

Figure 8.1 The choice-making cycle (adapted from Grove and McIntosh 2002)

but it is also important to note that the process also involves supporting the person to understand that may not always be able to have exactly what he or she want he or she (e.g. see the example of Andrew). Grove and McIntosh also provide a useful communication checklist for PCP, which includes thinking about the person, the information and the environment.

GOOD PRACTICE FOR PCP: SERVICE CONSIDERATIONS

Consideration of communication across all levels of services is clearly needed, with an explicit acknowledgement and statement that services have a duty not only to provide individuals with learning disabilities with appropriate communication forms but also to develop communication strategies to support effective partnerships (Bradshaw and Carnaby 2002). The City and Hackney Learning Difficulties Service are clearly working towards considering service user communication skills in all areas of their service. For example, according to their mission statement:

> The effort and time commitment involved in supporting someone's communication needs to be seen as a priority for the whole service in order for us to become truly 'person centred' and that everyone has the right to be given the opportunity to try out and access different and new systems of communication in order to achieve this... Anything impacting on people's

> lives should be communicated to them in a way that they understand. People have a right to be involved in their own reviews, and communication needs to be adapted to suit the individual to facilitate this. (City and Hackney PCT 2002, p.1)

The policy also stresses the transactional nature of communication and the importance of all involved using multimodal approaches which should be used in making everyday choices, reviews and assessments, in feeding back information to service users, and in service users feeding back information to the service.

In practice, this is being realised by the following actions.

- The creation of a database of photographs and multimedia resources. This pool of images will be used for communication books, visual calendars, increased accessibility of letters, reports and reviews (for example, the use of PowerPoint presentations with pictures), recording a service user's progress in groups or workplaces, job lists and shopping lists, to give some key examples. The team are already using standard appointment letters designed by their user involvement group with pictorial symbols, to make them more accessible to service users. Letters are also sent out with the team logo stamped on them, so that people are aware where the letter comes from to help them to choose the most appropriate person to read the letter for them if they need this support. Staff from different parts of the service will be trained to use the database which will be located centrally. All staff will have access to the service and will also be requested to add to the databank wherever possible. These resources are currently being successfully used in feedback to service users and their families about the individual's involvement in an arts and crafts project. A multimedia co-ordinator post has also been developed.
- The use of individual communication books for all staff members. These will contain photographs, symbols, written information and sign prompts relating to their role, where they work, what they are likely to do with a service user and their interests. This initiative will enable staff to give individual service users access to a range of formats and use those most useful to the person.
- Plans are also in place to build up communication profiles for all service users, detailing each person's communication strengths and needs in terms of the methods communication partners need to adopt and the support needed for that person. This will also use insights into communication skills from those key people who know the service user well.

- Finally, the service will be working towards building up a resource of templates to be used to create more accessible letters, reports, notes, questionnaires and so on.

In addition, the team are developing targets of accessibility, using information from an audit. Clearly, provision of training is also seen as essential and the team have highlighted the fact that the inclusion of multimodal communication within documents is not a magic solution but that they are there to assist. They are also exploring the possibility of employing people to work on making information more accessible.

SPEECH AND LANGUAGE THERAPISTS' EXPERIENCES OF PCP

Services commented that there was little agreement about the way in which this process could best be taken forward in their locality and that the multi-disciplinary team did not always feel that they had been trained in the approach. This sometimes led to them feeling unsure about their role, as was sometimes the case for front-line staff. Therapists commented that this lack of agreement and understanding about PCP had contributed towards some degree of cynicism among staff, with doubts about the impact that person centred planning will make in the light of service limitations. Though, in theory, PCP should inform service provision, this was not yet felt to have occurred.

Some staff commented that they were sometimes reluctant to become involved because they suspected that they would simply end up taking on the majority of the work (which was considerable in terms of time and resources) and that this was impossible given competing demands on their time. Many staff commented that their involvement needed to be considered at a managerial and service level if services were truly to work in a more person-centred manner. Local person centred planning implementation groups often involved or consulted speech and language therapists (SaLT). However, it was not uncommon for SaLT to only become involved in the later stages of the process, sometimes limiting the scope for influencing the ways in which communication, accessibility of information and ultimately involvement of the person were considered.

CASE STUDIES

Some of the issues discussed above are now illustrated using case studies. These outline ways in which communication issues are being addressed with people who have complex needs. They provide specific examples of ways in which some needs are currently being addressed within a continuous process.

The following case study is an example of circumstances in which a decision needs to be made on the person's behalf, using a clearly documented process.

Case study: Ken

Ken is 75. He has severe learning disabilities and a severe hearing loss. He lived with his mother, receiving few services, but as she grew frailer, Ken moved to an older persons' home nearby. He lived there for three years. There were some concerns about 'inappropriate behaviour' and 'aggression' and following an incident he was asked to leave. Two emergency placements followed in quick succession, the later to a complex of bungalows for older people with learning disabilities.

Communication skills

Ken's speech is very dysarthric and unclear to strangers. Attempts to use alternative means such as signs and symbols had always been limited by their lack of use in his daily environment. Ken spontaneously uses a lot of non-verbal communication including some signs and recognises many simple pictures, photos and symbols. His comprehension is limited to familiar phrases in context. Re-assessment of his hearing revealed a reliance on both lip reading and gestures. He was issued with new aids. He is a very friendly gentleman who uses his communication skills to ask familiar questions, express affection or give simple context-bound information.

The process

Initial work focused on the communication priorities for him at this transitional period and a care planning meeting was requested. It was agreed that initial SaLT input should be focused on establishing Ken's views on his current and future living options. See What I Mean (SWIM) guidelines (Grove *et al.* 2000) were used to gather information from key informants. The SWIM set of guidelines is designed to assist in the validation of the accuracy of interpretations of communication around decision-making. Informants were asked for their observations of Ken's past and present communication and behaviour. There was a high degree of confidence that this information revealed Ken's contentment with his current lifestyle.

Ken's involvement in the process was also debated. There was unanimous agreement that the only way for him to be involved actively would be to sample various options. This was deemed to be ethically unacceptable given the confusion this was felt likely to cause Ken and the distress he had experienced in his two recent moves. It was evident that the decision that Ken could be involved in meaningfully was to establish whether or not he was happy with his current situation for the foreseeable future.

Outcome

The collated findings led to the consensus view that Ken was extremely settled in his new home and it would be in his best interests for him to remain living there for the time being. The staff group at his new house are developing a personal portfolio for him, all about his past and current homes. Having a process to follow which was documented and shared by all seemed to be a positive way of ensuring commitment to Ken's future, while acknowledging there were restrictions to the options that could reasonably be offered to him.

In other circumstances, the evidence around the person's ability to contribute to that decision-making process may not be taken into account, leaving the individual very vulnerable to others' interpretations, as shown in the case study below.

Case study: Jane

Jane is 21. She lives in a local authority medium-stay respite home and accesses the local day centre five days a week. Jane has severe learning disabilities.

Communication skills

Jane has a good understanding of everyday routines and situational understanding. She sometimes seems to understand single words but has difficulties relating to things if they are not within her immediate environment. She does not seem to understand more abstract concepts such as time. Jane communicates through several non-verbal means. She nods or shakes her head to convey information and will also vocalise.

Both of these means of communication are sometimes difficult to interpret. Jane also uses facial expression and body movements and can point to things with great accuracy. She is able to use symbols and photographs but in order to be reliable, these need to be used regularly. She is able to request things, give basic information, indicate her emotions and greet people. Jane can make choices that are about everyday things that she can see. She can sometimes be extremely passive in her communication skills – for example, she may try and indicate that she needs support only by standing near someone.

Process

Jane had recently moved into the respite home due to her mother's illness, and her mother was expecting her to return home afterwards, although others believed that Jane was indicating that she did not wish to do this. The SWIM guidelines were used with a number of key people, with a focus on the level of decision-making and whether the decision was to be made by her or on behalf of her. Generally, people who knew Jane well felt that in terms of level of decision-making, Jane would disengage from a formal review meeting, either being only able to participate in a limited way or as a passive observer. All agreed that she would have feelings relevant to the discussion. Most people felt that the decision should be made on behalf of Jane. However one member of the team felt that the decision should be made with her.

Time was spent gathering information from significant others about Jane's likes and dislikes to ensure her preferences were taken into account, her ability to make choices (including current methods of offering choices, type of choices and response methods) and how she conveyed her emotions in order to come to agreement within the team about her interpretation of information. It was established that a collection of photographs would need to be developed for use with Jane.

The formal discussion with her took place in the day centre and was videoed to enable the team to be involved in interpreting the discussion. The discussion with Jane was based on Talking Mats (Cameron and Murphy 2002). A starter topic was used to allow Jane time to follow the format of the discussion. Jane then needed to indicate whether she liked or didn't like things. The team then went on to discuss Jane's general likes and dislikes – as gathered by the team. It became evident during the discussion that Jane was unable to fully comprehend some aspects, in that she was indicating that she liked several things that actually there was firm evidence that she strongly disliked.

Outcome

It was acknowledged by the multidisciplinary team that while Jane had feelings relevant to the decision that needed to be made, she would not be able to comprehend the overall picture. It was agreed that the decision around housing should be made on Jane's behalf. However, it was also acknowledged that the team will need to work together to fully support Jane to understand the changes in her life.

However, regardless of this work, the respite care home decided to fully involve Jane in their plans around closure of the home, persisting in asking her questions that she was unable to process and acting on their interpretations of her responses. A reviewing officer, employed by social services, interviewed Jane and commented that 'Jane...would probably like to live close to her friends...would wish to move out of home on a permanent basis.'

Services may consider communication from the start of the process and involve advocacy services from the early stages, as in Sally's case (below).

Case study: Sally

Sally is 35. She has moderate learning disabilities and has cerebral palsy. She lives in a group home. She moved out of home five years previously, a decision that her parents supported but did not instigate. It was felt that Sally had the capacity to consent. She attends two day services.

Communication skills

Sally communicates using light tech communication systems including communication books and the Talking Mats system. She previously used electronic digital aids but expressed frustration that the aids were unreliable and inflexible, and expressed a preference for lower technology systems. She has good verbal comprehension. She tends to try to respond to people that she likes in a way that she thinks will please them and this may have previously influenced the interpretation of some of the decisions she has made.

The process

The SaLT offered support to the physical disability service in developing an appropriate communication system. The service was encouraged to consider Talking Mats to involve Sally in discussions, initially to present her views on which of her communication styles were most effective, most valued by staff and also the communication styles those supporting her that helped her the most. In addition, the local advocacy service was contacted and became involved.

Outcome

Through the use of additional communication means, all involved recognised the need for an advocate to support Sally through the PCP process. In addition, it became apparent that though Sally appeared to want to attend all meetings and was supported to do so, she would understandably become frustrated when all in the meeting did not quickly pick up her attempts at communication. Meetings were adapted so that Sally was supported to use the Talking Mats system to give her views in meetings, where a limited number of people would attend. These people received training on how to use her communication system.

The following case study demonstrates how the PCP process may also be used to influence service provision.

Case study: Craig

Craig is a young man with autism and severe learning disabilities. He lives in a small NHS residential unit for people with challenging behaviour with four other service users. He is currently not receiving day services as they are not able to cope with his challenging behaviours. He is on a range of medication for his behaviour and this has recently been increased as a result of increasing episodes of challenging behaviours. These include pinching, pushing, self-injury, faecal smearing and masturbating in public places. Staff (including service managers) generally have negative views of Craig and his lifestyle is very limited.

Communication skills

Craig has good understanding of single words and a range of familiar phrases that are used in context. He is able to use nine or ten Makaton signs and his comprehension is enhanced by communication partners' use of signs. His social communication can be very appropriate but quickly deteriorates, particularly if the surrounding environment is chaotic. He experiences difficulties with proximity and appropriate initiation of communication.

The process

The SaLT instigated the PCP process as the existing process of intervention with clients was very service-centred – decisions regarding ways forward with the clients being made in terms of resources and assumptions about the intractability of their challenging behaviours rather than a focus on needs. Initially service managers wanted to use a care programme approach (CPA) model but, after discussions, it was agreed that a more person-centred approach was needed. This enabled all involved to look at the changes that were possible to achieve concrete improvements that Craig would notice rather than on focusing on what the service could currently deliver. It was agreed that all goals of PCP would be concrete enough to be shared in visual form with Craig. The intention was that these would be things that he could see changing and would therefore help him to see the purpose of an otherwise 'strange' meeting. For example, a goal might be for him to go swimming, or to have his own snack box in his room.

Outcome

Craig was encouraged to attend meetings and was given visual information on concrete goals. By using a PCP approach, it was possible to try to go beyond the boundaries that were set because of the presence of challenging behaviour and to think about 'what if…' rather than 'we can't because he might…'

The process of making information accessible may increase understanding of the need to involve the person at all stages, as in the following case.

Case study: Michael

Michael is 50. He has moderate learning disabilities and cyclical periods of mental health problems. He spent much of his life in a long-stay hospital but has lived in a supported home for the past two years, accessing local college courses.

Communication

Michael has a good understanding of concrete language. He is able to discuss familiar things outside of his immediate environment. He needs support in understanding time concepts – both in a day-to-day sense and in a wider sense. Michael has difficulties accessing everyday information such as the household shopping list. This is due to both his literacy skills and his ability to recall information. Michael communicates through using speech alongside non-verbal means of communication. He has difficulties with paralinguistic aspects of his speech such as rate, and has word-finding difficulties. Michael can communicate for many reasons. He is an extremely sociable person and his communication skills sometimes seem to be affected by those that he is with. When he has word-finding difficulties he will tend to go along with what others have said. He can also be quite a passive communicator in some settings and has a tendency to acquiesce when he feels that people are asking his opinion or offering him a choice.

Process

SaLT services have supported Michael for the last year around making daily information more accessible to him – for example, using a shopping list with symbols and through using a weekly photographed timetable to aid his concept of time. Michael has been involved in these processes from the start. During this time Michael's care co-ordinator requested support in putting symbols to his completed ten-page Essential Lifestyle Plan (ELP), in order that he could understand more of the plan. This involved discussions with his care co-ordinator and meetings with Michael and his support worker to piece together an accessible version. Michael was key in deciding what photographs and which symbols represented his plan – for example, in selecting which symbols made abstract concepts more accessible to him. Once it was finished, Michael kept the plan in his room and would initially refer to it on a daily basis. He would look through it when alone or with significant people such as his family and support workers.

Outcome

Throughout this process, all involved became increasingly aware of the importance of making information more accessible to Michael and though this had not been assumed necessary in the initial gathering of the information, it led to discussions about use of vocabulary, using visual information to ensure Michael has access to information in discussions, concepts that Michael may have more difficulty understanding, use of questions, Michael's ability to make choices and Michael's tendency to acquiesce in certain situations. This has made it possible for staff to adopt strategies to support Michael's communication throughout the ongoing process of person centred planning.

Therapists also commented on the importance of involving people at all stages in the process, for example in designing housewarming party invitations and delivering them in person. Therapists were also involved in the design of checklists with which the service user could be supported to evaluate options.

Case study: Andrew

Andrew, a young man with severe learning disabilities, was supported to develop a list, working through photographs, pictures and concrete symbols, of the top ten important things for him in a house. These were then put together in a checklist with yes/no boxes so that he could visit a house and tick yes/no according to whether it met his requirements. The idea was to use the checklist to compare houses, and realise that a compromise may be necessary but that nine out of ten of the requirements may be acceptable. Andrew's list included the following items:

- a big bedroom
- a cupboard for my clothes
- cable TV and video
- garden

- house with men and women
- no silly people
- in the town centre
- near to a special friend/family
- help with the shopping
- help to look after the house.

The social worker and key worker visited accommodation with Andrew and went through the checklist. They felt Andrew understood the limitations of this choice but he was clear he wanted to move there.

ACKNOWLEDGEMENTS

Thanks to the following speech and language therapists for writing the case studies and providing the service information used in this chapter: Sue Thurman and Della Money (Head SaLTs), Vicky Romilly and Lucy Conn (Specialist SaLT), Nottinghamshire Healthcare NHS Trust; Sue Smith, Principle SaLTherapist, West Hampshire NHS Mental Health and Learning Disabilities Trust/Southampton City Primary Health Care Trust; the Health User Involvement Group for the City and Hackney Learning Difficulties Team, and the City and Hackney Joint Learning Difficulty Service and Hackney Independent Living Team.

REFERENCES

Bradley, P. and Darbyshire, P. (1993) 'Helping with multiple handicap.' In E. Shabley and T.A. Starrs (eds) *Learning Disabilities: A Handbook of Care* (2nd edition). Edinburgh: Churchill Livingstone.

Bradshaw, J. and Carnaby, S. (2002) 'Talking normalisation: the role of communication in integration.' *Journal of Community and Applied Social Psychology 12*, 298–302.

Cameron, L. and Murphy, J. (2002) 'Enabling young people with a learning disability to make choices at a time of transition.' *British Journal of Learning Disabilities 30*, 105–112.

City and Hackney PCT (2002) *Communication Mission Statement and Good Practice for the Learning Difficulty Team.* London: City and Hackney Learning Difficulties Team Health User Involvement Group, City and Hackney Joint Learning Difficulty Service and Hackney Independent Living Team.

Department of Health (2001) *Valuing People: A New Strategy for Learning Disability for the 21st Century.* London: Department of Health.

Edge, J. (2001) *Who's in Control? Decision-Making by People with Learning Difficulties Who Have High Support Needs.* London: Values Into Action.

Emerson, E., Kiernan, C., Alborz, A., Reeves, D., Mason, H., Swarbrick, R., Mason, L. and Hatton, C. (2001) 'The prevalence of challenging behaviours: a total population study.' *Research in Developmental Disabilities 22*, 1, 77–93.

Foundation for People with Learning Disabilities (2001) *Learning Disabilities. The Fundamental Fact.* London: The Foundation for People with Learning Disabilities, The Mental Health Foundation.

Grove, N., Bunning, K., Porter, J. and Morgan, M. (2000) *See What I Mean: Guidelines to Aid Understanding of Communication by People with Severe and Profound Learning Disabilities.* Kidderminster: BILD/Mencap.

Grove, N. and McIntosh, B. (2002) *Communication for Person Centred Planning.* London: King's College.

McLaren, J. and Bryson, S.E. (1987) 'Review of recent epidemiological studies of mental retardation: prevalence associated disorders and etiology.' *American Journal of Mental Retardation 92*, 243–254.

McLean, L.K., Brady, N.C. and McLean, J.E. (1996) 'Reported communication abilities of individuals with severe mental retardation.' *American Journal on Mental Retardation 100*, 6, 580–591.

Millar, S. and Caldwell, M. (1997) *Personal Communication Passports.* Paper presented at SENSE Conference, University of Dundee.

Park, K. (1997) 'How do objects become objects of reference? A review of the literature on objects of reference and a proposed model for the use of objects in communication.' *British Journal of Special Education 24*, 3, 108–114.

Purcell, M., Morris, I. and McConkey, R. (1999) 'Staff perceptions of the communicative competence of adult persons with intellectual disabilities.' *British Journal of Developmental Disabilities 45*, 1, 16–25.

Yeates, S. (1995) 'The incidence and importance of hearing loss in people with severe learning disability: the evaluation of a service.' *British Journal of Learning Disabilities 23*, 79–89.

CHAPTER 9

Addressing Ethnicity and the Multicultural Context

Robina Shah

> Hi, my name is Sunil but I have been known as Steve. That wasn't my choice of name but when I was five and started special school the teachers couldn't pronounce my name, and one day the school driver said call him Steve and it stuck. As time went on neither myself or my parents thought about my name change and soon, wherever I went, whoever I was taken to or seen by, they all knew me as Steve; what was worse I even became Steve in my own home. I am now 20 and my name is 'Sunil'. It took me a long time to realise it but even I have the right to be known by my name of choice. The name given to me at birth which is a statement about me for me. Not a name that is for everyone else's convenience except mine. (Sunil, age 20 years)

INTRODUCTION

There are many people who have experienced a name change through convenience and not by choice. For some it will have no value, be unconsciously received and be treated as someone else's inability to pronounce a name properly. However, for others or particularly for people from minority ethnic communities with learning disabilities the quote illustrates a very strong message about identity, culture, and institutionalised behaviour and value systems. The inter-relationship between all of these facets and how they impact on services and the people who work within them is worthy of discussion. Inappropriate definitions of ethnicity and culture and their application to people from minority ethnic communities with learning disabilities may have serious implications in a service management context with far-reaching consequences.

This chapter will seek to address a few of these implications and consequences in relation to person centred planning (PCP) and care management for people with learning disabilities. The story of 'E' is about definitions of ethnicity and culture and how they have sometimes been used to the disadvantage of people with learning disabilities from minority ethnic communities. The ability to appreciate the subtlety of these definitions being used to negate rather than improve services for people from minority ethnic communities is an important one.

The debate although interesting is equally challenging to service providers and policy makers in a climate when social inclusion is still creating barriers by the continued establishment of specialist services for people with learning disabilities from minority ethnic communities. This is too often seen as the preferred option and undermines the necessity to address the integration of ethnicity and culture as an integral component of any health and social care policy, both nationally and locally and also of course within a wider European context. This perspective has never been more pronounced than now and can be embraced as part of the philosophy of *Valuing People* (Department of Health 2001) in shaping the management of person centred planning as an effective tool.

THE STORY OF 'E': DEFINING RACE, ETHNICITY AND CULTURE

A number of factors and considerations are associated with service design, in relation to the impact of ethnicity on the experience of people with learning disabilities from minority ethnic communities. Evidence from the ways in which race, ethnicity and culture are used within service planning and design suggests confusion about their interpretation. In discussions of research and service practice these terms have been confused or used interchangeably, resulting in reduced service outcomes for both carers and people with learning disabilities from minority ethnic communities.

It is therefore important that such terms are clearly defined, especially if they are being used to help explain the circumstances or life experiences of people with learning disabilities in minority ethnic communities. This is because assumptions about the importance of race, ethnicity and culture are likely to lead to very different outcomes for the planning and provision of appropriate learning disability services, staff development and professional practice (Shah 1994, 1995, 1997, 1998b; Shah and Hatton 1999).

What is race?

Race can be defined as a population distinguished as discrete groups on the basis of genetically transmitted physical features, such as skin colour (Betancourt and Lopez 1995). As the genetic characteristics used to distinguish racial groups are comparatively small and arbitrary (relating to a small number of physical characteristics), the concept of race has very little validity as an explanatory construct (Emerson and Hatton 1999). Similarly the eugenic political use of racist explanations of behaviour (Hernstein and Murray 1994) illustrates the negative consequences of using race as an explanatory construct for many people with learning disabilities (Smith 1995).

Furthermore, the identification of ethnic groups is complex and many contemporary perceptions of race and ethnicity have varied substantially over time according to the political use of such information (Desrosières 1998).

The 1991 Census of Great Britain constituted four broadly defined ethnic categories: White (Irish and non-Irish), Black (Black Caribbean, Black African, and Black Other), Asian (Indian, Pakistani, Bangladeshi, Chinese and Asian Other), and Other (Emerson and Hatton 1999).

Within each of these categories one would expect considerable racial, ethnic and cultural diversity. For example, the category 'American Indian' in the USA encompasses over 500 tribes (US Bureau of the Census 1992), whereas the UK category of 'Indian' encompasses important differences in religion, language and ethnic self-identification (Modood *et al.* 1998; Shah 1995, 1997, 1998c).

A major issue in the racialisation of service design and health research is that it is assumed that populations can be meaningfully divided into 'ethnic' or 'racial' groups, taking these as primary categories and using these categories for explanatory purposes. Stratification by class, income and so on is then seen as less important; issues of institutional and individual racism as determinants of health status or health care become peripheral at best (Ahmad 1993).

What is ethnicity?

Ethnicity too is often used interchangeably with race although the construct of ethnicity is essentially socio-political rather than biological. Ethnicity can be defined as a set of individuals who share a common and distinctive heritage, and who have a sense of identity as a group. However, ethnicity is not necessarily a monolithic construct. For example, Mink (1997) suggests that behavioural ethnicity (distinctive beliefs, values, norms and languages which underpin social behaviour) and ideological ethnicity (customs and beliefs which are observed, but are not central to the person's life) may be quite different. This distinction is particularly important when looking at person centred planning and choice.

Thus as Emerson and Hatton (1999) note, identification within an ethnic group may be associated with diverse beliefs and behaviours, which are subject to change over time as different ethnic groups interact with each other. Although there appears to be overlap between the constructs of ethnicity and culture, there are some distinctive differences between them in relation to ethnic identification, perceived discrimination and bilingualism. Therefore when considering ethnicity as an explanatory variable to plan specific services or improve services, it is important to identify which aspects of ethnicity are important and how they influence the overall outcome for people with learning disabilities from minority ethnic communities (Shah 1997, 1998c; Shah and Hatton 1999). In person centred planning this will be key to determining effective social and health-care strategies in the future provision of services for people with learning disabilities, irrespective of race.

What is culture?

As with ethnicity, culture is of little value as an explanatory construct without specifying which aspects of it are perceived to be important to users, service managers and policy makers, and how they influence behaviour. Most definitions of culture emphasise aspects of individuals' physical and social environment which are shared by a group, and are learnt or transmitted across generations (Betancourt and Lopez 1995). Of particular focus here is subjective culture: collective beliefs, values and social norms identified by individuals as shared. This has commonly been the vehicle for cultural stereotyping, where the experience of one person is perceived to explain and determine the care of other people perceived to be part of their shared cultural norm.

However, the important point to emphasise in relation to understanding how services perceive health and illness is to recognise that culture is a dynamic entity which changes to incorporate fresh ideas and perspectives as people develop new ways of responding to their environment. Those who oppose the use of the categories of culture and ethnicity, and the exploration of difference, are often described as anti-racists (Smaje 1995). They suggest that cultural analysis is a diversion from the more important issue of showing how racism is a common experience of all Black (non-white) people. This then becomes the major factor involving them in social disadvantage – for example, a higher rate of illness from a range of diseases and conditions (Ahmad 1993; Donovan 1986; Pearson 1983).

Cultural needs are also defined largely as independent of other social experiences centred on class, gender, race or sexuality. This means that a group identified as culturally different is assumed to be initially homogenous (Shah 1995, 1997). Anti-racists also argue that culturally based research using ethnicity as the independent variable has not led to much improvement of services for Black people or to an improvement in their health status (Ahmad 1993; Pearson 1983; Shah 1994, 1997). This view may be attributable to the structuralist position they propose, in which, to varying degrees, small-scale developments and improvements in attitudes that have taken place have been ignored.

In this way cultural awareness training may contribute to the reinforcement of stereotypes, unless the cultural awareness itself avoids stereotyping and shows the complexity of identity formation (Shah 1994, 1995). Therefore, the culture of a group does influence, but does not necessarily determine, the way that people live. Detailing such differences and the beliefs that they are based on can help break down crude stereotypical views of ethnic minority groups, indicating that the behaviours which social care and health professionals and others find hard to understand are based on their values and beliefs (Shah 1995). Hammersley (1995), in writing about the politics of anti-racism, accepts the view that research may in many cases do no more than attempt to correct common-sense assumptions. But this limited objective may be of real value if the findings of culturally based research are disseminated in ways which can influence practice (Shah 1994, 1997, 1998b, 1998c).

There is validity in the criticisms of culturally based research made by Donovan (1986) and others that it tends to concentrate on 'the exotic and unusual' and to identify the cultural practices of minority groups which are seen as harmful to their health.

The tendency to form judgements about others solely on the basis of racial, ethnic or religious identity lies at the heart of the processes examined in many studies (Chamba *et al.* 1999; Hatton *et al.* 1998, 2000; Shah 1995, 1997, 1998a, 1998b, 1998c; Shah and Hatton 1999), namely prejudice, stereotypes and discrimination.

These terms are often interchangeable with personal and cultural racism, which are enhanced through institutional racism. These three constructs help explain how racism may be reinforced within social work theory and practice. Institutional racism is embedded within an infrastructure, resistant to change as a result of policies and practices installed and perpetuated by white professionals working within the organisation (Dominelli 1998; Shah 1997, 1998a, 1998c). Institutional racism maybe endorsed in any institution, whether it be social work, health, education or in the voluntary sector, through a number of strategies which Dominelli identifies as: omission, denial, de-contextualisation, dumping, the colour-blind approach, the patronising approach and avoidance.

Ahmad (1993) has argued that discourses built around the concept of culture and cultural difference play an important part within the strategies of control of people from minority ethnic communities through state systems of immigration control, education, professional ideologies and practices. The effect of an emphasis entirely on cultural difference to explain inequalities and differences in health and social care services is to pathologise culture, making it the cause of as well as the solution to inequalities in social care services. Many studies openly challenge this school of thought by comparing the needs of Asian families to their white peers and arguing that culture is not rigid but changing for all people (Chamba *et al.* 1999; Hatton *et al.* 1998, 2000; Shah 1997, 1998a, 1998b, 1998c). These studies suggest that race is used to explain people's differences rather than looking at how cultural identity may be more important. For example, when parents seek explanations to understand their child's condition they may be influenced by cultural values irrespective of their racial backgrounds.

Smaje (1995) has drawn attention to the difficulties involved in distinguishing material and cultural factors in health and the problem of defining ethnic groupings. He suggests that while it cannot be said that the evidence produced by culturally sensitive research has clearly shown the validity of this approach for policy making, more such research is needed. This should attempt to produce 'more refined approaches to the dynamic interactions between culture, socio-economic status and health experience'.

One may argue that there are clearly conceptual and political differences, which will continue to guide both the practices of learning disability services and researchers, the interpretation of their findings, and the ways in which these are used. Being aware of the criticisms made by anti-racists of culturally based service design and research can begin to open the debate about how services should really be improved without always assuming the need to create specialist services as an answer (Shah 1997, 1998a, 1998c). In time, care management may also come to appreciate that ethnic differences can be used positively in ways that take account of how people in minority ethnic communities see themselves and wish to have services delivered to them.

Another practical concern raised in relation to the use of ethnic groupings is the problem of defining the boundaries of ethnic groups and deciding who is and who is not a member of a particular group (McKenzie and Crowcroft 1994). There is also the question of the appropriateness of categories such as 'Asian'. Such categories may be used to describe a homogenous group whereas there is in fact much diversity and distinctiveness between people who choose to identify themselves as 'Asian' (Shah 1995, 1997, 1998a). Such a categorisation may mean something different in different places. For a number of reasons it is the case that the ethnic labels sometimes used in care management may be crude or even inaccurate indications of what people with learning disabilities so labelled share, and what their ethnicity means to them as individuals, individuals with learning disabilities or members of wider communities. It is important to explore this to deconstruct the certainty, which is implicit in categories used in most epidemiological research.

IMPLICATIONS FOR SERVICES

If a service for people from minority ethnic communities with learning disabilities assumes that group differences are related to race, ethnicity or culture, a number of related questions will also need to be resolved. These include the needs of different groups for services and the quantity or intensity of service provision, as well as the types and range of service.

It is well documented that people from minority ethnic communities with learning disabilities living in the UK experience substantial inequalities, discrimination and disadvantage. For example, people from South Asian communities are more likely than their white peers to live in substandard housing in inner-city areas, to be unemployed (or if working to be employed in semi-skilled or unskilled jobs), to experience poorer physical and mental health, and to experience discrimination in education, health and social services (Atkin and Rollings 1996; Modood *et al.* 1998; Nazaroo 1997).

Such evidence therefore suggests there is much to be gained from looking at a wider service context in which approaches to PCP can help develop truly individualised service and care packages. Culture and ethnicity can be explored with people with learning disabilities as part of the discipline of creating an individualised service and will likely be central to their identity and service. However, to achieve this it is necessary to examine and acknowledge the process links and constraints between providing an individual service and the requirement for this to be sensitive and appropriate to culture and ethnicity.

BARRIERS TO EFFECTIVE SERVICES

The backcloth to developing such services is the general invisibility of service users from minority ethnic communities coupled with a poor record of routinely collecting and using information on race, ethnicity and culture. The imprecise understanding of race previously referenced, outside an understanding of ethnicity and culture, risks leading to inappropriate services and individual interventions or – worse – a conclusion that people with learning disabilities from minority ethnic communities neither want or need a service.

This is compounded by a lack of evidence-gathering to test established assumptions or beliefs coupled with little consultation about service need or service provision with people with learning disabilities themselves or others from minority ethnic communities. Even individualised forms of assessment and service planning can be Anglo-centric. Basing assumptions on service norms for the dominant group also wrongly suggests that only people from minority ethnic groups have ethnicity or culture and can become the route for reinforcing institutional racism and excluding people perceived to be different from mainstream service planning and development strategies. It is similarly concerning when equality or equity is defined as providing the same service to all, irrespective of need and with no acknowledgement of the impact of racism.

Within such essentially racist views is the perception that improving services for people from minority ethnic communities requires adding something extra to normal services rather than providing and improving services holistically, resulting in positive outcomes for all service users.

The assumption that culture and ethnicity are the primary determinants of people's beliefs, attitudes and behaviours also risks fear of doing the wrong thing as excuses for inaction by ignoring everything else that is likely to be important, such as poverty, housing, language, carer health, lack of transport and so on. This can sometimes also lead to providing 'specialist' services based on ethnicity.

On examination of the research evidence already described it is important to acknowledge that people with learning disabilities from minority ethnic communities and their carers report that the barriers to formal support for them include a failure to address language needs, the provision of poor information about services and access, services which are not culturally sensitive and a failure to acknowledge the impact of racism on individuals and families.

The historical solution has always been to establish specialist services based on ethnicity. It is readily appreciated why this response is perceived to be the right way forward because it demonstrates a commitment to focus services and service receipt for people with learning disabilities in a wider multicultural context. This is particularly the case with interventions such as care management or PCP, because of the client-centred focus. However, while the creation of such services may be of real benefit to some people they may not fully result in widespread improvements in the quality or quantity of service supports. Yet it may be argued that having a relatively quick response to the desperate situations of many families is an improvement. Also, ring-fenced resources are more likely to provide greater improvements for families and service users from a specific ethnic group as they are targeted and result in the specific appointment of staff from minority ethnic communities.

Yet setting up specialist services or service intervention such as care management or PCP in this way also risks a number of disadvantages. For example, specialist services attract short-term funding and are invariably vulnerable to funding cuts. Good services may not be sustained unless carers' and users' experiences are used to inform service design and planning. It is therefore important for all services to assess their functions appropriately making sure the confidence of their carers and users is retained. This will lead to a better uptake of service support and a reduction in poor access. There is also usually high staff turnover with a loss of skills to the service and little continuity between services and users themselves. Service staff may also lack confidence to work with diverse groups of people because they perceive such positions and work to reflect specialist 'ethnic experts'.

Another disadvantage is that mainstream services do not take the opportunity to learn or change in relation to the learning and positive outcomes from such specialist services, without learning being translated to mainstream service planning and provision.

THE STORY OF 'E' AND PERSON CENTRED PLANNING

Ethnicity is a construct that shapes all of our lives irrespective of race. Culture and ethnicity can be used positively to influence the way in which services are designed, planned, delivered and managed. People with learning disabilities from minority ethnic communities need to know that their cultural needs are addressed sensitively but are not seen as the only constructs which determine their lives. There is increasing ethnic diversity in the population of the UK and there is great variation within and between ethnic groups. The difference between being called 'Sunil' and 'Steve' is not just about labelling and the creation of an identity which does not fit. It is more about creating the opportunity for people to exercise real and valid choice about who they are and what they want from services. So what is the way forward?

Valuing People (Department of Health 2001) outlines a strategy which enables services and care management to think differently. Through PCP there is an opportunity to produce a truly individualised service which will routinely take into account the ethnic, cultural and religious needs of *all* people with learning disabilities. This approach challenges the notion of not assuming any 'norm' of a typical service user and can influence the way in which true partnership between all people with learning disabilities can acknowledge individual need within an individual's definition of what that need constitutes. To elicit a response the question must be asked about cultural or religious needs, and personal preferences and priorities of having those needs met sensitively. Aspects of gender, sexuality, religion, culture and ethnicity may indeed be intricately related and variable from person to person, so it will be important to take a holistic as well as individual view and not make assumptions about such questions.

The concept of person centred planning is not revolutionary, as the request for individual need assessments, care plans or service plans has been with us for a long time. What is unusual is the alignment of an individual approach through person centred planning which aims to integrate culture and ethnicity in the planning process. The advantages and benefits this will bring in the provision and planning of support services in the context of care management will be manifest in the development of mainstream services with the range of skills and resources needed to meet the full range of needs demanded of them.

SOME FINAL THOUGHTS

Outcomes for service users

The process should be flexible, easily accessed and offer good quality and frequency. Facilities are available to address the special, physical and emotional needs of all people with learning disabilities in the context of ethnicity and culture.

Care management, referral and assessment

The processes to respond to the initial contact or referral of people with learning disabilities should actively involve them in deciding how their needs will be met, what the person centred plan should look like and offer opportunities for change and support in meeting key priorities of care.

PCP and review

Reviews of the needs expressed in PCPs should be carried out in accordance with the needs of people with learning disabilities and where possible and with consent and positive outcomes shared as part of staff development. This approach should include the objectives and steps taken which enabled PCP to be most effective.

Establishing the evidence base

What do we know about the specific needs of people with learning disabilities from minority ethnic communities? What are their experiences of the assessment process, care planning, formal service support and different approaches to care management? What is unique to them and what is similar to the experience of all people with learning disabilities?

The lack of take-up of support services

What changes have led to improvements to the overall care management for people with learning disabilities from minority ethnic communities? How can this information be shared as good practice and inform the way in which PCP can be made more inclusive?

The lack of representation of relevant aspects of the life experiences of people with learning disabilities in the assessment and care management process, particularly, for example, racism

How does this impact on and shape the form and conduct of PCP? How do support workers, service managers and care managers reflect and acknowledge this in behaviours, attitude and values which underpin services?

Acknowledging that the assessment process may itself reinforce cultural and racial stereotyping

Discussion in staff development, with positive examples of how inclusive assessment can work in the care management and PCP process. How to make the approach inclusive for everyone, making connections as well as understanding unique differences between cultures and individuals. Supporting staff to have the confidence to think and behave laterally and address questions about culture in a safe and relaxed manner with all people with learning disabilities and their families.

Challenge and unlearn explicit learnt behaviour in which culture is seen to be exclusive to people from particular perceived cultural backgrounds

Recognising the value of an individual approach that understands that equality is not the same as treating people equally, and which acknowledges that people with learning disabilities have unique experiences.

> *What should the tool look like?*
> 'Same' is not equal so the 'E' story goes
> Discrimination and racism still flow
> But what matters too is that 'E' is entwined
> With person centred planning both yours and mine!

REFERENCES

Ahmad, W. (1993) 'Making Black people sick: "race", ideology and health research.' In W. Ahmad (ed) *'Race' and Health in Contemporary Britain.* Buckingham: Open University Press.

Atkin, K. and Rollings, J. (1996) 'Looking after their own? Family care-giving among Asian and Afro-Caribbean communities.' In W.I.U. Ahmad and K. Atkin (eds) *Race and Community Care.* Buckingham: Open University Press.

Betancourt, H. and Lopez, S. (1995) 'The study of culture, ethnicity and race in American psychology.' In N.R. Goldberger and J.B. Veroff (eds) *The Culture and Psychology Reader* (pp.87–107). New York: New York University Press.

Chamba, R., Ahmad, W., Hirst, M., Lawton, D. and Beresford, B. (1999) *On the Edge: Minority Ethnic Families Caring for a Severely Disabled Child.* Bristol: Policy Press.

Department of Health (2001) *Valuing People: A New Strategy for Learning Disability for the 21st Century.* London: Department of Health.

Desrosièr, A. (1998) *The Politics of Large Numbers: A History of Statistical Reasoning* (tr. C. Naish). Cambridge, MA: Harvard University Press.

Dominellis, L. (1998) 'Affirmative action: A counter to racial discrimination in international perspectives in social work: Countering discrimination in social work.' In B. Lesnick (ed) *International Perspectives in Social Work.* Aldershot: Ashgate.

Donovan, J. (1986) *We Don't Buy Sickness It Just Comes.* Aldershot: Gower Press.

Hammersley, M. (1995) *The Politics of Social Research.* London: Sage.

Hatton, C., Akram, Y., Shah, R., Robertson, J. and Emerson, E. (2000) *Suporting South Asian Families with a Child with Severe Disabilities: report to the Department of Health.* Manchester: Hester Adrian Research Centre, University of Manchester.

Hatton, C., Azmi, S., Caine, A. and Emerson, E. (1998) 'Informal carers of adolescents with learning difficulties from the South Asian communities: family circumstances, service support and carer stress.' *British Journal of Social Work 28*, 821–837.

Hernstein, R. and Murray, C. (1994) *The Bell Curve: Intelligence and Class Structure in American Life.* New York: The Free Press.

McKenzie, K. and Crowcroft, N. (1994) 'Race, ethnicity, culture and science.' *British Medical Journal 309*, 286–287.

Mink, I. (1997) 'Studying culturally diverse families of children with mental retardation.' In N. Bray (ed) *International Review on Research in Mental Retardation* (Vol. 20). San Diego, CA: Academic Press.

Modood, T., Berthoud, R., Lakey, J., Nazaroo, J., Smith, P., Verdes, S. and Beishon, S. (1998) *Ethnic Minorities in Britain: Difference and Diversity.* London: Policy Studies Institute.

Nazaroo, J. (1997) *The Health of Britain's Ethnic Minorities.* London: Policy Studies Institute.

Pearson, M. (1983) 'The politics of ethnic minority health studies.' *Radical Community Medicine 16*, 34–44.

Shah, R. (1994) 'Practice with attitude.' *Child Health Journal for Paediatric Nurses,* April/May, 245–251.

Shah, R. (1995) *The Silent Minority. Children with Disabilities in Asian Families.* London: The National Children Bureau.

Shah, R. (1997) 'Improving services to Asian families and children with disabilities.' *Journal of Child Care, Health and Development 23,* 1, 41–47.

Shah, R. (1998a) 'Addressing equality in the provision of services to black people with profound and multiple learning disabilities.' In P. Lacey and C. Ouvry (eds) *Addressing equality in the provision of services to black people with profound and multiple learning disabilities* (pp.194–204). Birmingham: University of Birmingham.

Shah, R. (1998b) 'He's our child and we shall always love him – mental handicap: the parents' response.' In M. Allott and M. Robb (eds) *Understanding Health and Social Care.* Buckingham: Open University.

Shah, R. (1998c) *Sharing the News with Asian Parents.* London: Mental Health Foundation.

Shah, R. and Hatton, C. (1999) *Caring Alone – Young Carers from South Asian Communities.* London: Barnardo's.

Smaje, C. (1995) *Health, Race and Ethnicity.* London: King's Fund Institute.

Smith, J.A. (1995) 'Semi-structured interviewing and qualitative analysis.' In J.A. Smith, R. Harre and L. Van Langenhove (eds) *Rethinking Methods in Psychology.* London: Sage.

US Bureau of the Census (1992) American Indian Population by Tribe for the United States Regions, Divisions and States: 1990, CPH-L-99. Washington DC: Department of Commerce.

Part 3

CHAPTER 10

Implementing and Reviewing Person Centred Planning

Links with Care Management, Clinical Support and Commissioning

Hector Medora and Sue Ledger

INTRODUCTION

The Royal Borough of Kensington and Chelsea, an Inner London borough, in partnership with the Foundation for People with Learning Disabilities (formerly the Institute of Applied Health and Social Policy at King's College), undertook a pilot project to promote the introduction of person centred planning (PCP) and develop an associated aggregation tool to help commissioning become more responsive to what local people with learning disabilities were saying through PCP. The subsequent project evaluation in Kensington and Chelsea also considered the implementation of PCP, its historical and policy context and identified wider lessons from other individualised systems. This chapter aims to share learning by describing some of the steps towards the development of a workable model and the issues that arose in relation to care management and clinical support systems, leadership styles and commissioning methods.

Valuing People (Department of Health 2001, p.44) identified the objective of enabling 'people with learning disabilities to have as much choice and control as possible over their lives through advocacy and a person-centred approach to planning the services and support they need'. The emphasis on people with learning disabilities exercising their own choices makes *Valuing People* very different from previous White Papers (Fyson and Simons 2003), with effective

PCP viewed as an essential cornerstone in delivering the four constituent principles, namely promoting the rights of people with learning disabilities alongside the availability of greater choice and opportunities for independence and inclusion. *Valuing People* also rightly recognised that people with learning disabilities had very little control over their lives, although almost all – including people with very high support needs – were capable of making choices and expressing their views and preferences (Beamer and Brookes 2001; Edge 2001), emphasising that 'people with learning difficulties should be fully involved in the decision-making processes that affect their lives' (p.51). This applies to decisions on day-to-day matters such as choice of activities as well as operational matters such as staff selection and strategic matters such as changes to eligibility criteria.

The challenge for public services such as ours in Kensington and Chelsea, as laid down in the White Paper, was therefore to develop a person-centred approach to both delivering and planning services: 'this means that planning should start with the individual (not with the services) and take account of their wishes and aspirations' (Department of Health 2001, p.49).

In Kensington and Chelsea, the team had welcomed the contents of the White Paper as offering a positive framework to further support the direction of the work we were undertaking alongside local people with learning disabilities and their families. We had already started some advocacy projects. People with learning disabilities had been training as quality assessors with the National Development Team (NDT)/British Institute of Learning Disabilities (BILD) Quality Network scheme and were helping audit services. We were experimenting with multimedia to increase self-determination for people with higher support needs and using a range of communication mediums to increase involvement in both individual meetings and strategic planning.

When we began the pilot PCP project in 2002 we were enthusiastic about and committed to the opportunities PCP presented but were initially very much feeling our way. How could we genuinely start the process of shifting power to users and families? How were we going to ensure really supportive links between PCP and existing systems such as care management, clinical support and commissioning? We consequently began to recognise the paradox between the apparent simplicity of PCP and the complexity of doing it well (Kinsella 2000).

Most agree that people with learning disabilities should have as much say in their lives as the rest of us, as we each have the inalienable right to think about and plan our lives in the ways we want. Ordinarily we regard choice and control as two basic human rights, yet there are some in society who are denied such fundamental rights. People with learning disabilities are often most disadvantaged and have least real choice and control over the way they would like to lead their lives. They are mostly dependent on relatives, carers, and an often well-meaning raft of supporters to make decisions about the most basic of human needs (Sanderson 2002).

Figure 10.1 identifies the issues that are important to all of us and shows that the way we manage our lives in interaction with others contributes to their quality.

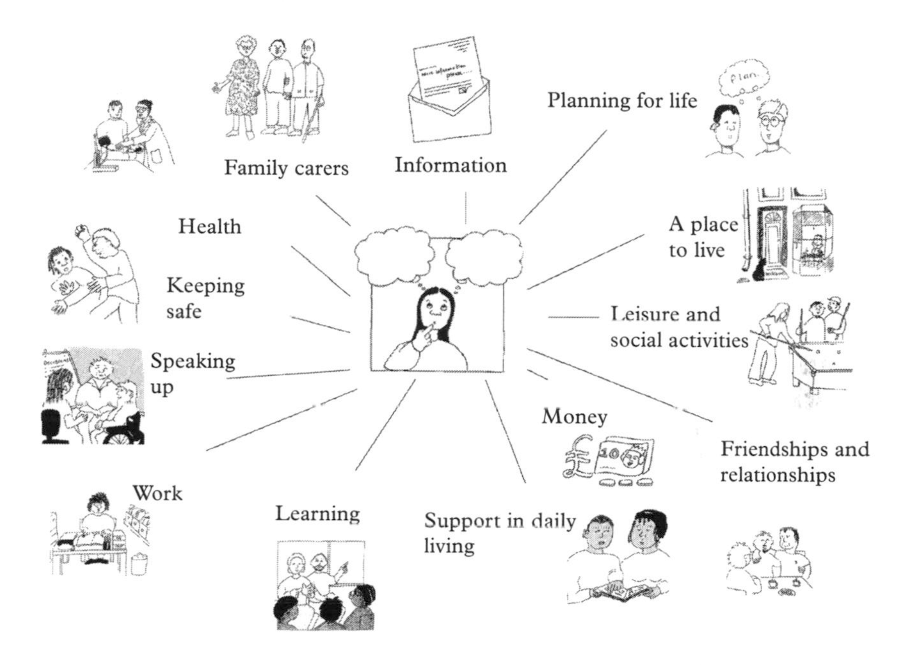

Figure 10.1 Ideas and wishes for living (Department of Health 2002)

HISTORICAL PERSPECTIVE: WHAT'S DIFFERENT ABOUT PCP AND WHAT WENT BEFORE?

Since the push for de-institutionalisation in the late 1980s and the development of markets in the 1990s, systems such as goal planning, individual care planning, individual service planning, individual programme planning and life planning have been developed and deployed (Cambridge 1999). As a broad concept, PCP is therefore far from new, having been developed in the mid 1980s 'as an effort to better understand people with disabilities, enhance their experiences, and facilitate effective problem-solving to achieve individualised and inclusive experiences' (O'Brien, O'Brien and Mount 1997). There have since been a number of different models, including Individual Service Design (Yates 1980), LifeStyle Planning (O'Brien 1987; O'Brien and Lovett 1992) and PATH[1] (Pearpoint, O'Brien and Forest 1993). All have one feature in common, namely that they are built around individual needs and preferences, putting the person not services at the centre of planning decisions, identifying responsibilities for action and reviewing progress (Holburn *et al.* 2000).

Sanderson (2002) describes PCP as a collective term for a family of planning styles which work with individuals to ask the question: 'What can we do together to achieve a better life for you now and in the future?' PCP is a process of continual listening and learning focused on what is important to someone now and for the future and acting upon this in alliance with his or her family and friends. Sanderson emphasises that PCP is not simply a collection of new techniques for planning to replace Individual Programme Planning but instead is based on a completely different way of seeing and working with people with disabilities which is fundamentally about sharing power and community inclusion. PCP is therefore an integral part of commitment to best practice in line with the social model of disability and new policy aims such as social inclusion and person-centred services more widely.

DEFINITIONS OF PCP

At the outset of our pilot project when training began for people with learning disabilities, staff and managers found that there was still a great deal of confusion between person-centred service reviews, care plans and PCPs. For this reason we felt it might be helpful to outline some of the key features we used to define PCP at the outset, drawing on Sanderson (2000, 2002).

Key features of person centred planning

- *The person is at the centre of everything that is arranged.* He or she is consulted about all planning, and chooses who to involve and the setting and timing of meetings.
- *Family members and friends are partners in planning.* Sharing power with families means seeking their active involvement and building a partnership. This has to be based on families and professionals getting to know and trust each other.
- *The plan reflects what is important to them, their capacities and what support they require.* PCP will also involve a rethinking of the role of the professional. People using PCP assume that the person is the first authority on his or her life and that a dialogue with other people can build on this. Therefore professionals are no longer in charge of collecting and holding information and making decisions about the person's life. Instead individuals and the people who care about them take the lead in deciding what is important, which community

opportunities could be taken or created and what the future could look like. In this style, professionals move from being 'the expert on the person' to being 'experts in the process of problem solving with others'. In PCP clinical or professional staff move from being the owners of the process, centre stage, to being backstage technicians, the people who know what is technically possible and how to make it happen.

- *The plan results in actions that have a bias towards inclusion.* PCP is not about standard service packages. Traditional planning has sought to fit people into existing models and solutions. PCP describes the support needed from the perspective of the person and then designs a unique arrangement for getting that support. People who practise PCP believe that communities benefit from including people with disabilities.
- *The plan results in ongoing listening, learning and further action.*

If individuals do not want, or for whatever reason are not able, to run their own PCP meeting they may entrust this to a family member or friend. This is what most of us do when planning changes in our own life. If individuals do not have the stamina to organise the process and have no one else in their personal network who can take this on, then they will need to rely on a paid member of staff. At the beginning of the pilot project we identified, through local consultation, self-advocates, advocates, family members, friends and paid supporters who were interested in receiving training and support in PCP facilitation.

The pilot also outlined the different approaches or styles of PCP, including Essential Lifestyle Planning, PATH, Maps and Personal Futures Planning.

WHAT MAKES FOR A GOOD PERSON-CENTRED PLAN?

We tend not to be known for the things we cannot do, yet we often see service users defined by their limitations. There is little value in offering people choices when they have no real notion of what that means. To ensure a good plan we must make sure that the strengths of the person are foremost in our minds and that any choices on offer are real. For example, if a person has only ever lived in a residential home then he or she should be given the opportunity to experience what it might be like to live independently in the community before making more permanent or life-defining decisions (Medora and Cambridge 2002).

During implementation, staff raised issues about independence, informed consent and risk-taking in the context of their developing roles and PCP, sometimes because existing organisational policies seem to offer contradictory guidance to the philosophy of PCP. For example, a number of accommodation support agencies had adult protection policies that stated that staff should never take service users to their own homes. In some cases staff participating in the project were keen to offer this as a means of developing networks for the people they were supporting. The support model of independence (O'Brien and O'Brien 1998) was found to be a helpful framework, defining independence as 'independence to choose and live one's own lifestyle, regardless of the amount and type of assistance necessary'. Independence would not be measured therefore by the number of tasks that people did without assistance, rather the quality of life a person had with whatever support he or she needed. PCP assumes that people with learning disabilities are *ready now* to do whatever they want, as long as they are adequately supported. Thus the 'making sure you are ready for independence model' is replaced by the 'support model'. We found that investing time discussing this concept at the outset was helpful in moving supporters away from the notion that people were required to receive assessments, training, core competencies and complex risk assessments before they were in a position to contemplate a new activity.

Similarly many issues of consent were raised in the pilot. Paid staff were often worried about evidencing consent for plans concerning people who did not use speech to communicate or had high support needs. Legally, people either have the capacity to make a decision or they do not, but the decision frequently goes untested in law (Joseph Rowntree Foundation 2001). The process of decision-making for and by vulnerable adults in England is currently under the spotlight. The Mental Capacity Act 2005 aimed to improve and clarify the decision-making process for those unable to make decisions for themselves. The act is underpinned by a set of five key principles, namely a presumption of capacity, the rights of the individual to be supported to make his or her own decisions, the right to make what might be seen as 'eccentric' or 'unwise' decisions, best interests and least restrictive interventions (Department of Constitutional Affairs 2004). How whatever is ultimately agreed will assist or hinder the use of supported-decision-making models is critical. In the meantime, those of us working with people with learning disabilities have a duty to ensure that the wishes of vulnerable people in our communities are clearly heard and acted upon.

Best practice in PCP implementation meant that we wanted to move away from assessment concepts such as whether people were deemed competent to make decisions, instead using a model of supported decision-making (Beamer and Brookes 2001; Edge 2001; Ticoll 1998) with reference to the Presumption of Capacity contained in the Good Practice Guidance (Holman 1997).

PCP IN KENSINGTON AND CHELSEA

At the start of the project, health and social care services had not formally integrated, and clinical and social care staff, although working towards integration, were located on separate sites and operating separate management systems. This changed in August 2003 when the Learning Disability National Health Service and local authority community teams and provider services were formally integrated.

In 1993, prior to the pilot PCP project, Kensington and Chelsea had established an accommodation monitoring team, which consisted of care managers experienced in working alongside people with learning disabilities and their families to conduct 'person-centred reviews' and monitor the care received by people living in a range of accommodation funded by the borough. This included people living in supported tenancies, registered care and nursing homes throughout the country. Review meetings had begun to make use of photographs, posters and multimedia to involve people in planning their futures and commenting on their current support packages. As a result of the work of this team, local residential service providers had been encouraged to involve people in their six-monthly reviews of service, support people to set their own agendas for their service reviews, and to use multimedia and advocates to increase their involvement in the process. As part of the service review, people were also encouraged to meet in places of their choice with their advocate, family member or circle of support, to be able to talk more privately about their plans and the care they were currently receiving.

At the time of the pilot, the borough had also set up a commissioner-led model of Quality Network reviews, a national quality audit tool developed by the National Development Team and BILD. This system was further developed and involved people with learning disabilities, all local independent sector providers, NHS and local authority staff working together as partners in quality assessment and planning. These stakeholders trained alongside each other in the borough as quality assessors and then visited people with learning disabilities in their own homes and with permission at their place of education, employment or leisure, spending extended periods of time alongside them to find out more about their lives. Findings were subsequently recorded in the form of a poster mapping the person's life with reference to the ten Quality Network Standards:

1. I make everyday choices.
2. People treat me with respect.
3. I take part in everyday activities.
4. I have friendships and relationships.
5. I am part of my local community.

6. I get the chance to work.
7. I take part in important decisions about my life.
8. People listen to my family's views.
9. I am safe from harassment.
10. I get help to stay healthy.

This approach appeared to work well as a person-centred quality tool, equally accessible to people who do not use speech to communicate, and had yielded some very powerful findings about current service user experiences and support. At the time of the pilot these were actively informing our commissioning strategies and strengthening user involvement in planning, audit and partnership working. The findings from consultation with partnership agencies in our Best Value Review consultation (Royal Borough of Kensington and Chelsea 2002) had emphasised that the scheme was highly regarded by our local independent sector partners. At the time of commencing the PCP pilot, we were planning our third Quality Network review and we were keen to retain the benefits of this system alongside PCP. We felt the two systems had potential to complement each other effectively but we were aware that when introducing PCP locally we needed to explain how we envisaged PCP fitting with Quality Network and service reviews. The Kensington and Chelsea system (see Figure 10.2) was developed as a pictorial aid for mapping out how PCP would fit with systems in Kensington and Chelsea.

The pilot project

To ensure that the pilot addressed the needs of as many groups of service users as possible, including the most vulnerable groups, a cross-section of service users was identified using existing commissioning data. This included those in 'priority groups' as highlighted in *Valuing People*, including people with complex needs and dual diagnoses, in transition from children's to adult services and to old age, from minority ethnic backgrounds, with communication difficulties, living with older carers and in out-of-borough placements. Initially 40 people from this sample and their support networks who had expressed an interest in taking part were approached with an invitation to participate in the pilot. Participation required an ongoing commitment to training and planning and 26 people and their support networks agreed to trial this model.

The Foundation for People with Learning Disabilities, with the Borough and representatives of independent sector providers, developed a training schedule, subsequently delivered by the pilot project team and designed to meet the needs of service users, carers, PCP facilitators, paid support staff, care managers and service managers.

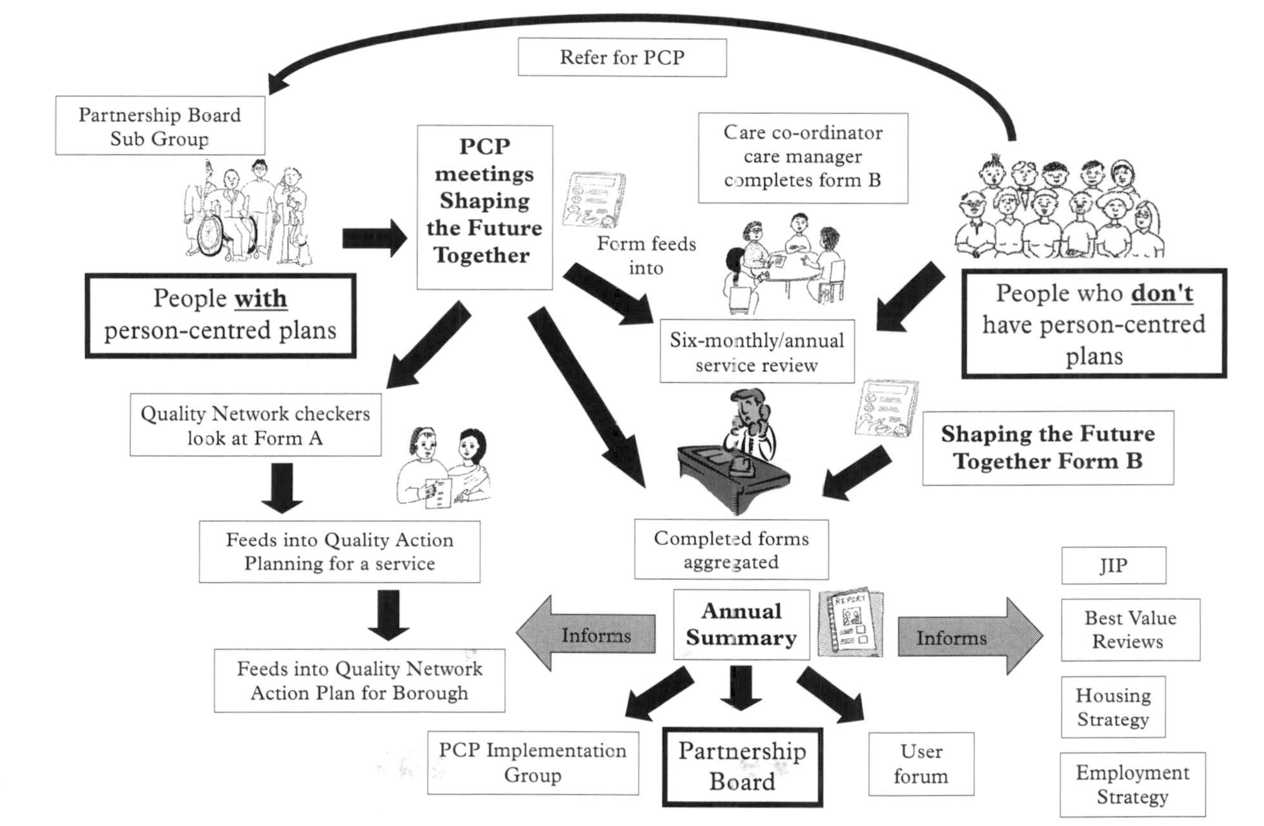

Figure 10.2 Linking systems – the PCP Aggregation Project

Supplementary training in communication for PCP (Grove and McIntosh 2002) was also developed and introduced to support the programme and to increase the involvement of people who did not use speech (Sanderson 1998). At the time of the pilot, the borough and five independent sector providers supplied services for people with learning disabilities. The independent sector partners participated in the pilot as did the people living at home with their carers and a small number located out of borough. The local advocacy service and Circles of Support project were also involved. Once the project was under way, learning opportunities took the form of teaching sessions, on-site visits to support staff, consultation and problem-solving and action-learning groups. A wide range of people with learning disabilities participated including people labelled as having high support needs and presenting significant challenges to services. Slowly person-centred meetings began to be set up and the first tentative steps towards a different way of working were taken.

It is interesting to note that independent sector agencies varied widely in the priority they gave to PCP, reflected in their commitment (training and financial) to implementing PCP, the extent to which they regarded it as a provider responsibility and the type of PCP formats implemented. Although there was genuine local support and enthusiasm for PCP, variations were also evident among clinical and care management staff in how much they regarded PCP as a key force for change in defining their future roles and the extent to which they assumed personal responsibility for its implementation.

With support from the pilot project team, care managers and direct support, staff began to encourage people with learning disabilities and their families and friends to assume greater ownership and control of where their PCP meetings were held. For example, people began to experiment and meetings were set up in cafés, local pubs, picnics in parks or held in spaces that the Circle had specially identified in order to include the individual in the meetings as much as possible (see Table 10.1). People also moved away from a 'who should be there' mentality to a 'who does the person want to be there' outlook and to recording meetings in different ways, such as in a PATH Plan, the PCP workbook, posters, flip charts and CD-ROMs.

Across the 26 participants a range of existing support networks and Circles arrangements were utilised. Some people had family members, friends and advocates keen to be involved. Others were starting from a very different position with no one but paid staff in their lives, and facilitators began by trying to trace ex-members of staff and former contacts from long-stay hospitals. Person-centred meetings happened in ways to suit the individual. An example from a care manager who was a member of the planning circle is illustrated in the case study of 'R' on p.160.

Table 10.1 Characteristics of PCPs and ISRs

Person centred plans (PCPs)

- Chaired by the person or the chosen facilitator
- Involving the most important people for the individual
- Recorded in whatever way is most helpful
- Taking place anywhere and at any time, such as weekends and evenings
- Owned by the person
- Start with an ideal world rather than current services
- There to bring about change, improvement and more choice and control
- Inform the individual service review
- Take place as frequently as required
- Not governed by statutory requirements
- Ideally chaired by a facilitator rather than service provider, care manager or team manager

Individual service reviews (ISRs)

- Usually chaired by a care manager, joint team member or provider manager
- Ideas, wishes and suggested actions needed to arise from the PCP
- The PCP facilitator helps decide what actions are relevant for discussion; the chair ensures PCP ideas are a part of the review
- There to make sure that the services being bought meet assessed needs and are working well for the person and whether new services are required
- Check if the person would like to convert services to a direct payment
- Check with the person that the services being offered at present are set up in a way that maximises his or her control
- Ensure the services being purchased are a high standard and that actions agreed for services happen on time
- A review action plan agreed with the individual about services should be written up
- Generally service reviews occur six-monthly for people in residential care/supported living and annually for people receiving day care
- Required by statutory and local guidance (good practice standards) and have prescribed methods of recording

Case study: R's story – extract from an emerging PCP

R is a young Filipino man of 27 years who has a learning disability, with high support needs and complex epilepsy. He does not use speech to communicate, but he will clearly let people know when he is happy – R is an energetic man with a range of interests. He communicates enjoyment and approval by running and jumping and rubbing his ears. R lived in a residential home with four others and had regular contact with his family. His first PCP meeting was designed as a type of party. His favourite food and lots of drinks were prepared and a room was chosen so he could move around – run, jump as he wished. His mother was initially asked if she would like to be the facilitator and told that she could be offered support through training if she wished but she felt a bit nervous about the process and the responsibility of this role, and thought this might happen at a later stage. The first meetings were initially facilitated by the care manager and then jointly with the key worker from the home.

The first meetings were very much focused on sharing the ideas that were most important for R's future. They talked a lot about health, family, cultural issues, religious festivals and holidays. A mixture of written plans, photographs and videos recorded the meetings. The difference between the service reviews and the PCP meetings was that there was no prescribed set agenda for the PCP meetings but people still brought lots of ideas and tried to be as creative as possible. As R couldn't say his wishes, everyone had to 'think' from his perspective – there were lots of things as a group we began to realise we thought he would like. One idea seemed to generate another and people became more creative and thinking of new ideas – R attended many more mainstream activities and events such as music festivals, pubs, Filipino restaurants and holidays, which no one thought he could access or enjoy before. R has severe epilepsy and lots of work was done by everyone to look at how his health could be supported better and eventually resulted in neurology appointments, better monitoring by all and as a consequence of all of this there was a dramatic improvement for him and a better quality of life.

For R the PCP process seemed to get people much more involved, especially his family; it got people motivated to make things happen and try new ideas.

With the 26 people for whom PCPs were being developed, people gradually began to think outside set categories, with needs for new types of support beginning to emerge: X wanted to revisit his country of origin to see a relative with whom he had lost touch; Y loves to paint but how could he access local studio space; massage could help Z when she feels tense; J has a family history of breast cancer and we needed to offer regular screening.

It became apparent that a mechanism was needed to link the individual voices from PCPs to the bigger picture of service planning and commissioning in progressing the inclusion agenda. We wanted a mechanism that would not lose the individual essence of PCP but would contribute to a broader canvas. The pilot steering group also felt it was very important that people with learning disabilities and those providing support, both in the Circle and in services, could see how personal changes were being implemented and actioned by care managers and clinicians and through commissioning.

Shortly after PCPs started, an aggregation tool was developed with the involvement of people with learning disabilities and carers (Figure 10.3) and was distributed to those working on PCPs with accompanying guidance for staff and managers. People with learning disabilities completed these with support, returning them to the relevant service manager for analysis and aggregation. The aggregation tool was also designed to be person-focused, with a picture of the individual attached to the front sheet. On subsequent pages the person identified his or her dreams and what he or she needed to do to achieve those dreams, in the areas of Learning; Leisure and Fun; Where and How I Live; Work; Choices; Controls and Rights; Feeling Well and Good About Myself.

At the time of the pilot, although we had 26 people participating in PCP, we were also mindful of the much larger group of people who were receiving services and not having the benefits of the intervention. We also designed a form for placement monitoring officers and care managers to complete following service review, with requests from service users to commissioners, so that we did not miss feedback from this group.

Findings

The following benefits and opportunities emerged:

- There was an emphasis on power residing with service users and their network.
- Feedback indicated that people with learning disabilities and their families enjoyed the experience of PCP.
- PCP is particularly helpful to people in transition from school to adult services and from one living situation to another.

Shaping the Future Together

Dear Managers and Planners,

Hello, I am ______________________ (full name)

Photo

Here is some information that will help you plan and develop the *right* opportunities, services and support *for me* in the future.

You need to take into account that:

my date of birth is _____________ I am ____ years old

my nationality is _______________

my preferred way of communicating is

my first language is (tick as appropriate)

☐ English	☐ Arabic	☐ Other
☐ Bengali	☐ Hindi	

I am (tick as appropriate)

☐ White UK	☐ African/Carribean	☐ Other
☐ Black UK	☐ African	
☐ Irish	☐ Asian	

I am (tick as appropriate)

☐ Church of England	☐ Muslim
☐ Roman Catholic	☐ Other

☐ I use a wheelchair

☐ I find it difficult or impossible to use stairs

☐ I have a visual impairment

☐ I have a hearing impairment

☐ I use communication equipment or sign language

Figure 10.3 Piloted material from aggregation tool – Kensington and Chelsea PCP Pilot Project (Cole and Lloyd 2003)

- PCP techniques lead to more creative solutions and a 'can do' approach, focusing increasingly on the whole person and his or her interests and aspirations, rather than his or her 'deficits'.
- PCP facilitators would ideally be people outside services, such as family members or friends.
- There are real benefits in moving away from traditional methods of recording (Gillman, Swain and Heyman 1997), allowing for increased flexibility. What is right is what works for the person – for example, laminated cards, posters and multimedia presentations.
- In the absence of friends, advocates or family members or direct care, staff and care managers were able to work effectively with people with learning disabilities, helping implement PCP and set up and facilitate circles.
- The involvement of independent sector partners in a shared vision of PCP was important, enabling statutory and independent organisations to work together to drive up standards and focus on service users.
- Care managers, clinicians, independent sector providers and direct care benefited from PCPs being distinguished from service reviews, mapping how they could complement each other and their respective characteristics. Definitions (see Table 10.1) were worked on as a group exercise with users, carers and the independent sector providers.
- PCP increased opportunities for social inclusion and links to mainstream services.
- Links between PCP and mainstream services – including leisure, housing and transport and specialist learning disability services – were improved with better planning information for use across a wide range of provision, in line with *Valuing People* (Department of Health 2001).

Aggregating information

Figure 10.3 shows the form used by people with learning disabilities and their circle of support to inform local commissioners of planning needs arising from PCPs. In Kensington and Chelsea, this was the first time that people with learning disabilities had been part of such a change process. If change is evidenced as a result, it has the potential of being very empowering for service users.

Even the start proved a very useful process, as it was positive that service users were being encouraged to think about their wishes, hopes and aspirations and how these might be realised. For commissioners the visual image of a photograph of the user at the beginning of the form proved a powerful reminder that they were planning for real people and were there to make a real difference in people's lives.

Some parts of the aggregation tool needed refining. The information on the front sheet was not always a useful record and barriers to achieving the wishes and hopes were often poorly stated or occasionally incomplete. The quality of some information was poor – for example, 'go out more' – requiring more specific detail to inform commissioning and help ensure success. Timeframes were not always clear and which issues were dependent on others being achieved first were sometimes not explicit. Frequently 'supporters' seemed to be using their own aspirations for service users, with some of the language underlining this.

It was surprising how many users' wishes and aspirations were limited and could easily be achieved with existing resources and equally puzzling why this had not already happened with the support of care managers, clinicians and providers. Were users not really experiencing the choices available? Was this an indication that the process of planning for users was not adequately woven into the care management and commissioning process? Whatever the shortcomings, there was clearly an imperative to improve.

Two final observations can be made. First, if PCP was to succeed in organisations then it needed to be simple and embedded in existing processes rather than a stand-alone system. Second, some form of manageable database was essential to do the donkey work of aggregation. Without addressing and resolving these concerns, PCP would suffer the same fate of many of its predecessors and rapidly fall into decline.

THE NEED FOR A SYSTEMS-WIDE PERSPECTIVE

PCP cannot exist in isolation, only within the broader service system and policy context locally and nationally. The evaluation will need to consider the links between PCP and a range of other new and existing management, practitioner, governance and quality initiatives, as these will ultimately influence PCP or the information it generates. The links between PCP and user advocacy services, health action plans, joint investment plans, managed competition and consultation through best value processes, care standards and the inspection of services are just some main examples (Cambridge 2002).

PCP cannot be evaluated as an intervention or analysed in terms of its effectiveness for the individual, particularly in relation to considerations relating to discrimination or anti-oppressive practice, unless its place in wider organisational systems or processes is considered (Cambridge 2002). Work was therefore commissioned to identify administrative and bureaucratic constraints on PCP and factors limiting its success within the organisation.

AN EVALUATION OF PCP IN AN ORGANISATIONAL CONTEXT

An interim evaluation of PCP was undertaken in Kensington and Chelsea and Westminster (Swift 2004) through in-house and independent services. Although the results of the final evaluation are awaited, findings indicate that while most staff had either heard of PCP or undertaken some training for it, only a relatively small proportion had any direct involvement in developing a person-centred plan. The principles of PCP and how it was implemented in practice consequently continue to present a challenge – it was often easier to say what it was not, reflecting a need to re-orientate from service considerations to individuals and their families.

The evaluation was positive about the commitment and goodwill of staff in implementing PCP. The principles of PCP co-existed well with the value-base of front-line staff, with respondents acknowledging the efficiency potentials of PCP, through partnership working in developing individual plans. There was a consensus that mainstream services such as leisure and transport were adequate, although access and funding continued to be problematic. Previous work on individual planning and facilitating choice appeared to have helped lay a solid foundation for PCP. There were positive examples of variety and flexibility in local services, underpinned by a relatively strong financial position. Staff valued the support of advocacy organisations and specialist communication available for promoting PCP, and the modernisation and reconfiguration of day services had provided further opportunities for the active use of PCP.

Other factors were seen to have inhibited the development of PCP. The pilot projects had encouraged a 'wait and see' attitude among some service providers who might have been more proactive in initiating PCP. Residential staff had not had a sufficient depth of training and staff were anxious about the potential of PCP to undermine their roles: 'It may be hard to hear that someone doesn't want to be here' and 'It is easier to see and hear about the things that we can do and influence.' Staff sought clarification about the implications of implementing PCP – for example, would it mean greater flexibility in support working hours? Professional staff expressed uncertainties about their roles in relation to PCP – whether they should remain detached and allow the circle to play a more active role. Also the relative lack of networks of families and friends was seen to make this complex. Staff in both boroughs expressed scepticism about the ability of services to deliver the objectives of *Valuing People* within timescales. There was a realisation that, however positively and proactively the principles were embraced, successful outcomes might take years and that their achievement would inevitably be subject to staff shortages, high turnover and budgetary uncertainty.

The early findings clearly indicated that PCP is still very much in its infancy and the benefits were therefore marginal. The changes had, in the main, encouraged service users to have more say in their care planning and although the influence of PCP on commissioning had been minimal, it had stimulated the use of payments.

Areas identified for further work and development

- PCP does not automatically guarantee access to resources – care management remains the statutory framework for allocating resources. To ensure successful links between care management and PCP this needs to be made explicit.
- Managers need to own the values of PCP and lead by example. Person-centred teams and person-centred leadership styles with reduced hierarchies are needed.
- Without a well thought-out infrastructure there is a risk of PCP becoming an isolated activity, undermining the potential of empowerment.
- Greater clarification is needed about the roles of care management and clinicians in supporting PCP, codified into organisational culture, recruitment, learning and performance systems.
- Primary care trust staff need further support to increase their awareness of PCP and how it relates to good health and health action planning.
- Confusion continued between PCP meetings and service review meetings. Managers and staff need to understand that PCPs are not improved service reviews. If done well, they are completely separate, although the PCP should feed into service review and redesign.
- Statutory organisations involved in the delivery of health and social care have not resolved the extent to which they make improvements to people's quality of life as opposed to meeting their more basic assessed health and social care needs. For example, a remit to direct resources to those most in need does not always fit with preventative work and long-term investment in improving quality of life.
- More work and political energy is needed to promote the social model of disability and to ensure responsibility is accepted by mainstream agencies for implementing *Valuing People* in its wider context.

- There is a tension between PCP and seeing staff as friends and circle members. For example, vulnerable adult protection and risk policies discourage paid staff from inviting people with learning disabilities to their homes or to social events outside their place of work.
- The experience of many people in the pilot suggested few family contacts and social isolation (Pitonyak 2003), with many having no one but paid staff in their lives. This may be replicated within PCP, containing many of the same people as more traditional service reviews.
- There is a need to build an evidence base for PCP, measuring outcomes and justifying further resources to demonstrate its effectiveness.
- Some family members are reluctant to train as facilitators and need considerable reassurance and support to take on this role.
- The needs of people from minority groups must not be compromised or overlooked. In terms of people from Black and minority ethnic groups, facilitators should have a good understanding and awareness of religious and cultural issues so that they are able to ask appropriate prompt questions (Khan, Rahim and Routledge 2004).
- Inner-city areas appear to have a high percentage of transient populations, both as staff and neighbours. Developing and retaining longer-term links is therefore difficult for people with learning disabilities, but can be done.
- Supportive frameworks and guidance are needed to enable service users to have integrated plans that work and to avoid the danger of a bureaucratic 'plan fest' (Cumella 2003; Routledge 2003), with service users and partner-agencies swamped in paper (Mansell and Beadle-Brown 2004).
- To do PCP well is time consuming and should not be rushed. There is a risk of a preoccupation with meeting *Valuing People* objectives at the expense of ensuring quality PCP practice and avoiding tokenism.
- There is a danger that local statutory and provider services may be tempted to short-cut by adapting and renaming existing assessment and review procedures rather than developing new and integrated PCP, as was the case with care management 12 years ago (Cambridge 1999).

Although we identified many areas of further development, the initial findings were encouraging, with evidence of the increased involvement of family and friends. There was more clarity about the interests, hopes and aspirations of individuals with learning disabilities and anecdotal evidence that they were more in control of the process. People with learning disabilities were developing and being supported to develop pictorial maps of their lives and their hopes and dreams which were feeding through to requests for trips back to the Caribbean to see relatives or tracing ex-members of staff. PCP contributed towards the planning process allowing commissioners, providers and health and social care staff to better deliver services that people wanted, helping ensure that real choices of services were available. Creative solutions appeared, with people tapping into a wider cross-section of mainstream resources. The time spent on planning for the future also appeared more focused.

More work needs to be done to make the process less complex and greater attention needs to be given to the promotion of direct payments and an increased awareness of personal budgets, giving service users and their circle of support as much control as possible in the planning process. Moving from individual needs to a strategic plan proved complex and the role of the partnership board in this requires further clarification. Organisationally, PCP needs to be embedded in existing processes for aggregating data if the process is to become manageable and succeed.

CONCLUSION

Valuing People (Department of Health 2001) is remarkable in its breadth and ambition. It is not just about learning disability services but seeks to take a much wider 'whole government approach', tying into a broader vision aligned to the social model of disability through eliminating social exclusion (Fyson and Simons 2003).

The pilot project highlighted both the real value of person-centred approaches for people with learning disabilities and their families and the fact that the implementation of PCP requires a radical and complex review and redesign of service delivery if real shifts in the power are to occur (Kinsella 2000).

As Sanderson (2002) emphasises, the effective implementation of PCP involves rethinking the role of the learning disability professional. People using PCP assume that the person is the first authority on his ot her life and that a dialogue with others can build on this. Professionals are therefore no longer in charge of collecting and holding information and making decisions about the person's life, but will remain key problem-solvers and critical allies in making things happen. It is essential that members of community learning disability teams, both care managers and clinicians, are given ongoing support and development opportunities to change their roles and responsibilities in supporting the successful implementation of PCP.

For direct care staff, care managers and clinicians to be effective in PCP, changes are also required to the organisational culture and hierarchy in which they operate. Effective PCP needs to take place with the support of person-centred teams. These see their purpose as supporting individuals to achieve the lifestyles they want as part of their local communities, characterised by a willingness to listen and learn continually and to value personal commitment and relationships with the people they support (De Pree 1997).

Person-centred organisations value staff and service users, devolve resources and authority to service users and staff and facilitate empowerment through direct payments and information sharing. They review themselves and not the people they support and involve staff in decision-making. They also tend towards non-hierarchical structures and management systems where managers link into practice by having contact with service users and supporting and empowering practitioners (Sanderson 2003).

Commissioning learning disability services requires the ability to balance not only complex budgets and resources but also complex and competing demands. If the *Valuing People* vision is to become a reality for more than a handful of people with learning disabilities, commissioners must also skilfully nurture and manage their local care markets in order that a wide range of innovative and flexible support packages are available to meet individual need. An aggregation of person-centred plans should help commissioners develop a blueprint for needs-led services. If PCP is properly embedded in strategic planning, then it will help reinforce self-determination, respect diversity and equality and contribute to the enrichment of the wider community.

NOTE

1 PATH (Planning Alternative Tomorrows with Hope) is a tool which can be used in person centred planning. Using the focus person's dreams as a starting point, a PATH is used to help plan the steps necessary to achieve those dreams.

REFERENCES

Beamer, S. and Brookes, M. (2001) *Best Practice and New Ideas for Supporting People with High Support Needs to Make Decisions.* London: Values Into Action.

Cambridge, P. (1999) 'Building care management competence in services for people with learning disabilities.' *British Journal of Social Work 29*, 393–415.

Cambridge, P. (2002) *Macro-Structures in Providing Services: Mainstreaming, Synergism and Specialisation. Observations and Arguments from the UK with a Focus on Experience in Kensington and Chelsea.* EU STEPS Conference Report, Organisational Structures in Learning Disability Services, Lidingo, May.

Cole, A. and Lloyd, A. (2003) *PCP Aggregation Project.* London: Kensington and Chelsea Social Services Department.

Cumella, S. (2003) 'Valuing assessments and reports? The impact of *Valuing People* on people with a learning disability.' *Journal of Integrated Care 11*, 2, 3–8.

Department of Constitutional Affairs (2004) *Summary of Mental Capacity Bill.* www.dca.gov.uk/menincap/bill-summary.htm

Department of Health (2001) *Valuing People: A New Strategy for Learning Disability for the 21st Century.* London: Department of Health.

Department of Health (2002) *Keys to Partnership Working: Working Together to Make a Difference in People's Lives.* See www.learningdisabilitiesuk.org.uk

De Pree, M. (1997) *Leading Without Power.* San Francisco, CA: Jossey-Bass.

Edge, J. (2001) *Who's in Control? Decision-making by People with Learning Difficulties Who Have High Support Needs.* London: Values Into Action.

Fyson, R. and Simons, K. (2003) 'Strategies for change: making *Valuing People* a reality.' *British Journal of Learning Disabilities 31*, 153–158.

Gillman, M., Swain, J. and Heyman, B. (1997) 'Life history or case history: the objectification of people with learning difficulties through the tyranny of professional discourses.' *Disability and Society 12*, 5, 675–693.

Grove, N. and McIntosh, B. (2002) *Communication for Person Centred Planning.* London: RBKC Project publication.

Holburn, S., Jacobson, J.W., Vietze, P.M., Schwartz, A.A. and Sersen, E. (2000) 'Qualifying the process and outcomes of person-centred planning.' *American Journal on Mental Retardation 105*, 5, 402–416.

Holman, A. (1997) 'In the absence of legislation follow the best interest guidelines.' *Community Living 10*, 3, 2.

Joseph Rowntree Foundation (2001) *Findings: Demonstrating Control of Decisions by Adults with Learning Difficulties Who Have High Support Needs.* York: Joseph Rowntree Foundation.

Khan, N., Rahim, N. and Routledge, M. (2004) *Person Centred Planning and People from South Asian Communities: Some Experiences From One Locality.* www.valuingpeople.gov.uk

Kinsella, P. (2000) *What are the Barriers in relation to Person Centred Planning?* www.paradigm-uk.org/pdf/Articles/jrfpcp.pdf

Mansell, J. and Beadle-Brown, J. (2004) 'Person-centred planning or person-centred action? Policy and practice in intellectual disability services.' *Journal of Applied Research in Intellectual Disabilities 17*, 1–19.

Medora, H. and Cambridge, P. (2002) *Person-Centred Planning: An Overview.* Paper presented at STEPS conference, Rotterdam, November.

O'Brien, J. (1987) 'A guide to lifestyle planning.' In B. Wilcox and T. Bellany (eds) *A Comprehensive Guide to the Activities Catalogue.* Baltimore, MD: Paul H. Brookes.

O'Brien, J. and O'Brien, C. (1998) *Little Book of Person Centred Planning.* Edinburgh: Inclusion Press.

O'Brien, J., O'Brien, L. and Mount, B. (1997) 'Person-centred planning has arrived... or has it?' *Mental Retardation 35*, 480–488.

Pearpoint, J., O'Brien, J. and Forest, M. (1995) *PATH* (second edition). Toronto: Inclusion Press.

Pitonyak, D. (2003) *Toolbox for Change – Reclaiming Purpose, Joy and Commitment in the Helping Professions.* www.dimagine.com

Routledge, M. (2003) 'Glass half empty or half full?' Response to Stuart Cumella.' *Journal of Integrated Care 11*, 3, 44–47.

Royal Borough of Kensington and Chelsea (2002) *Best Value Review of LD Services.* London: Royal Borough of Kensington and Chelsea.

Sanderson, H. (1998) 'A say in my future – involving people with profound and multiple disabilities in person centred planning.' In L. Ward (ed) *Innovations in Advocacy and Empowerment for People with Intellectual Disabilities.* Chorley: Lisieux Hall Publications.

Sanderson, H. (2000) *Person Centred Planning: Key Features and Approaches.* www.valuingpeople.gov.uk

Sanderson, H. (2002) 'Person-centred teams.' In J. O'Brien and C. Lyle O'Brien (eds) *Implementing Person-Centred Planning.* Edinburgh: SHS Ltd.

Sanderson, H. (2003) 'Implementing person-centred planning by developing person-centred teams.' *Journal of Integrated Care,* June, 18–25.

Swift, P. (2004) *An Evaluation of PCP in the Royal Borough of Kensington and Chelsea and Westminster (Interim findings).* Report to the EU STEPS Conference, London, May.

Ticoll, M. (1998) 'Working together for a change. Involving people with intellectual disabilities in the work of a public policy research institute.' In L. Ward (ed) *Innovations in Advocacy and Empowerment for People with Intellectual Disabilities.* Chorley: Lisieux Hall Publications.

Yates, J. (1980) *Program Design Sessions.* Carver, MA: Jack Yates.

CHAPTER 11

Person Centred Planning and Direct Payments

Opening Doors for People with Learning Disabilities

Julie Beadle-Brown

INTRODUCTION

Person centred planning (PCP) requires having the means available to translate the personal aspirations of individual disabled people into action. One of the most potent means of doing this is to provide funds directly to the individual so that he or she can purchase whatever services he or she needs or wants. This is the idea behind direct payments.

The history and definition of PCP, which had its origins almost 30 years ago in the USA, has already been reviewed in Chapter 2. Direct payments are a more recent phenomenon. The Community Care (Direct Payments) Act (Department of Health 1996) gave local authorities the power to make cash payments for community care direct to individuals who need services (effective from April 1997). The Policy and Practice Guidance (Department of Health 2000) states that the aim of direct payments was to:

> bring about improvements in the quality of life of people who would like to manage their own support. They promote independence, and they aid social inclusion by offering opportunities for rehabilitation, for education, leisure and employment for people in need of community care. (para.1, p.3)

As such there is a shared aim of both PCP and direct payments to enable people (including those with learning disabilities) to have as much choice and control as possible over their lives and the services and support they receive. There are many examples available in the popular literature about how both direct payments and PCP can have beneficial effects (Department of Health 2001b; Holman and Bewley 1999, 2001; Holman and Collins 1997; Ryan and Holman 1998; Sanderson 2000). Although there is little published work on combining these two potentially powerful tools, it is conceivable that the benefits of having both direct payments and a properly functioning person-centred plan would be multiplied. However, despite these conceivable benefits, there is evidence that neither PCP nor direct payments are being implemented to the extent initially envisaged in both quality and quantity.

IMPLEMENTATION

In 2000, only 216 people out of a total of 3700 receiving direct payments were people with learning disabilities (Department of Health 2001b). In 2002 government statistics reported that 736 people with learning disabilities were receiving direct payments out of a total of 7882 people across the whole of England. In 2003, a total of 9600 people were receiving direct payments, but a breakdown of the figures by client group and local authority was not (yet) available. In 2002 the figures across councils ranged from 0 to 61, with 40 councils not operating any direct payments for people with learning disabilities. However, three councils (Durham, Hampshire and Essex) were managing to run direct payment schemes for more than 40 people with learning disabilities. These figures illustrate an improvement in terms of the uptake of direct payments but given that there is an estimated 1.2 million people with mild to moderate learning disabilities living in England, they are only a drop in the ocean.

There are no similar statistics on PCP but it is generally accepted that this is also not happening to the extent envisaged. Black (2000) discusses whether PCP and person-centred approaches are happening for as many people and as well as one might like, concluding that when done properly PCP can be really effective but that there are many barriers to implementation in services. This is also an issue discussed by Kinsella (2000). One illustration of this is the case of 'Rosie'(Beadle-Brown 2002).

An attempt was made by her father to set up a trust fund for Rosie so that consistent input from trained support workers could be provided. However, a judicial review ruled that the local authority did not have power to do this. With the advent of direct payments in 1997 the family began to explore the option of a trust-managed direct payment for Rosie or an Independent Living Trust using money from direct payments (Holman and Bewley 2001). This would allow them to recruit trained support staff or provide training for workers, and develop a recruitment process in which Rosie would have a clear role. The aim was to provide carers who could operate a structured daily programme for Rosie, a programme that would allow her to follow a mixture of activities using the TEACCH system and incorporate activities of choice. In essence, Rosie would be in control of who supported her, what she did and when, with some guidance given by carers to ensure a balance of activities.

Case study: Rosie

Rosie is a 24-year-old woman with severe learning disabilities and autistic spectrum disorders. She has relatively severe challenging behaviour, often exacerbated by complex medical problems, and has relatively severe physical impairments. She is a very vibrant, strong-willed and for the most part enthusiastic young woman who appears to know exactly what she wants. She loves watching sport, loves to play games (on her own terms) and loves to spend time with her family and those she likes and trusts. She lives with her family (the limited residential options available in the local area were seen as undesirable by both Rosie and her family) and at present is cared for by a number of care aides provided by a local privately run organisation. However, the provision of care is unreliable – carers often do not turn up for shifts and replacements are often unavailable. Rosie's father has had to give up work to care for her and the family rarely get any respite due to a lack of reliable support. Because all of the carers are untrained in particular on autism and how to deal with challenging behaviour, Rosie's support often focuses on preventing challenging outbursts, rather than providing interesting, stimulating experiences for her. Only with the support of a family member, usually her father, can Rosie participate in community activities. (Beadle-Brown 2002, p.10)

Rosie would, of course, need substantial help in managing the money and personnel issues. For example, she could be involved in the selection of carers but would need someone else to manage the legal and contractual issues. She could also be assisted to sign pay cheques but would need help in managing the accounts and keeping records. This would likely best be done by her father or another member of the trust, with help to ensure that full precautions were taken to safeguard Rosie's rights and the rights of the carers employed. However, the local authority ruled that Rosie could not consent to direct payments using their guidelines and therefore could not have a direct payment. Six years on, Rosie is still struggling to get a reliable service that meets her needs and the needs of her family. She also does not have a person centred plan as such although she has had numerous care assessments. Through a combination of a direct payment and person centred planning, Rosie could be much more in control of her life, participate much more widely in activities at home and in the community and her family could have the respite from 24-hour care that would enable her family also to have a better life. It would also give Rosie the opportunity to develop and to have some security for the future – whether she remains living in the family home as she appears to want to or whether she chooses to move into her own home in later years.

So why, given the obvious benefits of both PCP and direct payments, is there not greater uptake of both direct payments and PCP and why in Rosie's case is it so difficult for her to benefit from a direct payment, when other people in a similar position with similar levels of need and ability have a direct payment from a different council?

BARRIERS TO IMPLEMENTATION

Kinsella (2000) identifies six main barriers to the effective implementation of person centred planning. First, there is a lack of evidence base for the effectiveness of person centred planning. In Chapter 2, Mansell and Beadle-Brown expand on this point to illustrate that there is a lack of evidence base for any form of individualised planning that has been introduced as a wider initiative. Second, although the concept behind PCP is a simple one, the process is a complex one, so much so that people are expected to go on special training courses to learn how to do it! Third, there is the historical issue, that many other types of planning systems (Individual Programme Planning, Goal Planning etc.) have failed to be implemented widely across services and there is evidence that even where they have been implemented the exercise can become a paperwork one or tokenistic (see Chapter 2). Fourth, there is a misconception that only one type of planning is possible, despite the fact that O'Brien and Lovett (1992) and Sanderson (2000) make it clear that different types of planning are appropriate in different situations. The fifth barrier to PCP in the UK in particular is that in this country PCP for an individual is often led by service staff with all the biases and difficulties that that introduces. PCP can become a service planning tool rather than really focusing on the individual. Finally, an additional barrier has been placed in its path, because PCP has not been taken onboard by advocacy organisations, parent organisations or family groups.

In addition to these specific barriers, there are also general barriers to implementing any sort of change in services such as low expectations of people, lack of imagination, separatist thinking, financial inflexibility and competition from other activities to name but a few (Black 2000). In terms of direct payments, barriers over the years can be summarised under four headings (Beadle-Brown 2002):

- lack of compulsion
- lack of guidance and readily available demonstration projects
- lack of flexibility and creativity
- lack of understanding of consent and ability to manage.

Lack of compulsion

Until recently, with the Health and Social Care Act (Department of Health 2001a), it was not compulsory for local authorities to offer direct payments and there were no consequences for authorities who did not support the use of direct payments for people with learning disabilities.

Lack of guidance and readily available demonstration projects

Although there is guidance on direct payments available, this is relatively general and fails to approach the issue of consent and ability to manage direct payments in detail, leaving interpretation of these up to individual authorities. In Rosie's case, this was the main stumbling block. Although some evidence exists that direct payments can work with people with severe learning disabilities, much comes from authorities that were creative and pioneering in all aspects of service organisation *or* from situations in which pioneering organisations such as Values Into Action have had an input. There has been some research looking at the forms of assistance people with learning disabilities need to be able to use direct payments (Swindon People First and Norah Fry Research Centre 2002) but results are not yet available. There are also a number of studies funded by the Joseph Rowntree Foundation, which illustrate the barriers people with learning disability face in obtaining direct payments but again many of these involved organisations such as Values Into Action (see www.jrf.org.uk).

What may be needed to convince the 'typical' local authority, working without specialised input, are more examples that shows that it is possible to use direct payments effectively, within their limited resources. Funding Freedom 2000 (Holman and Bewley 1999) provided some such examples, as did the 2001 White Paper *Valuing People* (Department of Health 2001b), but perhaps locally based demonstrations in which authorities are actually involved may be the most effective demonstration. These are now starting to emerge and the newly established Direct Payments Development Fund is encouraging authorities to be more creative. In fact, Denise Platt, the Chair of the Commission for Social Care Inspection (CSCI), in her keynote speech to the recent Disability Rights Commission Debate on a 'Right to Independent Living', notes that we now have many pilot projects and it is time for direct payments to become mainstream.

Lack of flexibility and creativity

There is generally something of a lack of flexibility and creativity in terms of service provision. In some authorities, there is a tendency to purchase institutional or out-of-area placements for people with challenging behaviour, usually due to a lack of flexibility and creativity within the service organisation and funding structure (Department of Health 1993; Mansell 1994). Setting up a direct payment especially for someone with a severe learning disability takes just such creativity and flexibility.

The care management system is partly to blame here. In general, there have been too few care managers and those that do exist therefore have too high a caseload to make care management work on the individual level initially intended (Cambridge 1999). In many places care management has become a tool for pigeonholing people into existing services and not for creatively meeting individual need. Individual care managers will have conducted an assessment but this assessment is often not implemented as no local services exist to meet that person's assessed needs – resources dictate that the person is required to fit into existing services or move to an area where such services exist. In addition, care managers are often inexperienced in working with people with intellectual disabilities and do not have the chance to get to know their individual cases due to caseload (Cambridge 1999). Where care management has worked well, comprehensive assessment has been backed up by creative service provision and commissioning and good review processes.

Lack of understanding of consent and ability to manage

The BILD Factsheet on direct payments (Northfield 2004) points out that initially people were being excluded from some schemes because local authorities were focusing on 'able' rather than 'assistance' in the initial guidance. It is very clear that as much help as necessary can be given to individuals to manage direct payments. Funding Freedom 2000 (Holman and Bewley 1999) notes that local authorities were more concerned about the issue of handing over control of money to individuals or trusts than the more fundamental issue of consent. However, recent government guidance on consent has helped to clarify the issue and Holman (2002) points out that the 'best interests' principle may serve to make the situation easier for people with more severe learning disabilities. Although Rosie may not be able to be judged capable of understanding all aspects of direct payments, she could show consent retrospectively, in terms of her satisfaction with arrangements through her behaviour as suggested as desirable for people with severe learning disabilities in

Funding Freedom 2002 (Holman and Bewley 1999). There are examples where authorities have worked on this basis already – for example, in Hampshire (www.hants.gov.uk/socservs/directpayments).

IS THERE A BRIGHTER FUTURE FOR ROSIE?

Recent developments both political and legal are important here and perhaps Rosie still has a chance of getting her direct payment or an Independent Living Trust, which will mean more independence, choice and control for Rosie and some respite and reassurance for her family.

Requirement to offer direct payments

Local authorities are now required to offer direct payments (Health and Social Care Act, Department of Health 2001a). In fact, in his speech to the Learning Disability Today conference on 26 November 2003, Stephen Ladyman, the Parliamentary Under Secretary of State (Community), challenged councils around their promotion of direct payments, reminding people that only 1 out of 100 people with a learning disability are using direct payments and that the vast majority of people should be able to do this. He pointed out that:

> Many Councils believe they have a duty to *offer* direct payments. They don't. They have a duty to *make* direct payments. That is what the law now says. And the assumption should be that all care will be delivered via a direct payment. (Ladyman 2003a, p.3)

He goes on to stress the importance of helping people to manage direct payments:

> Being properly supported to manage a direct payment is important for everyone. This support can be from the council, from a voluntary sector support service or from friends or family. But let me be clear. Councils should assume firstly that someone can manage and then look for ways to help them do so. (p.3)

New guidance on direct payments

The new guidance on direct payments, which was issued in September 2003, offers much more concrete advice than previous guidance. It gives local authorities examples of good practice for promoting, supporting and instigating direct payment schemes. There are examples of how PCP and direct payments can work together, and there is also an emphasis on advocacy and the empowerment of the individual with a disability. Some of the issues around consent are clarified and in particular ability to manage is dealt with in much greater detail, including the options of using a power of attorney or a user-controlled trust to help manage the employment and financial aspects.

Most importantly the new guidance deals specifically with the issue of supporting people with communication difficulties and in particular those with learning disabilities, emphasising the need to consider how best to empower people to make an informed decision about direct payments, including the use of people who know the person well and who understand how the individuals express preferences. For further information the guidance refers people to the publications of Values Into Action, which illustrate the possibilities for people with learning disabilities if authorities are creative and encourage the involvement of people's circles of support.

Direct Payments Development Fund

In October 2002, Alan Milburn, the then Secretary of State for Health, announced the establishment of the Direct Payments Development Fund. In July 2003, it was announced by the Department of Health that:

> £4.5m has been granted to 45 voluntary organisations over 18 months to create and build on support schemes for Direct Payments (cash in lieu of social services). Working in partnership with local councils, they will promote and engage people to exercise choice and control through the use of Direct Payments. (Ladyman 2003b)

This will, it is hoped, create more examples of good practice to guide local authorities and in particular find ways of enabling people with learning disabilities to take advantage of direct payments. However, as pointed out earlier, there is now a call for a move from pilot studies to making direct payments schemes mainstream.

Examples of good practice in person centred planning

In terms of PCP there are some examples of good practice in the guidance itself and a number of Department of Health publications that aim to help partnerships boards to implement and monitor how they are progressing towards the target of everyone having a person centred plan. Although, as illustrated in Chapter 2, there is little research on the effective implementation of person centred planning, there has been some work, mostly funded by the Joseph Rowntree Foundation, that has started to look at these issues. One such project is that reported by Sanderson (2003), which illustrated that people with severe learning disabilities could be meaningfully included in PCP meetings. However, these are small-scale, mostly anecdotal studies and larger-scale research-based studies are basically non-existent as yet.

Legal developments

In 2002 the Lord Chancellor's consultation paper stated that 'best interest' guidelines should be used with regard to direct payments – this may offer a way forward on the somewhat sticky issue of consent (Lord Chancellor's Department 2002). There have also been other legal issues which have arisen around the payment of family carers to provide care, if they are deemed to be best placed to provide for the individual concerned. Following airing of these issues in court (Care and Health, 2003) and discussion in other government forums, the government announced that direct payments could be used to pay relatives who do not live with the person to provide support for them without limitations, and that in exceptional circumstances they could pay a relative who does live with them to provide care if they and their local council decide this is the only satisfactory way of meeting their care needs (Stephen Ladyman, Department of Health 2004).

Increased lobbying for a right to independent living

In addition to the legal and political advancements in thinking around empowering people with learning disabilities to have more control over their lives, the lobbying also continues. In fact, the lobbying is now not just for direct payments to be available to people with learning disabilities but that direct payments should be extended into individualised funding for everyone (see Community Living and Emprise 2002). The recent (3 March 2004) Disability Rights Commission Debate focused on the 'Right to Independent Living' for people with disabilities. At this event there was a consensus that the way forward to ensuring independence for people was to give people a right to independence, so that residential care was seen as the last resort or the true choice of the person him- or herself. Attention was also drawn to the fact that special consideration needed to be given as to how to extend this right in practical terms to people with severe learning disabilities such as Rosie.

In summary, it is probably true to say that the future is looking brighter for people like Rosie. However, rather than the central issue being how to make existing systems such as care management responsive to direct payments and person centred planning, the main issue is actually how to increase the uptake of direct payments and PCP so that care management is not needed. The key intervention then becomes giving people a right to direct payments (and independent living) – a right which allows them to buy any service that meets their needs or allows them to achieve the aspirations highlighted in their person-centred plan. Steps in this direction are already being taken in a project led by Mencap in partnership with other organisations. Although still only a relatively small-scale study in 6 local authorities, the In Control project helps people with all levels of disabilities to have more control over their lives through a system of 'self-directed support' involving assessment, planning, individual funding and individual support. Funding is drawn from several social care sources to provide the money needed to meet the assessed needs and fulfil the person-centred plan. One of the main differences between self-directed support and direct payments is that the person is given the choice of how they would like to have their funding organised – this could be through a direct payment to themselves, to a Trust, to an agent or third party, to an organisation for individualised support or to be managed on an ongoing basis by the care manager. This means that personalised budgets can be used to purchase the support the person really wants even if in residential care – this is not an option with direct payments. It also means that people with intellectual disabilities don't have to manage the payments themselves, which may be one possible factor that has affected uptake of direct payments. Here in particular there is hope for people like Rosie to have truly individualised support that meets their needs.

ACKNOWLEDGEMENTS

Thank you to 'Rosie's' family for allowing me to use her story to illustrate the issues discussed here. Thank you also to Jim Mansell for his comments on earlier drafts of this chapter and to the editors and publishers for their patience and tactful reminders.

REFERENCES

Beadle-Brown, J. (2002) 'Direct payments for people with severe learning disabilities: a service case study and implications for policy.' *Tizard Learning Disability Review 7*, 4, 8–15.

Black, P. (2000) *Why Aren't Person Centred Approaches and Planning Happening For As Many People and As Well As We Would Like?* www.doh.gov.uk/vpst/pcp.htm

Cambridge, P. (1999) 'Building care management competence in services for people with learning disabilities.' *British Journal of Social Work 29*, 393–415.

Care and Health (2003) 'User independent trusts and the law.' *Care and Health: Legal Update*, April, 11–12.

Community Living and Emprise (2002) *Not Just About the Money: Reshaping Social Care for Self-Determination.* Community Living and Emprise. www.empire-international.com/njam.htm

Department of Health (1993) *Services for People with Learning Disabilities and Challenging Behaviour or Mental Health Needs: Report of a Project Group* (Chairman: Prof J.L. Mansell). London: Her Majesty's Stationery Office.

Department of Health (1996) *Community Care (Direct Payments) Act.* London: HMSO.

Department of Health (2000) *Community Care (Direct Payments) Act: Policy and Practice Guidance.* London: HMSO.

Department of Health (2001a) *Health and Social Care Act.* London: Department of Health.

Department of Health (2001b) *Valuing People: A New Strategy for Learning Disability for the 21st Century: Implementation.* London: Department of Health.

Department of Health (2004) *Increased choice of people who receive direct payments.* London: Department of Health. press release 2004/0028.

Duffy, S., Casey, J., Poll, C., Routledge, M., Sanderson, H. and Stansfield, J. (2004) *In Control: A national programme to change the organisation of social care in England so that people who need support can take more control of their own lives and fulfil their role as citizens.* See www.selfdirectedsupport.org/downloads/inControl_pro_bk.pdf

Holman, A. (2002) 'Direct payments: commentary and review.' *Tizard Learning Disability Review* 7, 4, 17–20.

Holman, A. and Bewley, C. (1999) *Funding Freedom 2000: People with Learning Disabilities Using Direct Payments.* London: Values Into Action.

Holman, A. and Bewley, C. (2001) *Trusting Independence: A Practice Guide to Independent Living Trusts.* London: Values Into Action and Community Living.

Holman, A. and Collins, E. (1997) *Funding Freedom: A Guide to Direct Payments for People with Learning Disabilities.* London: Values Into Action.

Kinsella, P. (2000) *What are the Barriers in Relation to Person-Centred Planning?* Paradigm. www.valuingpeople.gov.uk/documents/PCPJrfpcp.pdf

Ladyman, S. (2003a) Speech by Stephen Ladyman MP, Pariliamentary Under-Secretary of State for Community, to Learning Disability Today conference, 26 November. See www.dh.gov/newhome/speeches/speechlist/

Ladyman, S. (2003b) Press release by Stephen Ladyman MP, Parliamentary Under Secretary of State for Community, 21 July. London: Depart0ment of Health.

Lord Chancellor's Department (2002) *Making Decisions: Helping People Who Have Difficulty Deciding for Themselves. A Consultation Paper.* London: Lord Chancellor's Department.

Mansell, J. (1994) 'Specialized group homes for persons with severe or profound mental retardation and serious problem behaviour in England.' *Research in Developmental Disabilities 15*, 371–388.

Northfield, J. (last updated 2004) *BILD Factsheet: Direct Payments.* www.bild.org.uk/factsheets/direct_payments.htm

O'Brien, J. and Lovett, H. (1992) *Finding A Way Toward Everyday Lives: The Contribution of Person Centred Planning.* Harrisburg, PA: Pennsylvania Office of Mental Retardation.

Ryan, T. and Holman, A. (1998) *Able and Willing? Supporting People with Learning Disabilities to Use Direct Payments.* London: Values Into Action.

Sanderson, H. (2000) *Person-Centred Planning: Key Features and Approaches.* Valuing People Support Team. www.doh.gov.uk/vpst/pcp.htm

Sanderson, H. (2003) *'It's My Meeting': Finding Ways to Involve People with High Support Needs in Person Centred Planning.* Valuing People Support Team. www.valuingpeople.gov.uk/documents/My-meet.pdf

Swindon People First and Norah Fry Research Centre (2002) *Journey to Independence: what Self-advocates Tell us about Direct Payments.* London: BILD.

CHAPTER 12

Person Centred Planning and Risk

Challenging the Boundaries

Helen Alaszewski and Andy Alaszewski

INTRODUCTION

In this chapter we explore the significance of risk for person centred planning (PCP) and the ways in which such planning can be used to manage risk creatively. We start with a discussion of the ambiguous status of risk in services for people with learning disabilities and its association with negative and defensive practice. We then identify why it is important that risk is openly and explicitly acknowledged and managed. The chapter then goes on to examine how risk is currently defined and managed in planning and decision-making, finishing with a discussion of the ways in which risk can be used in PCP.

THE RISE AND FALL OF RISK IN SERVICES FOR PEOPLE WITH LEARNING DISABILITIES

Risk in its various guises has a long and chequered history in association with people with learning disabilities. The initial development of state concern and intervention in the lives of people with learning disabilities at the end of the nineteenth century was justified in terms of the risks they posed to themselves and society and the protection and safety that institutions provided (Alaszewski 1988).

Paradoxically the attack on institutional care especially in learning disability hospitals focused on the failure to manage risk effectively, as they neither provided a stimulating environment nor protected individuals from harm or exploitation. Contemporary accounts of institutions (Ryan with Thomas 1987), public inquiries into scandals (Ely Inquiry 1969) and individual recollection of institutions (Atkinson and Williams 1990) all emphasise the rigid, repressive controlling routine of institutions. Early experiments such as Tizard's Brooklands Unit demonstrated the ways in which children with learning disabilities thrived and developed when cared for in more stimulating environments (Tizard 1964).

In the 1970s advocates of alternatives to institutional care emphasised the importance of the opportunities afforded by ordinary living and enabling people with learning disabilities to take risks. For example, risk formed a prominent component of normalisation. Wolfensberger argued that services should treat all individuals with learning disabilities, including those with profound disabilities, as human beings with the capacity for growth and development:

> There is dignity in risk, and it is dehumanizing to remove all danger from the lives of the retarded and handicapped. After all, we take for granted that there is risk and danger in our lives, and the lives of our non-handicapped children! (Wolfensberger 1972, p.205)

While parents may now be less willing to accept that there is risk and danger within their children's lives, Furedi (1997) has argued that the development of a culture of fear is restricting opportunities for all children. Wolfensberger himself stressed the importance of accepting risk and danger even when some individuals were harmed. For example, reflecting on the death of Robert, a young man with severe learning disability who had died in a fire in his own home, he comments:

> Robert could have led a sheltered existence, perhaps in some residential haven for the retarded where no demands are imposed, and where risks are virtually eliminated. There, he might have lived to a ripe old age; but to me, in his charity-inspired and heroic death in the flames, he found greater dignity. (Wolfensberger 1972, p.205)

In Britain the Jay Committee argued that children and adults with learning disabilities had the right to 'assume a fair and prudent share of risk' (Jay Committee 1979, para.121). The committee argued that:

> The question of risk...is one of extreme delicacy for those who care. Staff are likely to receive harsh criticism when accidents or injury occurs, yet if we entirely cushion people against these dangers we immediately restrict their lives and their chances of development. This restriction can be cloaked in respectability and defended on the grounds of protecting mentally handicapped people and keeping them safe, but it can also endanger human dignity. (Jay Committee 1979, para.121)

Despite the Jay Committee's view that effective risk management is an important component of care, in current policy statements risk is implicit rather than explicit. For example, in the White Paper *Valuing People* there is no explicit discussion of risk. The main emphasis is on empowering people with learning disabilities through rights, independence, choice and inclusion (Department of Health 2001, para.2.2). In the linked working papers on *Planning with People* this emphasis is maintained. For example, in the web-based *Accessible Guide* the headline definition of PCP is provided by a self-advocate: 'Person centred planning is about being in charge of what happens in my life and getting people I want and trust to help me make things happen' (Department of Health 2002, p.1).

Emphasis on empowerment is evident in the White Paper's discussion of performance measurement and quality assurance, which indicates that agencies should 'put the needs and wishes of the persons using the service at the centre of their quality assurance system (empowerment)' (Department of Health 2001, para 8.2, p.91).

The negative dimensions of risk and potential for harm are addressed in current policy guidance in terms of protection from abuse, namely from the actions of others but not from the consequences of the individual's own actions. This emphasis on the vulnerability of people with learning disabilities is seen in *Valuing People* which states that 'people with learning disabilities do not always receive adequate protection from abuse and exploitation' (Department of Health 2001, para.8.2, p.90) and in the focus on measuring both the level of abuse and the actions taken to protect individuals from abuse to: 'enable people with learning disabilities to lead lives safe from harm and abuse' (Department of Health 2001, para.8.2, p.91).

This relative silence on risk appears to be a result of the misuse of the term. As we will discuss later, agencies and professionals use risk in restricted and restrictive ways. For a number of commentators risk management has become a form of abuse. For example, Booth and Booth, in their ethnographic study of children who were growing up with parents with learning disabilities, identified a risk paradigm which:

> Encourages practitioners to look for what is going wrong rather than what is going right in the lives of children. It is not surprising that people trained to look for problems usually manage to find them. This is why the at-risk label, like other negative labels, might itself be regarded as a risk factor. (Booth and Booth 1998, pp.205–6)

In the next section we argue why risk should form an important part of PCP and also identify the dangers of neglecting it.

THE IMPORTANCE OF RISK

Risk assessment and risk management can be neglected if there is complete certainty about the outcome of actions and full agreement over values. However, in the real world, where there is both uncertainty about outcomes and disagreement over values, risk cannot be neglected. It should form an important part of PCP so that the type and nature of uncertainties and disagreements over values can be identified and managed creatively.

While uncertainty forms an important part of everyday life, most of us choose to disregard it. Thus while we may be aware that commonplace environments such as the home or everyday activities such as crossing the road are potentially harmful we do not anticipate harmful consequences and usually do not take special precautions to protect ourselves. Most people live in a 'protective cocoon' of basic trust which they believe will ensure their safety. Indeed without such trust we become paralysed by anxiety (Wilkinson 2001). Giddens has described the development of basic trust in the following way:

> The possibility of bodily injury is ever-present, even in the most familiar of surroundings. The home, for example, is a dangerous place: a high proportion of serious injuries are brought about by accidents in the domestic milieu... Within the setting of daily life, basic trust is expressed as a bracketing-out of possible events or issues which could, in certain circumstances, be cause for alarm. (Giddens 1991, pp.126–7)

As Giddens points out, 'basic trust is an essential component of the "uneventful" character of much of day-to-day life' (Giddens 1991, p.127). However, in modern society such trust cannot be taken for granted and most individuals develop it through sustained learning and 'skilled watchfulness' (p.127). An important part of 'growing up' in modern society is developing the skills that underpin basic trust. The problematic status of basic trust presents a number of challenges when developing personal care programmes:

- It cannot be assumed that adults with learning disabilities have developed basic trust and it is likely that any major change in their lives may call into question the existence of basic trust.
- Assisting adults with learning disabilities to develop basic trust requires an explicit and systematic approach to the type of knowledge and skills which underpin performance of everyday activities. While individuals can 'bracket out' risks when they perform an activity themselves, when they are responsible for the welfare and safety of another person such 'bracketing out' is no longer acceptable.
- Individuals who are developing basic trust often challenge the boundaries which those seeking to help them may set. Giddens notes

> that such deliberate exposure to risk forms an important part of early socialisation as the 'mastery of such dangers is an act of self-vindication and a demonstration, to self and others, that under difficult circumstances one can come through' (1991, p.133).

The uncertainties of everyday life are compounded by potential disagreement over values. While people with learning disabilities wish to achieve goals that are culturally valued, there are no difficulties in giving precedence to their desires. However, if such desires are seen as problematic within a particular cultural environment then there are likely to be major problems. This can be seen in a number of areas – e.g., diet, consuming alcohol and drugs, and in sexual relations. For example, if a person with learning disability chooses to consume large amounts of convenience food or alcohol then there may be serious negative consequences for his or her health, mobility or behaviour and his or her carers. Day and Hollins have noted that carers' *laissez-faire* attitude to diet can have serious health consequences:

> 'They miss out so much that other people can enjoy.' 'Let her eat what she wants.' Such attitudes quickly lead to dietary imbalance, perhaps to vitamin deficiency, obesity, dental caries or constipation. (Day and Hollins 1985, p.393)

The difficulties created by failing to recognise and manage risk are perhaps most clearly seen in the case of men with learning disabilities who are sexually abusive. Thompson has examined the harmful consequences of failing to effectively identify and manage the risks associated with men who are sexually abusive (Thompson 2000), noting that many agencies do not have an agreed or consistent approach to the sexual rights of individuals with learning disabilities. As a result responses vary according to the attitudes of individual members of staff or the specific practices of a unit (Thompson 2000, pp.34–5). Such inconsistencies mean that services can tolerate the sexual activities of abusive men, failing to prevent men with known histories of sexual abuse from perpetrating further abuse (Thompson 1997). Such tolerance can have harmful consequences for the victims of the abuse. Thompson notes that services tended 'to be more tolerant of sexually abusive behaviour if the victim was another person with learning disabilities' (2000, p.38). It may also have harmful consequences for the perpetrators of the abuse. While services may be initially tolerant, if the abuse increases and can no longer be contained within the service – for example, the victims are outside the service – then tolerance may be aggressive intervention: 'When men with learning disabilities receive sanctions for their abusive behaviour they may find themselves punished more harshly than other men who have committed similar crimes' (Thompson 2000, p.38).

Comment

It is important that people with learning disabilities have their fair share of the risks of everyday life. Taking reasonable risks is important for learning and developing a personal sense of identity and worth. For those seeking to support such reasonable risk-taking, the uncertainties associated with everyday life and the potential for conflict over values mean that a structured approach to risk assessment and risk management is an indispensable component of PCP. The next section considers approaches to framing risk within the context of such planning.

FRAMING RISK IN PCP

One of the difficulties of using risk creatively in developing PCP is that risk is difficult to define in an objective and universally accepted fashion. Risk means different things to different people and varies according to context, with inconsistency between agencies, professionals and carers in use and approach.

Within health and welfare agencies this inconsistency is particularly evident in different areas of activities. Agencies which provide support for individuals with learning disabilities emphasise the importance of empowerment, and in research conducted in 1998–99 (Alaszewski, Parker and Alaszewski 1999) we identified statements and practices which were designed to provide users with the confidence to articulate and make choices. The prime focus of such systems was care planning or PCP. All the agencies in our study had some form of individual care planning which provided opportunities for user participation. For example, one service manager indicated that:

> If clients can self-advocate, they are given the opportunity to discuss their own care and they do that through essential lifestyle planning systems, for they have involvement in developing their own needs and goals. (Alaszewski *et al.* 1999, p.21)

Where users were unable to self-advocate, many agencies were encouraging the use of outside advocates. Such PCP systems encompassed philosophies and values which supported user empowerment and procedures which provided for wider user participation. For example, one health service trust manager identified the ways in which users participated in agency decision-making:

> We've got service users on our clinical audit committee. We're getting a service user on our ethics committee, we have service users on most interview panels now. You know, when we are looking at the future of day services and quality within the organisation, we always have users there. (Alaszewski *et al.* 1999, p.20)

While all the agencies in our study were committed to empowering users, they also accepted that safety was a prime objective not only of users but also the staff they employ and for the wider public. Indeed respondents in our study tended to see risk very much in the context of safety. They saw risk assessment and risk management as activities which they were obliged to undertake to ensure safety and came under the general umbrella of 'health and safety'. This umbrella included a range of policies designed to ensure personal safety such as fire procedures, manual handling and adult abuse (Alaszewski *et al.* 1999, pp.18–19).

Most agencies had both empowerment and health and safety policies but the two were rarely integrated. For example, one manager in the independent sector indicated that:

> We have our health and safety policy and procedures which entail a lot obviously of risk assessment, risk management. Then also in our standard practice manuals we have a policy called 'taking positive risks', which is specifically aimed at a positive way of helping residents develop new skills, through risk taking. *It's not coming from the health and safety angle, it's coming from the good life-planning angle.* (emphasis added, Alaszewski *et al.* 1999, p.27)

This tension between a client-centred approach and a 'health and safety' approach was also evident in the following statement made by an independent sector manager: 'Within supported living, we don't have quite as many policies as we would for residential care. We try to make them a lot more user friendly' (Alaszewski *et al.* 1999, p.19).

Only very exceptionally did we find agencies in which safety and personal development issues were considered together and for user-centred planning:

> On admission, on their care plan, it defines whether they are at risk in any particular area of their life because it goes through all the areas of living. We accept that it is our responsibility to minimise and create a safe environment within which our residents can continue to live as unrestricted and active a life as their age and disabilities will allow. (Alaszewski *et al.* 1999, p.27)

The tensions between the 'health and safety' and client-centred approaches are exacerbated by the different definition of risk evident in each area. In the 'health and safety' area there was a narrow and restricted approach in which risk was viewed in negative terms as something dangerous and to be avoided at all cost. For example, one private sector manager defined risk in terms of:

> the possibility of either a resident, a member of staff, contractor or a visitor actually being open to catching a contagious disease or of being abused or of being attacked or whatever it is, or electrocuted or at risk of slipping on the floor. (Alaszewski *et al.* 1999, p.24)

In client-centred discussions there was less immediate and obvious use of the term risk but when it was used the emphasis was on the normality of risk and its part in everyday life:

> Risk is a normal part of life and responsible risk taking and risk assessment is or should be a normal part of life for tenants that we're supporting... It talks about risk...in relation to all sorts of things; financial matters, relationships, choice of activities, medication...interaction in the community, all sorts of thing. (Alaszewski *et al.* 1999, p.24)

Such differences in defining risk are not restricted to these specific areas of policy and practice but can be found in carers' and professionals' discussions of risk. For example, in 72 interviews with nurses providing support for vulnerable adults living in community settings we found major variations in the ways in which these nurses defined risk (for a fuller discussion see Alaszewski *et al.* 2000).

Although most nurses saw risk in terms of outcomes of actions or decisions, they primarily saw it in terms of danger or hazard (59/72: 82%). One student on the learning disability branch of a registration degree used the following example to illustrate his definition of risk: 'Giving someone the opportunity to do something which might have harmful consequences: making cups of tea; running baths; using hot and cold water; crossing the road; promoting independence' (Alaszewski *et al.* 2000, p.43).

This approach tended to predominate among nurses supporting people with mental illness. One qualified mental health nurse defined risk in the following way: 'Risk to me connotes something negative, danger, needs something doing about it, it's dangerous, it's negative and something awful is going to happen' (Alaszewski *et al.* 1998, p.26).

A minority of nurses (22/72: 31%) stressed a more positive aspect of risk, although acknowledging that things can go wrong, focusing on the positive aspects of the process, rather than potential negative outcomes. They saw risk as a learning or therapeutic process that was beneficial for the users of services and used a more positive definition. A nursing student specialising in learning disabilities provided the following definition:

> There is risk in everything and it is what is 'acceptable'. Taking a gamble – the idea of being bad being more fun than being good. It's an aspect of life which most people enjoy – a bit of fear, getting the adrenaline going can be a good thing. If you would account for all your actions you wouldn't develop at all. If you knew what was going to happen before you did it there would be no point in doing it. (Alaszewski *et al.* 1998, p.27)

The following dialogue between these students emphasised the importance of risk in developing the skills to manage everyday life (please note that the unreferenced quotes in this chapter are taken from interviews that formed part of the ENB-funded study of risk, Alazewski *et al.*, 1998):

Student A:	It's like when you're teaching somebody how to be independent and take a bus themselves...
Student B:	Or crossing the road.
Student A:	...when do you actually leave that person to get on that bus themselves say and meet them at the other end or whatever; those kinds of risk came to my mind which...
Student B:	Particularly road safety; I was thinking of that.
Student C:	Yes, a service user learning to cross the road for instance.

Approximately half of the respondents (38/72: 53%) acknowledged both the positive and negative aspects of risk and therefore saw risk as a balancing process in which probability was of crucial importance. Thus, if taking a risk could have a harmful consequence while not taking it would be a missed opportunity, the issue of choice and the probability of different outcomes was of central significance. A qualified learning disability nurse used the example of developing skills in everyday living to illustrate the importance of balancing positive and negative outcomes:

> Balancing...[clients] don't have insight into all the areas that you're talking about and would choose to go off when they've got no road safety skills. You know that's their choice but with a duty of care you'd have to balance that with what the risk was and your responsibility to ensure that they were [safe].

Another qualified learning disability nurse also emphasised the importance of balance:

> Well, risk is a very important area in learning disability and anybody working in that area needs to be concerned with it. It is enabling the people you work with to do something but taking into account the risk that may be involved...for example, you might have somebody who is suffering from epilepsy and you may want them to take part in a certain activity – you need to make a judgement about what the risk to that person is and that's got to be balanced with the experience that they get by taking part, so it's taking account of the risk involved without devaluing the person by not letting them take part.

These differing definitions of risk are a source of much confusion in welfare agencies and in PCP. It is important that a common approach is adopted and a uniform approach agreed. While risk can be either defined negatively as hazard or positively as personal choice, our preference is for the more balanced approach that recognises both the benefits of individual risk-taking and also the potentially harmful consequences. Such an approach would in our view avoid the muddle which appears evident in the following example:

> A real life example is...a girl I worked with some years ago who was able and made friends with some men in a pub and two of them invited her to a party and she really wanted to go. It was like no, but in the end she did because she's got a right to go. But it was like thinking it through. [It was] not a case of what I allowed her to do but...what has she let herself in for basically.

Comment

There is a danger that within agencies providing support for individuals living in the community setting, the positive components of risk management, empowering individuals to make choices and take risks, are separated from the more negative components, identifying and minimising hazards. In such circumstances there is a danger of inconsistency: for some individuals in some circumstances precedence will be given to choice and empowerment whereas for others or in different circumstances concerns with safety will be used to restrict choice or even enforce control and restriction of activities. It is therefore important that PCP considers not only the potential benefits of risk-taking but also identifies the potential hazards. Reasonable risk-taking involves balancing the potential benefits against the possible harmful consequences and needs to be based on transparent and sound decision-making and it is to these issues that the discussion turns in the final section of this chapter.

RISK, DECISION-MAKING AND PCP

While adopting an agreed and consistent approach to risk should form an important part of person centred planning, this will not, of itself, facilitate a process which effectively balances the threats and benefits of risk. Risk needs to be embedded within the process of planning. One way of doing this is to see PCP as a process of decision-making and to examine how the quality of decisions can be improved.

It is one of the major paradoxes of caring that while it is universally acknowledged that decision-making is important, there appears to be little explicit and formal training in decision-making (see, for example, Alaszewski *et al.* 2000, pp.131–56). It is assumed that while adults with learning disabilities may need help with making decisions, professionals and other carers are competent adults who know how to do so, yet there is little evidence to support this. High-profile incidents such as the failure of surgeons at Bristol Royal Infirmary have undermined the government's confidence in the quality of professional decision-making and underpin the development of mechanisms such as clinical governance designed to reassure the public about the quality of such decisions (see Alaszewski, 2002).

The starting point needs to be the actual components of decisions. To give some indication of the type of decisions which need to be made, we have selected an example from one of the diaries completed by nurses in the community (Alaszewski *et al.* 1998, p.48). The example is based on the decisions that a learning disability student nurse had to make when he took a client to visit a shopping centre. The decision to make the trip was made by the student and his mentor. However, when the student encountered problems he had to use his own judgement to analyse and manage the risks.

The agreed plan was that the student nurse would accompany the client to a shopping centre, where the client would first shop for clothes and then as a 'reward' would visit a café in the centre for refreshments. However, when the student and client entered the shopping centre the client became distressed and screamed. He indicated that he wanted to go straight to the café. The student decided to go straight to the café and then continue the visit and report the incident when he returned.

This incident highlights some of the typical features of the real world within which plans and decisions are made, where things are not clear-cut and may be messy, with one thing leading to another. This decision formed part of a set of linked decisions, as the events forming the basis of the diary entry were a product of an earlier joint decision in which the student had participated in assessing the hazards of the trip:

Interviewer: What was your personal involvement in this decision?

Student: To pick the actual client who went out. I was part of a group of three who decided that. We went through firstly asking which people wanted to go out that day and this person was one of them. Then we looked at physical capabilities, we took that into account, whether they were capable of walking which would amount to about one mile in total, the environment that they would actually be going in, were they capable of climbing steps and things like that. We also looked at whether they would act socially, any sort of adverse behaviour, if they did have any history of verbally being aggressive or physically being aggressive. Then after that when we had gone through that criteria then basically it came down to...whose turn it was, which person hadn't gone out for a fair while.

Furthermore when things do not turn out as anticipated, professionals need to be able to assess situations and make decisions quickly, using their own judgement. Such decisions are based not only on probabilities of outcomes and valuation of different outcomes and in this example the agreed plan for the visit was that the student and client should go shopping first and then visit a café. The client had agreed to this plan but during the visit changed his mind. The student perceived a dilemma: giving in to the client's demands might undermine the client's development by reinforcing bad behaviour, but not giving in could create an incident that might endanger the client and others and add to the stigma of people with learning disabilities. Thus the student was concerned with assessing the risk of different courses of action:

Interviewer: Was there a structured way for making the decision?

Student: Well I ran through a structured way in my own head, I ran through safety for the client first alongside my own safety as well, safety for the public so I took in the environment we were in...I was conscious at the time that that little incident, people, the public might be looking at that incident and thinking it's reinforcing their negative thoughts that they have already so I took that into consideration as well.

Interviewer: Had your training prepared you for making this decision?

Student: I drew on my own life experiences. Mostly I did feel that my training gave me the confidence, the theory to be able to say 'yes I can rationalise why I have done that or made the decision'.

It is clear that PCP should form the overall framework within which risk is managed and decisions made. While such a framework needs to leave scope for individual judgement, it is possible to identify the key elements of planning and decision-making. As Dowie (1999) argued, decisions require both information, about the probability of certain outcomes, and value systems, which are used to assess the desirability of different outcomes. He gives a hypothetical analysis of the choices facing nursery rhyme character Humpty Dumpty (see Figure 12.1).

> Any decision tree is one possible model of a decision. That drawn up by Humpty's consultant sets out two options as Sit on the Wall (top Branch) and not Sit on the Wall. There are three uncertainties on the top subtree... Each of the uncertainties must be quantified... Five outcomes are produced by these scenarios... Humpty's strengths of preferences for the outcome states had to be quantified in terms of their 'utilities' (desirabilities) for him. (Dowie 1999, p.44)

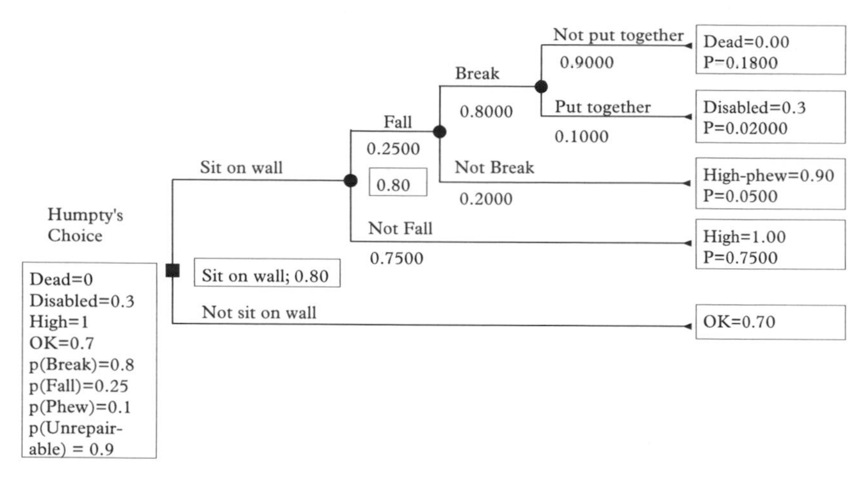

Figure 12.1 Humpty Dumpty's decision tree (Dowie 1999). Reproduced with permission.

This analysis does not 'make' the decision; it is merely a way of making the issues clear. In Dowie's example, the consultant's preferred option would have been for Humpty to sit on the wall, but as events turned out it would have been better for Humpty to stay on the ground.

This approach does provide some guidance about who should do what. Professionals should have evidence and experience on the likely outcomes of different courses of actions. Such information should form an important component of PCP. However, judgements also need to be made about values. In PCP primacy should be given to the values of the individual at the centre of the planning system. However, there may be circumstances in which these values can and should be overridden. For example, if by pursing such values someone is very likely to be harmed, either the person with learning disability or a third party, then serious consideration needs to be given to overriding the individual's values and substituting a default set based on minimising harm.

FINAL COMMENT

While we would not want to be prescriptive about how risk is managed within the context of PCP we hope that such planning:

- recognises that risk is an important issue and needs to be explicitly addressed
- considers PCP alongside aspects of risk management such as health and safety

- is based on an agreed and consistent definition and approach to risk, preferably one which emphasises opportunities and threats and seeks to balance them in the interest of users
- recognises the important role of professionals and their ability to provide information about probability, gives primacy to the values of the person with learning disabilities but also recognises that in some exceptional circumstances there may be a need to override these values and substitute a default set resolving them.

REFERENCES

Alaszewski, A. (1988) 'From villains to victims: a short history of changes in attitudes in official policy.' In A. Leighton (ed) *Mental Handicap in the Community* (pp.3–13). Cambridge: Woodhead-Faulkner.

Alaszewski, A. (2002) 'The impact of the Bristol Royal Infirmary disaster and inquiry on public services in the UK.' *Journal of Interprofessional Care 16*, 4, 371–378.

Alaszewski, A., Alaszewski, H., Ayer, S. and Manthorpe, J. (2000) *Managing Risk in Community Practice: Nursing, Risk and Decision Making.* Edinburgh: Baillière Tindall.

Alaszewski, A., Alaszewski, H., Manthorpe, J. and Ayer, S. (1998) *Assessing and Managing Risk in Nursing Education and Practice: Supporting Vulnerable People in the Community.* Research Reports Series No. 10. London: ENB.

Alaszewski, H., Parker, A. and Alaszewski, A. (1999) *Empowerment and Protection: The Development of Policies and Practice in Risk Assessment and Risk Management in Services for Adults with Learning Disabilities.* London: The Foundation for People with Learning Disabilities.

Atkinson, D. and Williams, F. (eds) (1990) *'Know Me As I Am': An Anthology of Prose, Poetry and Art by People with Learning Difficulties.* London: Hodder and Stoughton.

Booth, T. and Booth, W. (1998) *Growing Up with Parents Who Have Learning Difficulties.* London: Routledge.

Day, S. and Hollins, S. (1985) 'The role of the dietitian.' In M. Craft, J. Bicknell and S. Hollins (eds) *Mental Handicap: A Multi-Disciplinary Approach.* London: Baillière Tindall.

Department of Health (2001) *Valuing People: A New Strategy for Learning Disability for the 21st Century* (Cm 5086). London: The Stationery Office.

Department of Health (2002) *Planning with People – Accessible Guide.* www.doh.gov.uk/learningdisabilties/planning.htm [accessed 27 August 2002].

Dowie, J. (1999) 'Communications for better decisions: not about risk.' *Health, Risk and Society 1*, 41–53.

Ely Inquiry (1969) *Report of the Committee of Inquiry into Allegations of Ill-Treatment of Patients and Other Irregularities at the Ely Hospital, Cardiff,* Cmnd. 3975. London: HMSO.

Furedi, F. (1997) *Culture of Fear: Risk-Taking and the Morality of Low Expectations.* London: Cassell.

Giddens, A. (1991) *Modernity and Self-Identity: Self and Society in the Late Modern Age.* Cambridge: Polity Press.

Jay Committee (1979) *Report of the Committee of Enquiry into Mental Handicap Nursing*, Cmnd. 7468-1. London: HMSO.

Thompson, D.J. (2000) 'Vulnerability, dangerousness and risk: the case of men with learning disabilities who sexually abuse.' *Health, Risk and Society 12*, 1, 33–46.

Ryan, J. with Thomas, F. (1987) *The Politics of Mental Handicap* (revised edition). London: Free Association Books.

Tizard, J. (1964) *Community Services for the Mentally Handicapped.* Oxford: Oxford University Press.

Wilkinson, I. (2001) *Anxiety in a Risk Society.* London: Routledge.

Wolfensberger, W. (1972) *The Principles of Normalization in Human Services.* Toronto: Leonard Crainford.

CHAPTER 13

Person Centred Planning and the Adult Protection Process

Hilary Brown with Karen Scott

INTRODUCTION

This chapter explores the potential and limitations of person centred planning (PCP) with a particular focus on the needs of people with learning disabilities who have experienced, or are at risk of, abuse or neglect. It examines how far PCP provides a helpful set of principles in such situations but also suggests ways in which ordinary safeguards could be introduced into PCP 'thinking', to take account of the lessons learnt in the field of adult protection. The chapter also challenges some of the assumptions which have become attached to the current models of PCP and tries to make explicit where the ideology – as opposed to the ideals – of PCP might act as a barrier to achieving balanced outcomes.

BACKGROUND TO THE PROJECT

The ideas in this chapter arose out of, and have been tested by, a group of care managers in Kent Social Services who met eight times over a year in parallel to receiving training in PCP principles and practice. The group was self-selecting on the grounds that they were working with individuals whose wishes and needs were being assessed against the backdrop of complicated or unhelpful family and community dynamics. It may be that this group stretch a model which has been primarily designed around the needs of more profoundly impaired individuals on whose behalf circles of support have more often been formed. These workers were more concerned with a group of clients whose learning disabilities were mild to moderate but who were struggling, alongside their families, with poverty and debt, with the result that their lives were often dragged down by poor housing and impoverished neighbourhoods as well as, or more than, by any specific impacts of their learning disability.

In line with *Valuing People* (Department of Health 2001a), PCP remains an ideal within the local authority which sponsored this project and although there is much commitment to its implementation, this work suggests that in its 'pure' form, PCP might not be enough to address these pervasive disadvantages. Reliance on informal networks may be an effective strategy when such networks themselves have resources and skills but when those around a vulnerable person are also battered, or in conflict, proactive intervention is essential.

Faced with these issues the group has tried to work towards an understanding of the optimum relationship between the various planning and monitoring mechanisms in the lives of people with learning disabilities who seem to be most at risk. They have grappled with the contradictions in their own multiple roles as facilitators of PCPs, assessors under care management and, potentially, investigators in relation to adult protection concerns. Moreover, they have challenged some myths that seem to underpin a too-rigid adherence to this model of support. Case studies are used to illustrate their concerns and the dilemmas they have been grappling with over this period.

CORNERSTONES OF PERSON CENTRED PLANNING

It is helpful to recap on some essential features of PCP in order to evaluate its potential in situations of risk and exploitation. It would be easy but not helpful to set up a straw-man to knock down. In the Department of Health's formal guidance it is described as a 'family of approaches' and 'a process of continual listening and learning' embarked on 'in alliance with their family and friends' (2001b, p.12; see also Sanderson *et al.* 1997).

Mansell and Beadle-Brown (2004) identify the *specific* properties of PCP as opposed to other systems of individual planning as:

- a focus on aspirations as voiced and prioritised by the service user
- inclusion of family members and of their wider social network
- support to achieve goals in the present rather than waiting on a person to develop skills that will allow them to function without assistance in the arena(s) of their choice (p.2).

It is arguable whether these put much 'blue sky' between PCP and other sensitively applied care management systems but important to note the shift of emphasis towards involvement of families and social inclusion.

Although PCP purports to be new, it undoubtedly builds on a long history of attempts to individualise service provision and create flexible but accountable structures. Mansell and Beadle-Brown (2004, p.4) set out the common threads in a number of individual planning mechanisms as being 'intended to reflect the unique circumstances of the individual person with intellectual disabilities in both assessing and organizing what should be done' (2004, p.2). But they marshal evidence of problems in 'coverage, quality and outcomes' (p.4) in these previous systems: plans had only ever reached a minority of service users, many had not been reviewed, or they had been put on file without being used in practice. Mansell and Beadle-Brown also criticise the emphasis on person centred *planning* and advocate person-centred *action* instead. A shift in this direction might be particularly relevant to people with learning disabilities whose family relationships are unpredictable or chaotic, where the balance between anticipating and reacting might need to be reversed.

Meanwhile O'Brien (1994, p.13) lists five hoped-for outcomes of the person centred planning process:

- aligning the person and his or her allies around a common understanding of current and future wants
- supporting informed choices
- generating creative solutions to overcoming constraints and barriers
- finding ways of accessing local mainstream provision and
- updating and revising their shared understanding.

These outcomes would not look out of place on the agenda of a meeting held under adult protection procedures designed to lead to a personal protection plan – although this would have been preceded by a more formal investigation and analysis of risk. An adult protection referral raises the profile of a case with other mainstream agencies, particularly the police (including community safety) and health. Moreover, with the exception of resource issues, it might also serve as a manifesto for much of what takes place under the banner of care management. It is entirely appropriate that there is a common core of values underpinning practice across all three systems but important to note the overlaps in order to co-ordinate them better in the interest of vulnerable people.

These hoped-for outcomes do, however, present particular challenges in the kinds of cases members of the group had been dealing with. For example, a number of cases involved situations in which key pieces of information must remain confidential or where conflict had arisen which had yet to be resolved. Understandably, the main thrust of the guidance surrounding PCP has been to emphasise the importance of working alongside families and respecting their long-term commitment to their relative with learning disabilities but it is also important that, in its implementation, there is room to acknowledge the possibility that the person's family or network might be a source of exploitation or violence rather than, or perhaps as well as, support. Adult protection cases investigated by social services departments as a matter of routine make it clear that, for an unlucky minority, this is going to be the case.

WHERE DOES PCP FIT IN WITH OTHER SYSTEMS?

O'Brien (2004, p.12) distinguishes between the support provided by mainstream service provision, specialist service provision and what he calls the citizen sector. In practice we found that where cases were predominantly being dealt with using PCP there was a tendency to marginalise professionals, even those who would later be closely involved in implementing elements of the plan. Ongoing care management was more often used in those cases where there was some element of disagreement about what was best which had to be actively managed or mediated. In adult protection cases, access to mainstream services (especially the criminal justice system and victim support agencies) was actively facilitated but sometimes family members were marginalised, particularly if there were signs that their care had been abusive or neglectful. It is as if each system can really only handle one sector rather than provide the necessary bridges across them. This weakens the position of vulnerable people on whose behalf the active involvement of all three sectors is needed to provide a system of 'checks and balances', each empowered to call the other sectors to account.

Although PCP features heavily in the recent White Paper (Department of Health 2001a) it is not part of a statutory framework and nor does it provide a gateway to funding, professional input or service provision. Commentators have pointed out the risk that this will provide a rationale for shifting the cost of care from the collective purse to individual families. This reliance on informal supports also hugely disadvantages those whose families are themselves poor or fragmented, creating major issues of inequity. Instead of providing these individuals with more, they risk getting a lot less if they are left to their own or their family's devices. Care management is the mechanism that is designed to produce fair access to available resources and to generate the data to underpin planning of future provision on the basis of aggregated assessments of need. As long as these functions are left out of the PCP process, a parallel planning and rationing system will be needed.

The adult protection process is also mandated (Department of Health/ Home Office 2000[1]) and leads to co-ordinated interagency assessment and investigation backed up by a protection plan which seeks to prevent further abuse or neglect and put in place supports to aid recovery. Mechanisms are in place to monitor individual outcomes and patterns of abuse across each local authority with a view to building in safeguards, screening the workforce and preventing unacceptable risks. Proposed new mental capacity legislation will strengthen the rights of people with learning disabilities to receive proper information, or family members and direct care staff to take day-to-day decisions on behalf of people with learning disabilities who cannot handle aspects of decision-making on their own; it will also provide a formal route for adjudicating in situations where it is necessary to take action in a person's best interests which override his or her immediate wishes or the immediate wishes of his or her relatives (see, for example, Darren's case).

In many ways this legislation supports the stronger emphasis being placed on informal carers, which is also at the heart of the current model of PCP. The belief that unpaid, voluntary networks are preferable to, or can do the same or even better than, professional supporters is key to the way PCP is being formulated. To quote from Mansell and Beadle-Brown, 'The social network is seen as a richer source of imagination, creativity and resources than the service system, not least in the area of forming and maintaining social relationships' (2004, p.3). But unfortunately this cannot be assumed for all people, all of the time. The cases discussed in this group seriously challenged this proposition.

Evidence suggests that people with learning disabilities often have very limited networks partly as a result of their difficulties in communicating, relating and/or managing their behaviour. The 'natural' exchange in relationships based on reciprocity ceases to hold and it is the resulting isolation that PCP seeks to remedy. But what is in it for these unpaid recruits? If, as Mansell and Beadle-Brown suggest (2004, p.3), 'tradition and duty are less important than they might once have been in recruiting and sustaining a "circle of support" then other sources of motivation are important'.

Altruism and the social rewards of belonging to a 'circle' come into play here. But the ethos around PCP tends to downplay the potential for negative motivation – for example, an intention to sexually or financially exploit someone. PCP acolytes often chafe at the need for safeguards, regulation and screening as if these were superfluous bureaucracy, but in doing so they ignore research studies into abuse of vulnerable adults. For example, research demonstrates that sexual exploitation is perpetrated in equal numbers by men (usually) from community, family and professional networks (Brown, Stein and Turk 1995; Brown and Turk 1992). These men do not turn up on the doorstep wearing a large label, more often posing as 'pillars of the community' in a bid to disguise their true purpose. Moreover clients, especially those living independently in social housing projects, are more often housed on problem estates than in communities seen through rose-tinted lenses.

If what it takes for PCP to work is a supportive family and resourceful neighbourhood, and if PCP is to become the main plank of the future organisation of services, then this raises major issues of equity in that those with the most problems may miss out on getting the support they need. A person like Anne, who finds herself at the centre of a network that she cannot control or manage, needs someone to do more than facilitate a meeting. The PCP process cannot proceed on the basis that the person is being *supported* by those around him or her, if he or she is actually being undermined or exploited by family or neighbourhood contacts. Where this is the case, excluding professionals and agencies that have a statutory responsibility to act cuts across a competing set of values about proactive sharing of information and interagency working that is mandated within adult protection procedures and care management systems. It is case *co-ordination* that has repeatedly been called for in these situations.[2]

CASES WHICH STRAIN THE PCP MODEL

The nature of the cases being managed by workers in the group

The following vignettes illustrate the complexity of the cases that were being managed by group members and the nature of the risks their clients faced. All names and some details have been changed to preserve anonymity but the dilemmas are all too real.

Case study: Maria

Maria is a 50-year-old woman who lives in a housing association flat across the road from her mother who is 85. Mrs Smith is increasingly frail physically although she is still very dominating emotionally. Maria does not seem to have control over any day-to-day decisions – for example, over what she cooks or eats – nor does she have access to her money, which her mother manages for her. Mrs Smith also recently stopped her going to a work placement, which she liked, because she was getting dirty and having to spend money on her lunch.

To save money, her mother has decided that Maria should use all the amenities in her house so Maria has to come over the road to her mother's house to use the phone and hot water and in winter because her flat has no heating.

Her mother has fallen out with the rest of the family so Maria has no contact with her brother and sister.

Implications for person-centred plan

Two workers are involved with the family and are treading on eggshells, having been shut out twice. They have talked to Maria and she doesn't want to force the issue or have a row with her mother who is the most important person in her life. So instead of a PCP, the workers have worked round Maria's mother and have managed to fix up day services for three afternoons a week and are actively trying to facilitate her befriending an older woman who attends the centre and who lives in her neighbourhood. They are trying to get her a 'pay as you go' mobile phone for Christmas from one of her siblings.

Case study: Anne

Anne is a 40-year-old woman with learning disabilities who has a 14-year-old daughter. Her mother also has a learning disability/mental health problem. Anne lives in her own rented accommodation managed by a housing association. Her brother lives with her too and uses her benefits sometimes to buy drugs. She knows this isn't right but she does not want to throw him out or get him into trouble and in other ways he helps her with her daughter. She has two outstanding loans at very high interest and she has also been 'sold' various insurance policies which are not good value. She buys clothes for a new 'friend' she has made and has rented four TVs because of special offers from persuasive door-to-door salespeople.

Implications for person-centred plan

This family have been known to social services for a long time. The children and families team are involved in respect of Anne's daughter and their views about what should happen is taking precedence over other planning. Under some duress (because it was made clear that otherwise her daughter would be taken into care) Anne has agreed to be rehoused but still the learning disability worker involved is expecting there to be an issue of boundaries and doubts whether Anne can keep her brother away from the household or keep her benefits for her own use.

Case study: James

James is 45 and lives with two other residents with moderate learning disabilities in supported accommodation: they all have tenancies and receive support in their home. A recent financial audit revealed that there had been systematic abuse of all the residents, but particularly of James, by the husband and wife team who ran the service. His key worker had acted as a whistleblower and was then forced to leave because of the bad atmosphere so James is experiencing a major disruption in his support and is exhibiting very anxious behaviour.

Implications for person-centred plan

There is an ongoing adult protection investigation and it is expected that the case will come to court. A protection plan was drawn up under these procedures but many of the issues need to be dealt with at a systems level. His family are now involved and have been supportive but say that this proves that he cannot manage his money and that they will withdraw him from the service unless they get a 'cast-iron guarantee' that social services will monitor all expenditure in the house from now on.

Case study: David

David is a 44-year-old man with severe learning disabilities who has always lived at home with his parents as the main carers. He has had chronic health problems and after a recent three-month stay in hospital, extensive assessments concluded that he could no longer swallow safely so he had a feeding tube fitted. His parents were clearly told that he could not be given food or drink but when they visit, or when he goes home, there has been concern that he may have been offered a drink. When he left hospital he was placed in a residential placement via continuing health care.

David is still in residential care and his parents are still having problems accepting the situation.

Implications for person-centred plan

A planning meeting was held around David which had to focus on his health issues: this was necessarily a professional meeting more than a PCP circle although a network of professionals and carers are supporting him. There is ongoing conflict with David's mother, who despite advice from specialists insists that she wants him to be given small amounts of food and drink.

The speech and language therapist wanted to find ways of explaining to David why he has to be fed by tube but his mother keeps butting in and confusing the issue saying that he could eat and that she will bring him something: this is cutting across any real involvement from him in how he wants his condition to be managed.

An adult protection alert was logged and a brief investigation carried out but no one was assigned to mediate between the parents and professionals, which is what had been hoped for. That referral is now closed but it has actually left an atmosphere of suspicion that is making things worse. The home has been advised to get in touch with social services if they suspect the parents have been offering him food.

Case study: Darren

Darren has difficult sexual behaviours which he exhibits both on his own and when he is with others; this has led him to be seen as an abuser on two occasions. He also cross-dresses and has been found in situations that suggest that he has practised auto-erotic asphyxiation.

Implications for person-centred plan

A PCP approach has been used to try to build up positives in Darren's life as he is currently being quite restricted as the result of an informal strategy of 'chaperoning' him whenever he goes out and at all times in the residential home. He is clearly a risk and at risk and although his family are generally supportive Darren did not want them to know about his behaviour and the reason for his recent moves of placement. But they have to know about risks he poses to children in the wider family network so he had to be overruled in this respect. Without accurate information it would be very difficult to involve them in what should happen next or to alert them to the nature of the risks he faces. His younger sister, who has just had a child, is currently very important to Darren but there is concern that she might not maintain contact if she is told about his behaviour.

Case study: Emily

Emily is 19 and is about to finish her time at a boarding school where she was placed when she was 13 after an allegation that she had been sexually abused by her stepfather. The investigation was inconclusive and formal child protection proceedings were never instigated. She has been consistent in saying that she wants to return home and says that she really likes her stepfather because he lets her sit in the front seat of his car.

Implications for person-centred plan

PCP has been used as an approach through the transition process but it has been difficult to negotiate the necessary supports or set up opportunities for informal monitoring within the network without making this history explicit. The result is that the move is having to go ahead on the basis of a wing and a prayer and professional monitoring and review will need to be ongoing to assure her safety. In other ways the PCP was very helpful and a number of opportunities have been identified for community involvement, including a part-time job and membership of a local sports and leisure centre.

Case study: Derek

Derek is living in a supported living placement with a support package. Although he can manage his money on a week-by-week basis, he was the victim of financial abuse when the brother of one of the other tenants (a woman who Derek believed to be his girlfriend and whose brother is a drug user) asked him for a loan and took him up to the cash machine late at night and with a mixture of pressure and persuasion got him to withdraw £250 before midnight and another £250 afterwards. This only came to light when the support worker checked over the bank statement but by then three other such withdrawals had been made. Derek still believes that his 'friend' will give the money back. His parents are furious: they are on a low income themselves and had saved very carefully to be able to put this money into his account to help him get started.

Implications for person-centred plan

A PCP meeting was held, facilitated by his care manager and attended by the service provider, parents and Derek himself. Derek does not want to 'make a fuss' and is angry about his parents making such a big deal out of this. He thinks they are interfering in who his friends should be and still thinks that it is okay that he lent them the money.

Derek's parents are very angry with social services for not picking up on this earlier and are in the process of making a formal complaint. This is cutting across any other planning on Derek's behalf.

Case study: Andrea

Andrea is in her mid-thirties and lives at home with her mother. She has moderate learning disabilities. The house belongs to her parents and she is a carer to her mother even though she has never got on with her. However, she was very close to her father when he was alive. Her disability prevents her from understanding other people very well and she feels that she cannot express herself well. She self-harms and opens up wounds on her arms and legs. This has resulted in her often being absent from work at the day centre, and from her job in the canteen at a local department store. She says she is feeling bored and undervalued.

The service provider believes that there is some element of risk and exploitation in what is going on.

Implications for person-centred plan

Andrea's PCP has been facilitated by the day service provider and has been successful in drawing in her sister and brother-in-law to take her out occasionally but there is also an underlying sense that they do not want to rock the boat too much as Andrea is currently preventing her mother from going into residential care and this preserves the capital in the house which will be their inheritance.

Case study: Jack and Diane

Jack and Diane have been married for seven years and live in a rented flat, receiving five hours of support each week. There has been a long history of domestic violence in their relationship which sometimes boils over and causes Diane huge distress but she does not want to leave her husband or go to the police. Jack gets very angry if anyone mentions this and has asked support workers to leave on several occasions in an intimidating way.

Implications for person-centred plan

At Diane's meeting it emerged that Jack was forcing her to have sex and that the violence was escalating. There was a disputed view of the seriousness of this between health and social services staff. When asked about her aspirations they all centre on them staying together but she has enormous difficulty in addressing the situation as it actually is. An adult protection alert was raised but it was inconclusive in that when she described recent events it was unclear whether she was talking about real force or clumsiness on Jack's part. He has been referred to the community learning disability team for follow-up sex education. Some support workers are overtly afraid of visiting the home when Jack is there and this is making it difficult to sustain their package of support.

Case study: Stewart

Stewart is 22 and was housed as a joint project between the leaving care team and the learning disability service. He has mild learning disabilities and is living in a rented flat. He has two groups who have befriended him – a local church group and a group of lads at the local pub. He is drinking heavily and over the last three months has made himself ill through binge drinking on four occasions – once he was found unconscious in the street and ended up in accident and emergency. This in turn uses up his money so that he is not eating well. He feels 'caught' between his two groups of friends and is very confused about his behaviour and feelings. He doesn't know what is right.

Implications for person-centred plan

Stewart does not want to get his friends together. He enjoys the activities he can join in at church but feels more comfortable with his mates. His care manager is concerned to get him a referral to a local voluntary agency which provides services for people experiencing problems with alcohol but so far he will not admit to there being a problem.

These snapshots illustrate the complexity of the cases being dealt with in relation to risk and protection issues. Some of the problems have arisen as a result of the severity of an individual's impairment, health status or challenging behaviour (for example in David's case) but more often the difficulties can be traced to ongoing tension and ruptures in family relationships, to the paucity of their collective resources and their community's lack of social capital. It is these social factors that have eroded relationships and alliances.

Implementing a PCP process in these circumstances is not straightforward. For service users like Anne a 'circle of support' seems inappropriate because she already has a network, albeit one which is difficult to manage; likewise Diane has an 'ordinary' violent marriage to navigate. For Darren and Emily there are major issues of confidentiality that strike at the heart of the 'shared understanding' on which PCP is presaged. While inclusion is seen as critical, for Maria, Anne and Derek there are issues about keeping people 'out' of their lives rather than 'in' them. For James and David there are serious conflicts between professionals and family members that cut across helpful planning relationships. For Maria and Andrea there are major issues about their role in their families and about being dominated by their relatives' views or needs, leading to difficult judgements about when to play down or work around such intransigence and when to confront it openly in the interests of the person who is the primary service user (see also Williams and Robinson 2001).

Where adult protection procedures have been formally invoked this has sometimes left a sour taste in people's mouths that has created a difficult backdrop for PCP. As Grant, Rachmaran and Flynn (2002, p.21) remark in the context of individual planning:

> The premium on high trust relationships was crucial and anything that undermined this – staff turnover or questions of perceived professional competence for example – was likely to nullify person-centred-ness.

It may also have revealed system failures as well as personal culpability on the part of staff, family members or community allies.

Is the meeting essential in these situations?

Despite its newness there is already a sense of orthodoxy in the process of PCP which revolves around a meeting of family and friends as the main forum for hearing the person's wishes and aspirations. It should be remembered however that this 'set-piece' does not need to take place in a rigid format. Sanderson *et al.* (1997) remind us that the individuals can think about their life on their own, or with whomever they feel comfortable to share. As adults many of us plan our lives while keeping our parents and families only partly in the loop, or even deliberately choosing to shut them out of decisions which they might find controversial. Although the more usual mode is one of trying to involve and include everyone concerned in these meetings, for some of the people featured in these case studies, keeping people at bay and setting appropriate boundaries would have been a more appropriate aim and was the thing they found most difficult. Case workers were then often drawn into black and white thinking that they had to *either* exclude difficult family members and shut them out completely *or* include them and bow entirely to their whims and wishes. It was as if they could not 'do' person centred planning if key family members were not there. A more normative model would be to help individuals plan what aspects of their lives they wish to share with different family members and/or to work with them in ways that weave planning into everyday conversations rather than as an 'event' that stands out and runs the risk of exacerbating existing tensions.

This flexibility is demanded in Maria's case. In theory she clearly has human rights that should be upheld independently of her mother but in practice it would cause her enormous (di)stress to challenge her mother's wishes in an open and confrontational manner. Her mother is the most important person in her life and at 85 is unlikely to change significantly. What is key is that Maria is helped gradually to operate outside of her mother's influence and prepare for a time when her mother cannot play such an important role in her life. Meanwhile Maria's mother is adamant that she will not attend or allow meetings, she has fallen out with Maria's siblings and is not talking to her neighbours, and she also objects forcibly to Maria doing a range of things such as getting dirty by attending the gardening project or having her own phone. If the emphasis is placed on the planning mechanism itself then Maria's mother acts as a barrier to any of this work being done; if the emphasis is placed on action and outcomes then an experienced case worker can chip away at these prohibitions and work round them.

Hence person-centred *action* in this situation requires tact and stealth as well as, or instead of, a one-size-fits-all 'circle of support'. If drawn, Maria's network would not look like a circle, more like a restricted galaxy, with bright spots (siblings who are not talking to mother), small planets (a potential boyfriend at the activity club she attends), distant comets (in the shape of an older neighbour who attends the same activity centre) and a lot of very empty sky. If joining the dots is a prerequisite to action then Maria's 'stars' don't hold out much hope. If joining some dots could instead be conceptualised as a possible outcome then work can be done now. Ongoing casework seems to be a more viable way of progressing these goals than set-piece planning.

New models of care, which have been set up to maximise autonomy, may also need to grapple with risks as Derek's situation demonstrates. Direct payments and/or enhanced benefits have been shown to provide flexibility and autonomy to disabled people (Glasby and Littlechild 2002). But in these cases there were often major concerns about whether or how money was deployed on behalf of the person concerned – benefits disappeared into the family budget (in Maria's and Anne's cases), bank accounts were accessed wrongfully (in Derek's and James's cases) and accommodation intended for the person with a learning disability was shared or taken over by other family members or acquaintances (in Anne's and James's cases). Care managers expressed considerable concern about the monitoring arrangements for direct payments and adult protection inquiries have raised issues about misuse of the appointeeship arrangements within the benefits system. New mental capacity legislation will clarify boundaries by making these arrangements more formal, but challengeable if those managing a person's resources are not using them in hir or her 'best interests'. But if professionals are squeezed out of such service provision there may not be anyone able to challenge such breaches of boundaries. Care managers are far better placed to make such judgements and to initiate such challenges than members of a 'circle of support' where social norms may well inhibit confrontation or questioning of the motivation of other parties.

We think it helpful to reflect on the implications of these cases, and others like them, for PCP. We have used them as worked examples, which test a number of potentially unfounded working hypotheses which underpin the PCP process, including the following:

- 'unpaid people always act in the vulnerable person's interests or are less likely to be following their own agendas than paid workers'
- 'communities are always supportive' – sometimes they are predatory: it is always the vicar who features in the PCP literature and never the loan shark!
- 'the network will agree about important areas of a person's life' – often there are active disagreements about a range of issues, for example, about how to address healthcare needs (see David's case) or attitudes to sex or drinking
- 'inclusion is best for everyone' – sometimes it is exclusion or at least sound boundary setting which allows someone to move on
- 'people with learning disabilities are not actively trying to manage their own networks' – for example, Anne runs her own household even though she struggles and Stewart tries to keep his incompatible friends apart; and in these cases the facilitator has to be careful to bolster and not to usurp their role at the helm
- 'PCP is the only, or even the best, mechanism for achieving person-centred goals' – other systems including transition planning, care management, adult protection, ongoing case work or advocacy can also be effective.

INTEGRATING SAFEGUARDS INTO PERSON CENTRED PLANNING

If these case studies test the model of PCP in exceptional ways we have also been concerned to explore how far ordinary safeguards and protection can be integrated into PCP as a strategy to prevent abuse and neglect in the future. Proponents of PCP have tended to work on the basis that abuse and neglect are rare aberrations rather than commonplace occurrences. Local adult protection committees routinely produce information that could inform those facilitating PCPs about potential risks. In this authority, arrangements have recently been set up for the partnership boards to routinely receive an annual report on cases of abuse involving people with learning disabilities so that they can take this into account when planning and commissioning new services.

The lack of engagement between these two systems seems to be another example of the unhelpful 'splitting' which has often dogged learning disability services. It is as if a false dichotomy has been created with protection on the one hand and empowerment on the other. With one eye on the legacy of institutional services, commentators leap to the false conclusion that it is 'protection' that has stopped people with learning disabilities from doing the things they want to do. But drab, unfulfilling lifestyles and empty hours never provided safety, being the hallmark of a service structure that was restrictive and sometimes negligent but not remotely protective and certainly not 'overprotective' because so many people were harmed while under its auspices.

The result of this history is that 'protection' is painted into a negative corner whereas the reality is that we all build protection into our lives and the lives of people we care about. 'Looking out for each other' is a part of what we do as friends, partners, parents and lovers. We urge each other to eat sensibly, to exercise, give up smoking and be safe in the sex we have. We warn people about safe routes across town, pass on information about acquaintances whose motivation might not be what it seems and we even (gently) impose boundaries such as suggested bed-times, times to be home from work, numbers of nights out in the pub and so on. This mutual risk assessment and risk management (although of course most people would not explicitly name it as such) is an essential part of ordinary caring relationships. If you live alone you do it for yourself, often more obsessively!

In the training we developed on safeguards in PCP we designed participative exercises that demonstrated to everyone how ingrained and automatic these processes of risk assessment are and therefore how perverse it is to leave it out of the planning we do on behalf of people with learning disabilities. We did an exercise in which participants quickly evaluated potential risks in a number of interesting activities and made plans to avoid trouble. No one found it difficult. We all do it every day. The plans were easy and the protective mechanisms were very 'ordinary' – taking out insurance, drawing maps, getting a mobile phone, using condoms, buying a chain for the door – you can work backwards to see the kind of situations we worked with which shows just how commonplace this kind of planning is. The problem is that it is so commonplace it is invisible – these are ordinary solutions to ordinary problems. They don't stop us doing things, rather they *allow* us to get on and lead the interesting and varied lives most of us take for granted. This thinking needs to be made integral to PCP meetings and thinking so that people with learning disabilities are not exposed to risks that other people would find unthinkable.

Occasionally if an activity carries particular risks we make particular provision – for example, we buy protective clothing such as lifejackets or cycle helmets or we take out extra insurance such as holiday insurance or extra cover for valuable possessions such as jewellery, cameras or computers. Very dangerous activities prompt more even more explicit planning just as services which aim high require detailed risk management systems and meticulous planning of supports. For example, if I were going to do a parachute jump I would make very sure that the safety harness was in order – people with high aspirations do not trade off safety against enjoyment. Nor can you average them out so that you have a bit of safety and a bit of excitement. To do so would leave service users with boring *and* unsafe activities when we should facilitate innovative and richly connected experiences which avoid harm to users through sensitive and age-appropriate safeguards.

So when protection gets the blame for stopping people with learning disabilities from doing things they want to do, it is easy to see why the reaction is to ignore risk and brush it under the carpet. To do so is not only naive but dangerous and more to the point it is not how other valued citizens live their lives. The end point is that people with learning disabilities are not (and never were) *over*protected – rather they are in fact often shockingly *under*protected.

CONCLUSION

O'Brien (2004) warns against 'cynicism or pessimism' and this is a problem we have engaged with in this group. We began to characterise the practice of PCP, as it is currently being implemented, as an exercise in inspired optimism (see Seligman 1991 for a definition of learned optimism). The circle meetings act as a necessary means of galvanising enough momentum to overcome depression and barriers, whether to mainstream service provision or greater acceptance in, and support from, people's networks and neighbourhoods. The prevention of abuse, however, requires a kind of disciplined pessimism, one which uses both common sense and reputable evidence to anticipate risk with a view to preventing harm or resolving conflict. They should not be seen as mutually exclusive but as complementary.

Mansell and Beadle-Brown (2004, p.6) raised the spectre that, in the absence of appropriate resources, PCP might become 'a kind of displacement activity, using staff energy, time and resources but not making any difference to people's lives'. In this chapter I have argued that where people with learning disabilities are struggling with issues of exploitation, abuse or neglect, PCP also risks deflecting from the ongoing responsibility of social services to assure their personal safety and to uphold their human rights. Despite the myth building, the reality is that most people with learning disabilities rely on family, community *and* professional supporters who together make up the essential fabric of their lives. For those whose families or communities are too frayed to play their part, a functioning and supportive professional network needs to step in. In practice these experienced workers were not using an orthodox model of PCP with their clients but more of an enhanced form of care management to contain ongoing situations of risk, coupled with skilled casework and family mediation to mend the rifts that could be mended. In short they were engaged in what used to be called 'social work'.

That does not mean that the PCP training has been wasted in relation to these perplexing situations. It has done much to raise the stakes so that it is clear that whichever system we are working within, the focus will be on placing the wishes, rights, welfare and integrity of service users at centre stage. Person-centred outcomes might then be achieved through a number of routes just as prevention of abuse can be built into PCP without compromising its ethos.

NOTES

1. Issued as guidance under Section 7 of the 1970 Local Authority Act.
2. For example, the Criminal Records Bureau searches or checks against the Department of Health's list of those who are barred from working with vulnerable adults, known as the Protection of Vulnerable Adults (POVA) list.
3. Interestingly, although user involvement is regarded as vital in mental health services, relying on informal networks is not a strategy that has been advocated or adopted in relation to high-risk clients in mental health services: instead assertive outreach teams work on the explicit basis that their role as professionals is to engage with, and sustain their engagement with, clients whose lives are chaotic, unstructured or unsupported.

REFERENCES

Brown, H., Stein, J. and Turk, V. (1995) 'The sexual abuse of adults with learning disabilities: report of a second two year incidence survey.' *Mental Handicap Research 8*, 1, 3–24.

Brown, H. and Turk, V. (1992) 'Defining sexual abuse as it affects adults with learning disabilities.' *Mental Handicap 20*, 2, 44–55.

Department of Health (2001a) *Valuing People: A New Strategy for Learning Disability for the 21st Century* (Cm 5086). London: HMSO.

Department of Health/Home Office (2000) *No Secrets: Guidance on Developing and Implementing Multi-Agency Policies and Procedures to Protect Vulnerable Adults From Abuse.* London: Department of Health.

Glasby, J. and Littlechild, R. (2002) *Social Work and Direct Payments.* Bristol: Policy Press.

Grant, G., Rachmaran, P. and Flynn, M. (2002) *What are the Foundations of Person-Centred Support? Links Between Individual and Person-Centred Planning.* Sheffield University School of Nursing and Midwifery.

Mansell, J. and Beadle-Brown, J. (2004) 'Person Centred Planning or Person Centred Action: Policy and Practice in Intellectual Disability Services.' *Journal of Applied Research in Intellectual Disabilities 17*, 1, 1–9.

O'Brien, J. (2004) 'If person centred planning did not exist, *Valuing People* would require its invention.' *Journal of Applied Research in Intellectual Disabilities 17*, 11–18.

Sanderson, H., Kennedy, J., Ritchie, P. and Goodwin, G. (1997) *People, Plans and Possibilities – Exploring Person Centred Planning.* Edinburgh: SHS.

Seligman, M.E.P. (1991) *Learned Optimism: How to Change your Mind and Your Life.* New York: Pocket Books.

Williams, V. and Robinson, C. (2001) 'More than one wavelength: identifying, understanding and resolving conflicts of interest between people with intellectual disabilities and their family carers.' *Journal of Applied Research in Intellectual Disabilities 14*, 30–46.

CHAPTER 14

Considerations for Making PCP and Care Management Work

Summary Observations and Concluding Remarks

Paul Cambridge and Steven Carnaby

In this final chapter we aim to provide a summary to the book by identifying key themes emerging from the span of discussion and issues identified by the authors in their different chapters. In so doing we primarily draw on this material but also aim to locate it in a wider analysis and discourse.

IMPLEMENTING AND REVIEWING PCP

It is clear that local authorities and partnership boards across the country are mapping and navigating the implementation of person centred planning (PCP) in various ways, as are practitioners and people with learning disabilities themselves, and examples from this book point to the different approaches being employed and demands encountered which influence the process of development. In terms of the national policy agenda for PCP, it is noteworthy that the work conducted on PCP in Kensington and Chelsea and described by Hector Medora and Sue Ledger (Chapter 10) is connected to a national evaluation of PCP (also see below), so there is the potential of comparative findings to reflect upon in due course. It will be important that all local authorities review the development of PCP based on experience elsewhere as well as its relationship with care management and other organisational systems. Most importantly, it will need to be reviewed on the basis of the experiences of service users, which is why the work conducted in Kensington and Chelsea provides a model, where work of the 'It's My Life' group informed approaches to PCP. Self-advocacy and other good models of advocacy clearly need to be developed alongside PCP if it is to achieve its maximum potential.

When reflecting on the best practices witnessed 12 years ago in the management of de-institutionalisation in the Care in the Community projects (Cambridge, Hayes and Knapp 1994; Knapp *et al.* 1992), there is convincing evidence that the effectiveness of PCP (and possibly that of other micro-organisational interventions such as care management and direct payments) hinges on its objectivity and independence. Experience also suggests that effectiveness is often related to newness. Even if well designed and executed and initially functioning well, PCP risks decay and institutionalisation in the long run, also underlining the imperative of longer-term review. Jim Mansell and Julie Beadle-Brown (Chapter 2) also underline the need to draw and reflect on experience with other individual planning systems that have been used, with varying success, in the past. If we fail to learn from past experience we risk not only reinventing the wheel but making the same mistakes in turning the wheel.

An early version of an individual planning and case review process was developed by the Care in the Community team at the Personal Social Services Research Unit (PSSRU) and implemented by all the pilot projects. It undoubtedly helped to manage the difficult transition and change in people's lives and services as they moved from hospital to the community. It also represented an early person-centred approach to service development, interestingly, implemented alongside new care management arrangements for all the pilot projects. However, such arrangements sometimes drifted into routinised practice, with person-centred action depending on enthusiastic individuals and champions for change in services, rather than on the systems themselves. There is an inevitable risk that PCP will fall victim to such decay at the individual and general levels. As Steven Carnaby and Patricia Lewis explain (Chapter 6), young people and adults with learning disabilities need good PCP to help navigate complex changes in their lives and the fractures in services and support encountered when moving into adulthood. This also suggests, however, that PCP needs to be seen as a long-term intervention with the capacity to sustain action and ensure the maintenance of outcomes. It needs the ability to focus attention, effort and resources on periods of transition in people's lives, such as from children's to adults' and from adults' to older people's services and supports, as much as it needs the ability to focus on those features of everyday life which are relatively ordinary but important to individuals. Consequently PCP also needs the capacity to be flexible, variable and robust and link into resources and planning systems at the macro-level, which is also why connections to care management and commissioning are so important.

DEVELOPING A SYSTEMS PERSPECTIVE

The critical importance of making sure innovations such as PCP are connected productively and efficiently to wider systems operating in services is also stressed in this book. One of the key messages from Simon Duffy and Helen Sanderson (Chapter 3) is that care managers need to work in constructive and creative ways with PCP but also on a broader front, to promote the wider self-determination of people with learning disabilities, which is also in line with the objectives of PCP. Similarly, David Dick and Karin Purvis (Chapter 7) identify and map how total communication can underpin PCP and wider person-centred approaches, with other work utilising total communication demonstrating its potential to involve people traditionally excluded from consultation (Cambridge and Forrester-Jones 2003). Hilary Brown and Karen Scott (Chapter 13) make a number of transferable observations about PCP when examining adult protection and related processes – in particular the powerful point that good PCP cannot necessarily rely on informal supports and in many cases strong interventions and supports from practitioners such as care managers will be essential to protect people, as well as promote productive PCP. Too often we find components or functions of service systems operating in different directions and to different goals for individuals or even challenging each other's territories.

The observations of Hilary Brown and Karen Scott also stress the potential relevance and importance of risk management in PCP, and as Helen and Andy Alaszewski argue (Chapter 12), risk management can only be neglected if there is certainty about actions and outcomes. Certainty is unlikely – and arguably unwanted – in person-centred change management, where people take control from practitioners and move in new and often uncharted directions in their lives. But this clearly brings associated risks and, echoing some of the observations of Hilary Brown and Karen Scott (Chapter 13), we need to acknowledge that for some service users, such as men with learning disabilities who sexually abuse, risk management (as the Alaszewskis point out) will need to be central to PCP.

Although care management has the potential to operate as a constraint as well as a vehicle to promote PCP, other systems level instruments are also relevant to the successful operation of PCP. In examining direct payments, Julie Beadle-Brown (Chapter 11) points out that PCP requires the means to promote change and that PCP and direct payments have the shared aim of enabling people to exercise as much choice and control as possible in their lives. In a society institutionalising capital, direct payments clearly provide a potential vehicle for PCP. Conversely, direct payments also require a strategy and plan to make them effective in producing the desired changes and outcomes in people's lives and PCP offers such a possibility.

PCP AND THE SOCIAL CARE MARKET

A fundamental question running through much of the evidence and discussion in this book concerns the location within the social care market and its relationship with the responsibilities of commissioners and providers. Although the principles of commissioning and contracting risk the exclusion of service users (Cambridge and Brown 1997), individual contracts, as argued by Julie Beadle-Brown (Chapter 11), can help shift power and control towards service users. Hector Medora and Sue Ledger (Chapter 10) also demonstrate how commissioning can link into advocacy to help develop person-centred services and action. In our work with men with learning disabilities we have developed therapeutic, counselling and psycho-educational approaches, but all put the person and his or her life and interests at the centre of the work and all help construct a bridge between the interests of purchasers and providers and the rights and interests of individual service users. PCP can also help develop such a bridge.

There is no doubt that practitioners and staff have long striven to achieve truly person-centred work supporting people with learning disabilities but the constraints upon them are multitudinous. For example, time constraints, administrative and managerial demands and simply the personal limits to coping all place restrictions on individual work. Our experience suggests that it is often only from outside services that person-centred work can be truly delivered or become truly effective. This is because it is generally resourced separately and has the capacity to address the interpersonal and power dynamics operating in services in a way that is difficult or impossible from within. Often, this approach reduces to a dual role of independent advocate and negotiator for the person and facilitator for change for the service, mirroring what is likely to be required for productive PCP interventions. It also mirrors the role often promoted for care management in the early experimental approaches in Britain in the 1980s, where care management was seen as a device for helping co-ordinate services around individual needs across an increasingly mixed economy of provision and where care managers could perhaps function as professional advocates for their clients. The emphasis of action may have shifted to the service user, but the conditions and constraints are all too familiar.

PCP AND SOCIAL NETWORKS

The fact that New Labour promoted social inclusion and PCP reflects the brutal realities in the lives of many people with learning disabilities. Their relatively sparse social networks, isolation in services and lack of participation in their communities (Forrester-Jones *et al.* in press) reflects relatively impoverished social networks, predominated by paid staff and other service users. Self-advocacy, circles of support and alliances such as the 'It's My Life' group are indeed evidence of the need to take action on a broad front to help combat such exclusion. Robust social networks require reciprocity and organic evolution (Bulmer 1987), features often lacking for people who use services due to their relative isolation and lack of power. While a reasonable objective would be to acknowledge and address all of the above as part of facilitating productive PCP, we also need to ask whether it is reasonable to expect the care management process, key workers or support services in general to construct broader social networks for people with learning disabilities. Doris Clark, Robert Garland and Val Williams (Chapter 5) explore this question in the context of their work and experience developing circles of support for people with learning disabilities. They illustrate how people at the centre of PCP can stay in control of the process and how their supports can be extended and opened up, despite wider social exclusion.

Maybe the learning point is that we need to acknowledge that PCP makes more sense when people live with supportive and safe families and are known to be safe, and less sense when care managers have to deal with the hard edge of services. Hilary Brown and Karen Scott articulate this tension (Chapter 13), and we clearly need to develop more robust and assertive social interventions where vulnerability and risk feature high or where mainstream or specialist resources and competence are lacking. Examples of situations where more focused intervention within and alongside PCP are likely to be required include people with challenging behaviours or those who simply do not fit into a community, such as people returning to their original local authority area or sent away to out-of-area placements. These interventions will primarily need to help protect people from neglect and isolation or abuse and it is here that care management has a particularly important and vital role to play. Indeed care management can sometimes be the only real scrutiny over the services and quality of life for some individuals. Such work falls within what is likely to emerge as a family of person-centred arrangements.

In order to promote social inclusion in its widest sense, PCP also needs to operate in culturally appropriate ways. What is culturally appropriate to a white male heterosexual service user will not necessarily be culturally appropriate to an Asian woman service user. Although individual interventions have the capacity to be culturally respectful and sensitive, we need to remember that, as a general rule, PCP is likely to be a product of hierarchies of power within and outside social care organisations and that institutionalised power has the potential to perpetuate sexism, racism and homophobia and exclude those on the margins of society and services, such as people with challenging behaviours, men with learning disabilities who sexually offend, or Black or Asian service users. Robina Shah (Chapter 9) unpacks PCP in a multicultural context signalling considerations for ethnicity and other areas of potential exclusion. In a similar vein, Jill Bradshaw (Chapter 8) focuses attention on service users traditionally excluded due to the severity of their disabilities and discusses ways accessible information and the creation of more meaningful choice-making processes can be advanced. David Dick and Karin Purvis (Chapter 7) in turn consider the role of a total communication approach, itself an inclusive intervention.

PCP AND CARE MANAGEMENT

If we are demanding the things from care management articulated above and more widely in this book we also need to be sure that care management itself has the necessary capacity and competence to carry out such complex tasks, which require a level of involvement and knowledge of individual cases seemingly left behind with the mainstreaming of care management as a policy instrument in the early 1990s. The risk that PCP will become diluted by the 'new wine into old bottles' approach – as explained by Jim Mansell and Julie Beadle-Brown (Chapter 2) – is undoubtedly high. The same observation was indeed made of care management when it was first introduced as a mainstream policy instrument (Davies 1992). We have since witnessed the dilution and diversification of care management for people with learning disabilities (Cambridge 1999), largely as a consequence of it losing sight of more intensive and productive ways of working with service users at the expense of organisational, administrative or cost-led demands. Tony Osgood (Chapter 4) effectively illustrates the tension between organisational and individual interests in the development of PCP. As a consequence of its profile in *Valuing People* (Department of Health 2001) and the subsequent work of the Support Team, PCP has become a prominent policy instrument for developing user-centred community care and for wider forms of user involvement. As such, it is beginning to achieve, much as care management did, the status of a policy outcome in its own right. It might be helpful for politicians and organisations to assess PCP in this way, but we need to put emphasis on the final outcomes for service users rather than on intermediate outcomes for organisations or practitioners.

In our experience, where services are under-resourced or are in impoverished communities, care managers often find themselves simply fire fighting – managing crises such as placement breakdowns or overwhelmed by adult protection on their caseloads. This risks a drift towards resource-led decision-making, impeding long-term work with individuals. Under such a scenario, case review becomes an administrative process, often conducted by correspondence, with decisions about resources forwarded to the duty desk or team leader, creating even more distance between practitioners and service users. Such organisational and professional paralysis removes any chance of care managers getting to know the people on their caseloads. If PCP is to stand any chance of working productively with care management, as many resources need to be directed towards intensive work with service users in care management as are currently directed to administrative processes.

There is no doubt that if PCP is to be effectively implemented, in most contexts it will require underpinning by effective care management and resource management for individuals, as illustrated by Simon Duffy and Helen Sanderson (Chapter 3). It is essential therefore that PCP and care management, including individual planning and review, do not operate as totally separate systems (Cambridge *et al.* in press). Wider information from care management is needed as a backcloth for PCP, although it should not constrain it. Conversely, information from PCP is needed to inform and drive individual service planning and review in care management, making some integration essential. Figure 14.1 summarises four possible models for the relationship between PCP and care management. Models 1 to 3 illustrate the three main approaches that are currently emerging (Cambridge *et al.* in press). It is, however, essential that we sustain movement towards model 4, where actions and priorities in care management are determined by PCP – where PCP forms the larger picture within which care management operates. This will require a major reorganisation and reassessment of care management, and PCP facilitators will need to be more than helpers with individual planning and care managers more than service co-ordinators, but such a reassessment of care management is anyway long overdue in most places.

PCP AND MACRO-ORGANISATION

The new language of partnerships, joint working and joint teams reminds us of the new language associated with the early days of care management and the community care reforms initiated in the 1990s – a sort of Orwellian New Speak, with a tendency to imply the opposite of what it is purporting to promote. Choice often means predetermined options. Partnership often means an alliance to exclude others. Person-centred is often translated to asking people for their views. Participation is sometimes a euphemism for inviting people to attend meetings. Empowerment is sometimes interpreted as consulting with people.

We need to sit down together as service users, policy makers, care managers, practitioners, commissioners and service managers and think very carefully about how macro- and micro-organisational systems (like partnership boards and PCP and care management) fit and work together and what we need to do to make them work together efficiently and well. This process might seem basic and laborious but it should lead to real structural efficiencies in the ways services are planned and organised, how effectively resources are matched to needs and

PCP replaces individual service planning and review as a core task of care management

Model 1: PCP integrated within care management

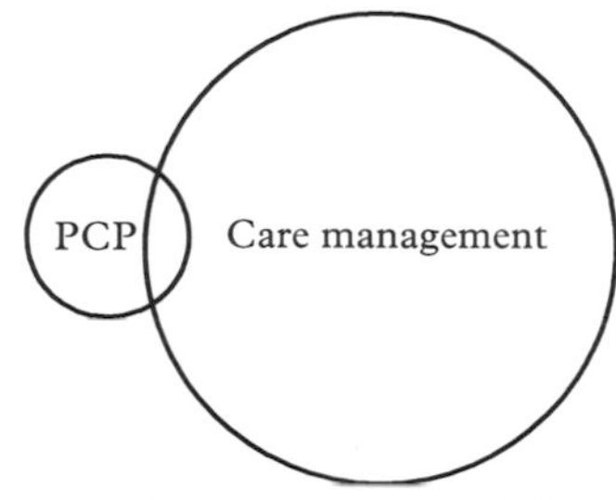

PCP and care management are connected operationally by professionals, carers and organisations involved

Model 2: Operational connections between PCP and care management

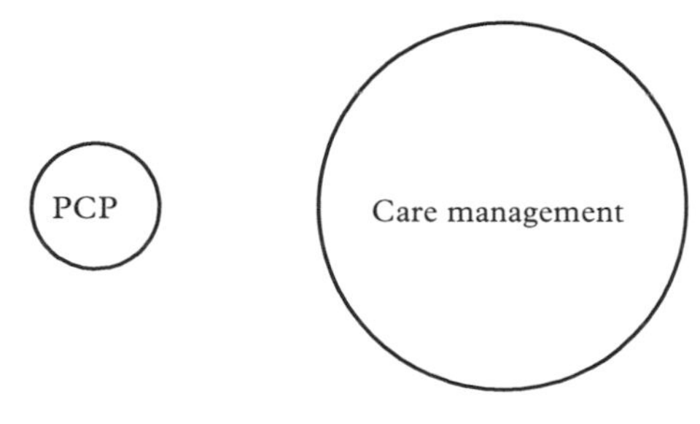

PCP and care management operate as seperate systems necessitating information exchange and co-ordination

Model 3: Separate PCP and care management

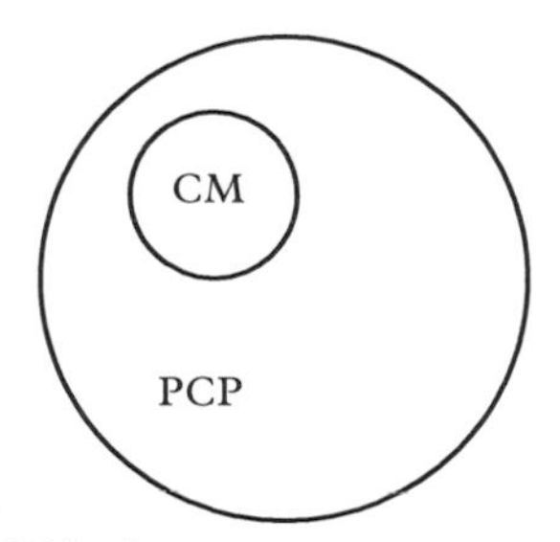

Care management becomes an integral part of PCP and operates according to PCP objectives

Model 4: PCP leads care management

Figure 14.1 Key models for the relationship between PCP and care management

the outcomes they achieve for service users as well as others involved in the system. Simon Duffy and Helen Sanderson offer just such an assessment (Chapter 3), mapping the various connections and options across aspects of micro-organisation. The process also implies that local people need to form alliances with stakeholders outside the system – statutory (education, housing, employment and health), independent (providers) and voluntary (advocacy, campaigning groups and other interest groups) – and that power is shared between these stakeholders.

This is true partnership working and partnership boards have the capacity to begin to bring such diverse interests together. David Dick and Karin Purvis with their focus on total communication (Chapter 7) illustrate how change can be implemented at different levels in an organisation and Hector Medora and Sue Ledger (Chapter 10) demonstrate the ways partnerships can be developed to make such an approach possible. Yet only recently have we begun to learn some of the limits, complexities and preconditions to successful partnership working, such as the importance of leadership, mediation and conflict resolution (Audit Commission 2002; Frye and Webb 2002; Huxham and Vangen 2000). Such rationales are also needed for helping understand how to ensure PCP, which is also partnership working at the micro-level, can work effectively.

A CROSS-NATIONAL FOCUS ON PCP

PCP in Kensington and Chelsea was the focus for the English partnership in the STEPS European anti-discrimination project in learning disability (Ernst 2002). Each national partnership (Germany, England, the Netherlands, Sweden and Spain) was between an academic institution, a service administration and service providers and was locally based (Hamburg, London, Rotterdam, Lidingo and Barcelona) with a different local anti-discrimination and participation initiative. At the final STEPS conference in London in May 2004, observations on PCP from the London partnership were provided as part of the recommendations to the project. While cross-national comparison in such areas is challenging, it is possible to develop supportive comparative frameworks to aid the task (Cambridge and Ernst 2004), and an aim of the exchange was to develop potentially transferable lessons.

It was noted that work on implementing PCP in London and elsewhere in the UK has largely been a natural experiment. As PCP was formally introduced by *Valuing People* (Department of Health 2001), it can be seen as a cultural directive as much if not more than an evidence-based policy initiative, although the key value of inclusion that underpinned *Valuing People* also means that PCP is effectively a policy instrument, implying that if implemented well it can facilitate the wider inclusion of people with learning disabilities – not only in developing their own services and lives but by developing networks of support in the wider community. The London evaluation for the STEPS project was consequently largely qualitative and interpretative, based on mapping process and approach and reporting experiences and key issues. The wider evaluation led by Eric Emerson and involving Paul Swift and Barbara McIntosh (see Chapter 10) includes PCP in Kensington and Chelsea and neighbouring Westminster and will be providing comparative findings using a longitudinal research model.

Two overarching observations were made regarding the material presented on PCP by the London partnership at the STEPS conference. The first was the importance of value-led initiatives. This means that services need to value staff and service users as well as their development work in PCP and that staff value the people they work alongside and support. It was amply evident that such a culture existed in Kensington and Chelsea. The second concerned the location and redistribution of power within social care organisations and considerations of power and powerlessness more widely in society, alongside attitudes to disability. To work well it was recognised that PCP requires that power and authority be devolved, not only to practitioners but also to service users in new ways.

In conclusion, seven key dimensions for helping ensure PCP works effectively were identified:

1. Person-centred organisations
2. Circles and networks of support
3. Advocacy and empowerment
4. Independent location
5. Communication and inclusion
6. Links with wider systems
7. Promoting competence.

Person-centred organisations

To work most effectively PCP needs to operate in truly person-centred organisations. As implied above, these should value staff and service users, devolve resources and authority to service users and staff, and facilitate direct payments. Structures will also tend to be non-hierarchical, with lateral management systems – managers linking into practice by supporting practitioners and having contact with service users and decision-making by agreement. Oxfordshire learning disability services have introduced the concept of 'person-centred teams' (also see Sanderson 2003), arguing that person-centred approaches can only be delivered if providers themselves are person-centred in their operation as well as their thinking.

Circles and networks of support

Broad social networks and alliances are required by PCP if it is to maximise its impact in changing people's lives for the better in sustainable ways. Change is difficult to effect without the support of others in people's lives and the wider community. Alliances such as circles of support provide for a more open system in situations where people with learning disabilities are isolated or have sparse social networks. The different interests and stakeholders involved in PCP provide allies for the person and the professionals in his or her life. Alliances and collective action are generally more effective than individual representation, especially in situations where people have traditionally been excluded or are socially or economically marginalised.

Advocacy and empowerment

PCP at its best is a form of self-advocacy or a combination of self, citizen and professional advocacy. However, PCP and the user voice can be significantly strengthened by constructing broader links between PCP and wider advocacy arrangements in services for people with learning disabilities, further empowering service users. For example, PCP can productively inform service commissioning, with service users as auditors and inspectors or represented on partnership boards, strengthening users' collective knowledge about services and consequently choice. PCP can help promote self-advocacy and play a part in redistributing power and resources within organisations.

Independent location

If PCP is to avoid becoming administratively driven – as has largely been the case with care management, which was also meant to deliver choice and change – then some independence from services is required. Administrative and managemment walls between PCP, social services departments and provider organisations are required to help ensure that the interests of the local state and key players in the social care market do not hijack PCP. Consequently, PCP should be organised at arm's length from care management and commissioning. Indeed, it may ultimately require ring-fencing and separate funding, an arrangement argued for care management in the early 1990s through the establishment of independent care management agencies.

Communication and inclusion

PCP is a key instrument for promoting the direct participation and wider social inclusion of people with learning disabilities. For such opportunities to be maximised, PCP needs to be culturally sensitive, personally relevant and where necessary operate using non-standard ways of recording and communicating information. It is essential for example that PCP is capable of engaging and representing people with complex needs. It should be conducted at the pace of the person and arrangements should be durable and sustainable as well as individualised and flexible overall. Total communication provides a relevant model.

Links with wider systems

PCP cannot effectively work in isolation of other service systems and processes. While it should not be tied to care management, productive links are required for negotiating resources or linking into wider service planning and commissioning. As such, PCP also has a part to play in best value reviews and in informing service audit and inspection. In order to fulfil its potential, PCP therefore not only needs to be connected to wider local government and NHS trust systems, but to outside functions such as inspections from the Commission for Social Care Inspection.

Promoting competence

PCP will work best in competent organisations but can also help organisations gain wider competencies, and a two-way relationship with staff training and development has the potential to develop wider organisational skills. Moreover, PCP can help promote individual competence through user empowerment and the promotion of positive self-images for people who use services. It can also help to promote flexible and accountable actions and responses and develop a more holistic approach to intervention and support.

CONCLUSION

A number of overarching lessons can be drawn when interpreting the arguments and material presented in this book. It is clearly evident that PCP is no panacea to facilitating user involvement or building person-centred services. There are good and less good approaches, effective and less effective methods, and useful and less useful techniques for developing person-centred approaches and actions. PCP is already varying in its form and approach – how it involves and is built around service users, the different processes employed and its links with care management and other micro- and macro-organisational systems. Individual (service user) and local (service systems) factors are therefore combining to create variability in form, design and process. While making comparisons of effectiveness is difficult, this variability also provides opportunities for comparison, determining what works well and why under different local and individual circumstances.

More widely we also need to be brave enough to ask how realistic PCP is and whether we also need to be seeking to develop a wider collection of person-centred techniques and arrangements, in some cases to complement PCP and in others to replace it. Perhaps it is more about philosophy and values than it is about a planning system *per se*, however individualised. We can more easily use a particular technique than address the fundamental issue about values and how these determine the way we support people with learning disabilities. PCP certainly risks becoming an administratively driven process or paper exercise, as argued by Jim Mansell and Julie Beadle-Brown (Chapter 2) and Tony Osgood (Chapter 4). This raises the thorny question as to whether we invest effort and resources in developing systems or in getting to know people with learning disabilities (Brost and Johnson 1982). This largely depends on what we really think about people and how we value them, but also on how we build effective systems beyond PCP, as discussed by Simon Duffy and Helen Sanderson (Chapter 3).

We believe that one of the most inhibiting characteristics of formal learning disability services (by which we mean services commissioned for people with learning disabilities which are funded from the public purse and provided by a range of statutory and non-statutory organisations) is the professional distance that often emerges between those who work in services – the paid labour of the managerial, professional and support workforce – and those who use services. Dependency relationships are institutionalised in services through hierarchies of power and promoted by guidelines and policies that effectively distance workers from service users. We construct administrative and operational policies and processes that create professional space and fractures in the social and sometimes the practical support we provide. This is a real dilemma, because services have a responsibility to protect people from undue risks (for example, sexual abuse or self-harm) but also a responsibility to support people in emotionally empowering and productive ways.

We fear and perhaps over-rationalise touch and we provide advice in perhaps overly structured ways. On the one hand we promote privacy and dignity but on the other commission services which are intrusive in people's lives, where communal spaces predominate or leave people isolated in the community. There is no doubt that these factors inhibit truly person-centred work. Just as budgetary responsibility within care management limits opportunities to develop professional advocacy, so professional responsibilities in service provision inhibit the development of close social relationships and exchange with service users. PCP has the potential, but only that, to help bridge these fractures and reduce social inequities in services for people with learning disabilities.

REFERENCES

Audit Commission (2002) *Developing Productive Partnerships.* London: District Audit.

Brost, M. and Johnson, T. (1982) *Getting to Know You: One Approach to Service Planning and Assessment for People with Learning Difficulties.* Madison, WI: Wisconsin Coalition for Advocacy, distributed in Britain by Chimera.

Bulmer, M. (1987) *The Social Basis of Community Care.* London: Allen and Unwin.

Cambridge, P. (1999) 'Building care management competence in services for people with learning disabilities.' *British Journal of Social Work 29,* 393–415.

Cambridge, P. and Brown, H. (1997) 'Making the market work for people with learning disabilities: an argument for principled contracting.' *Critical Social Policy 51,* 27–52.

Cambridge, P., Carpenter, J., Forrester-Jones, R., Tate, A., Knapp, M., Beecham, J. and Hallam, A. (in press) 'The state of care management in learning disability and mental health services twelve years into community care.' *British Journal of Social Work.*

Cambridge, P. and Ernst, E. (2004) *A Framework for Comparing National and Local Service Systems and Arrangements for People with Learning Disabilities in Europe: the Experience of the STEPS Anti-Discrimination Project.* Canterbury: Tizard Centre, University of Kent at Canterbury.

Cambridge, P. and Forrester-Jones, R. (2003) 'Using individualised communication for interviewing people with intellectual disability: a case study of user centred research.' *Journal of Intellectual and Developmental Disability 28,* 1, 5–23.

Cambridge, P., Hayes, L. and Knapp, M. (1994) *Care in the Community – Five Years On.* Aldershot: Ashgate.

Davies, B. (1992) 'Lessons for case management.' In S. Onyett and P. Cambridge (eds) *Case Management: Issues in Practice.* Canterbury: University of Kent, PSSRU.

Department of Health (2001) *Valuing People: A New Strategy for Learning Disability for the 21st Century.* London: Department of Health.

Ernst, A. (2002) 'STEPS – Structures towards emancipation, participation and solidarity: a European project to combat discrimination against people with learning disabilities.' *Tizard Learning Disability Review 7,* 4, 4–9.

Forrester-Jones, R., Cambridge, P., Carpenter, J., Tate, A., Beecham, J., Hallam, A., Knapp, M., Coolen-Schrijner, P. and Wooffe, D. (in press) 'The social networks of people with learning disabilities living in the community twelve years on.' *Journal of Applied Research in Intellectual Disabilities.*

Frye, M. and Webb, A. (2002) *Effective Partnership Working.* London: Public Enquiry Unit.

Huxham, C. and Vangen, S. (2000) 'Leadership in the shaping and implementation of collaboration agendas: how things happen in a (not quite) joined up world.' *Academy of Management Journal 43,* 6, 1159–1175.

Knapp, M., Cambridge, P., Thomason, C., Beecham, J., Allen, C. and Darton, R. (1992) *Care in the Community: Challenge and Demonstration.* Aldershot: Ashgate.

Sanderson, H. (2003) 'Implementing person-centred planning by developing person-centred teams.' *Journal of Integrated Care 11,* 3, 18–25.

The Contributors

Andy Alaszewski is Professor of Health Studies and Director of the Centre for Health Services Studies at the University of Kent. Andy is an applied social scientist who has been involved in research and service developments for vulnerable adults for over 30 years and in the past 10 years has focused on the ways in which risk is assessed and managed in health and social care. He is author of nearly 300 publications including: *Risk, Health and Welfare* (Open University Press 1998, with Larry Harrison and Jill Manthorpe); 'Learning disability nursing: user and carer perspectives', *Journal of Learning Disabilities 7*, pp.119–135, 2003 (with J. Manthorpe, B. Gates, S. Ayer and E. Motherby); 'Towards integrated health care and social care for older people: a European review', *Journal of Integrated Care 12*, 1, pp.3–8, 2004 (with J.R. Billings and K. Coxon). Andy is also editor of the international journal *Health, Risk and Society.*

Helen Alaszewski is a Research Associate in the Centre for Health Services Studies at the University of Kent. She is a qualified nurse who for the past ten years has been engaged in research on the care and support of vulnerable adults. Currently she is working on a project funded by the Stroke Association which explores younger stroke survivors' experiences. Her publications include *Assessing and Managing Risk in Nurse Education* (ENB 1998, with Andy Alaszewski, Jill Manthorpe and Sam Ayer), *Empowerment and Protection* (Mental Health Foundation 1999, with Andy Alaszewski and Alison Parker) and *Managing Risk in Community Practice* (Baillière Tindall 2000, with Andy Alaszewski, Jill Manthorpe and Sam Ayer).

Julie Beadle-Brown has worked at the Tizard Centre since 1995 and is currently a Lecturer in Learning Disability and Convenor of the MSc in Analysis and Intervention in Learning Disabilities. Her main research interests are service design and implementation and autism. She has developed an interest in direct payments and combines this with her interest in person-centred approaches such as person-centred active support and person centred planning. She has over ten years' experience working with people with learning disabilities and their staff and families, and in addition to her teaching and research is an active consultant, working on the assessment of capacity to consent and manage a direct payment.

Jill Bradshaw worked as a speech and language therapist in a multidisciplinary team in services for people with learning disabilities, before being appointed as a lecturer at the Tizard Centre in 1995. She has a particular interest in communication and people who challenge services and has published a number of articles and book chapters in this area in both the professional and academic press. Jill left the Tizard Centre in 2003 and is currently studying for a PhD at Manchester Metropolitan University. Jill retains an honorary lectureship with the Tizard Centre and continues to contribute towards teaching on a number of their programmes.

Hilary Brown is Professor of Social Care and a Consultant in Adult Protection based at Salomons, which is a faculty of Canterbury Christ Church University College. She has written and researched on issues of vulnerability and protection over many years and has worked with national and international agencies to further this agenda. Her recent work includes 'Safeguarding adults and children with disabilities from abuse' for the Council of Europe (2002) and (with Margaret Flynn and Sophie Burns) 'Dying matters' (2004) which explores the service needs of people with learning disabilities who are dying, for the Foundation for People with Learning Disabilities. Hilary is also training to be a psychotherapist.

Paul Cambridge is a Senior Lecturer at the Tizard Centre at the University of Kent, teaching an MA course in the Management of Community Care and a BA course in Health and Social Care Practice. He also undertakes development work with services and individuals using services. His research has included a Department of Health funded study on the long-term outcomes and costs of Care in the Community for people with learning disabilities and mental health problems, care management and micro-organisation, sexuality and HIV, intimate and personal care, gender and caring roles and cross-national work on learning disability in Europe. He has published widely on these subjects in the academic and professional literature and has also developed a wide range of educational and staff training resources in learning disability. Paul also co-edits the *Tizard Learning Disability Review.*

Steven Carnaby is a clinical psychologist at City and Hackney Teaching PCT and Oxfordshire Learning Disability Trust, and Honorary Lecturer in Learning Disabilities at the Tizard Centre, University of Kent. Steven's background is in the direct support of people with learning disabilities, working in both residential and day services. His main clinical interests are work with people with severe and profound disabilities, and his current research interests include intimate and personal care for people with complex needs, transition for young people leaving special school and the use of Intensive Interaction in supporting people with profound disabilities. He is editor of *Clinical Psychology and People with Learning Disabilities* (published by the BPS Faculty for Learning Disabilities), joint editor of *Tizard Learning Disability Review*, and principal author of the *Learning Disability Awards Framework* materials developed by the Foundation for People with Learning Disabilities, the Tizard Centre and Pavilion Publishing.

Doris Clark lives in Bristol and works for Circles Network as a Development Officer. In her role at Circles Network she assists in facilitating various training courses around the country and promoting the work of the organisation.

David Dick qualified as a social worker in 1980. He worked with people with learning disabilities in Nebraska, USA, in a pioneering scheme to move people from hospital to community settings. David has also worked with people with learning disabilities in a variety of accommodation, day services, work preparation and leisure settings. Since 1987 David has worked for the learning disability service in Somerset, initially as a social worker, and is now Operational Manager of a service that supports over 1650 adults with learning disabilities, many of whom receive services provided directly by the social services department. David is currently overseeing the departmental strategy for person centred planning. Ensuring that person-centred approaches are encouraged through implementing communication development plans is an integral part of this strategy.

Simon Duffy leads In Control, a national programme to promote self-directed support for disabled people. In the past he has set up several organisations, including Inclusion Glasgow and Altrum, to help people with learning difficulties achieve their own homes, support systems and lifestyles. He is the author of *Keys to Citizenship* (Paradigm 2003) and has a PhD in moral philosophy. His primary research interest is in ensuring that disabled people are better valued by moral and political theory.

Robert Garland lives in Barry, South Wales, and undertakes regular work as a presenter for Circles Network, especially in Wales and Bristol. He has also been a member of the Circles Network Core Group and carried out administrative work for the organisation.

Sue Ledger has had a long and varied career in the field of learning disabilities. She is currently the Joint Manager of the Learning Disability Community Health and Social Services Team in the Royal Borough of Kensington and Chelsea. Sue has been a member of a number of international, national and local projects and has been the driving force in developing oral histories for people with learning disabilities and more locally in Kensington and Chelsea in establishing person centred planning and Quality Networks.

Patricia Lewis is Head of Upper School and Special Needs Co-ordinator at Shepherd School, Nottingham, where she has taught Sixth Form students since 1998. Part of her role is working with students on issues such as self esteem, self assertion, and self and circle of peer/staff advocacy. Patricia has also been developing a communicative approach to preparing for Transition, beginning with the Year 9 Transition Review Meetings, and is actively involved in the development of 14–19 curricula.

Jim Mansell is Professor of Applied Psychology of Learning Disability at the Tizard Centre, University of Kent. He is a Fellow of the British Psychological Society and a Chartered Psychologist, and has been involved in the research and development of community-based intellectual disability services in England and Wales since 1970. He has been a consultant, teacher and adviser to many organisations, including the Department of Health, social services departments, health authorities, trusts and voluntary organisations in Britain, and governmental and non-governmental organisations in the USA, Australia and Europe. He is a Trustee of the charity United Response and a Commissioner for Social Care Inspection. His publications include the books *Deinstitutionalization and Community Living* (Chapman and Hall 1996), *Severe Learning Disability and Challenging Behaviour* (Chapman and Hall 1993) and *Developing Staffed Housing for People with Mental Handicaps* (Costello 1987); and the Department of Health report *Services for People with Learning*

Disabilities and Challenging Behaviour or Mental Health Needs (1992). Jim founded the *Tizard Learning Disability Review*, of which he was editor until 1998.

Hector Medora is Head of Disability Services in the London Borough of Camden and Camden NHS Primary Care Trust. He formerly worked as Head of Disability Services (and Head of Joint Learning Disability Services) in the Royal Borough of Kensington and Chelsea. He has worked on a range of projects here and abroad in the field of disabilities and vulnerable adults. His first contact with people with learning disabilities was in 1966 when he worked as a volunteer with Mencap and the National Federation of Gateway Clubs. He was a founder member of Kensington and Chelsea Mencap (now Equal People).

Tony Osgood works as a Behaviour Specialist for an NHS trust and is also Lecturer in Learning Disability at the Tizard Centre, University of Kent. He has worked in both private and statutory services, starting his career as a support worker in a Special Development Team service, and later working as a Registered Manager in Learning Disability, Physical Disability, and Mental Health services. His interests include behaviour analysis, person centred planning and positive behaviour support, as well as the organisational influence on human service outcomes.

Karin Purvis has been a specialist speech and language therapist for adults with learning disabilities for 14 years. She is currently Head of the Speech and Language Therapy Service for Somerset Partnership NHS and Social Care Trust. She supports a team of specialist speech and language therapists who are based in four joint health and social services community teams for adults with learning disabilities across Somerset. Karin has been instrumental in ensuring that communication has become integral to service planning and strategic change. She has also been involved in the design and implementation of communication development plans across Somerset to ensure that communication issues are considered at all levels within the organisation. Karin also is part of the Deciding Together Working Group that agrees with service users the priorities, protocols and formats for all key communications between service providers and service users.

Helen Sanderson is the primary author of *People, Plans and Possibilities: Exploring Person Centred Planning* (SHS 1997), the first book on person centred planning in the UK that emerged from three years' research. *People, Plans and Practicalities* (SHS 2003) followed this in 2003. Her PhD is on person centred planning and organisational change. Together with Martin Routledge, she has written guidance on person centred planning for England's Department of Health. Helen is also an Essential Lifestyle Planning mentor trainer, and much of her work is around the practice and development of person centred planning with families and in services. She also works as part of IAS, a service provider in Greater Manchester, helping develop a person-centred organisation.

Karen Scott is a Research Assistant based at Salomons, which is a faculty of Canterbury Christ Church University College. She has worked in consultancy settings such as Health Service Management, focusing on mental health, learning disabilities and professional development within the NHS and statutory services. Karen has an MSc in Occupational Psychology.

Robina Shah is a psychologist, research fellow and trainer. She has been working with children, young people and families for 15 years. During this time she has written many publications, the most notable being *The Silent Minority* and *Sharing the News*, which describe the experiences of parents finding out about their child's disability. Robina was appointed to the Valuing People Support Team at the Department of Health in 2002 as their specialist adviser on cultural diversity and learning disabilities. She is also involved in various public services, and is a magistrate and Chairman of Stockport Acute NHS Foundation Trust.

Val Williams is a research fellow at the Norah Fry Research Centre, University of Bristol, where she has worked since 1997. The Centre carries out academic research that aims to make a practical difference, and Val has been particularly involved in developing inclusive research methods, where people with learning disabilities do their own research or take part in projects. She has published widely in academic and user-led literature about these and other topics. The Centre has also developed accessible information, so that people with learning disabilities can understand the academic work about their lives. In the spirit of ghost authoring, Val has worked with Doris Clark and Robert Garland to produce the chapter for the present volume. In a voluntary capacity, Val is also a member of two trusts that help people with learning disabilities to live the life they want through person centred planning and direct payments.

Subject Index

Author Index

Printed in Great Britain
by Amazon.co.uk, Ltd.,
Marston Gate.